WASHIN

Confidential

BY JACK LAIT

AND

LEE MORTIMER

CROWN PUBLISHERS, INC.

NEW YORK

Printed in the United States of America
American Book–Knickerbocker Press, Inc., New York

The Confidential Contents

Part Two—THE PEOPLE (Confidential!)

WASHINGTON CONFIDENTIAL

P-S-S-S-T!

Here we go again—Confidential.

We turned New York inside out; but we both live there. We turned Chicago upside down; but we were both raised there. We descended on Washington not quite like Stanley invaded Africa, because in our combined 75 years of newspaper work we had been in the capital hundreds of times. It intrigued us because we never could understand it. So we decided brashly to do a Lait-Mortimer operation on it from scratch. Our principal discovery was that nobody understands Washington—the *city*, not the nation's nerve-center.

By the time we went through it—its avenues, its alleys, its cat-houses, its dumps, its mansions, its hotels, its police stations, its jails, its courts, its clubs, its closets, and its catacombs, we knew more about it than anyone who lives in it, and finished the job which stymied Lincoln Steffens 40 years ago; for that classic muckraker who turned up the shame of the cities recoiled in bafflement when he attempted to "do" Washington.

It was our toughest task of digging, but we turned up plenty. We think we have X-rayed the dizziest—and this will amaze you, as it did us, the dirtiest—community in America.

We are not reformers. We are reporters. As such we will take you with us through a metropolitan area of 1,500,000, living in what should be a utopia, but which is a cesspool of drunkenness, debauchery, whoring, homosexuality, municipal corruption and public apathy, protected crime under criminal protection, hoodlumism, racketeering, pandering and plundering, among anomalous situations found nowhere else on earth.

Washington is a made-to-order architectural paradise with the political status of an Indian reservation, inhabited by 800,000 economic parasites; no industries but one, government, and the tradesmen and servants and loafers and scum that feed on the highest average per capita income in the world, where exist the soundest security, the mightiest power, and the most superlative rates of crime, vice and juvenile delinquency anywhere. And this in a seat of intelligence, the cross-section of the whole United States, where women far outnumber men.

It leads the country in the percentage of the native-born. There are no peasants, factory-workers or slums as they are known in every other city of magnitude.

The paternal form of local administration in this disenfranchised and politically castrated community should eliminate ward and district bosses, vote-buyers, grafters and gangsters, all of whom elsewhere thrive primarily on controlling votes. Yet in this magnificent planned city of majestic proportions, the official heart of the richest and greatest and freest land in the history of mankind, we found corruption and perversion, organized and individual, that dazed a pair of hardened characters who considered themselves shock-proof after their groundwork for the books that debunked New York and deloused Chicago.

We spent many months in Washington. We made contacts in our own surefire way, which opened up sources not usually available to the reporters there, who regard affairs of their town as chickenfeed, and who dream of becoming syndicated columnists who can pontificate on Congress, the Cabinet and the White House.

We know plenty about those, too. But we will stick to the Lowdown on the Big Town, which has become our trademark.

We will not even attempt to be comprehensive. We have no hope or aim to make Washington a better place to live in. We don't give a damn what kind of a place it is to live in, except that the kind of place we found furnished us with that sole commodity in which we deal—copy.

Everything interested us, but we will limit this to what we think will interest you. This is no guide-book. This is no preachment and no appeal, not even a lesson. As we said in the introduction to *Chicago Confidential*, "We have nothing to sell except books." And we sold plenty of them and are still selling them.

This will be the stripped-down story of a queen who turned into a street-walker.

That's why we were born—to tell you what you couldn't find out without us—Confidential!

PART ONE

THE PLACES
(*Confidential!*)

1. DISTRICT OF CONFUSION

THE NATION'S CAPITAL is a bastard born of a compromise and nurtured on a lottery.

The founding fathers, whose infinite wisdom gave us a Constitution and form of government well nigh perfect, located the seat of that government in a stinking, steaming swamp. This was a peace offering to recalcitrant Southerners, who were that way then just as they are now.

The first funds to build and improve that city were raised by selling real estate by lottery. With such ancestry, it is no wonder today that "numbers" make one of the biggest businesses in Washington. The policy racket far exceeds bookmaking, the Number 1 source of gambling revenue in all others parts of the country.

Before the plane which brings the arriving traveler to Washington lands at the National Airport, on the Virginia side, it swoops gracefully over the city in a salute. The tall, needle-like Washington Monument and the familiar dome of the Capitol arise through a sea of green, to dominate the landscape.

They and the other public structures, which alone form the skyline in a city where buildings over 110 feet high are banned by law, are the symbols of Washington. It is an old-fashioned, tree-shaded Southern town, delightful and gracious, taken over by a gigantic governmental apparatus which, though founded on Colonial Virginia's tradition of personal freedom, has mush-

1

roomed into the world's greatest bureaucracy, humpbacked and bow-legged under tons of laws and endless regulations.

The spacious avenues, the tree-shaded lawns, the green which one sees wherever he looks, is a symbol too—that Washington is dominated by the rural mind.

It is the only capital of any world power where there is no variety of humanity. London, Paris, Berlin, Buenos Aires, Tokyo, these are great commercial centers where national government is incidental. Washington is inhabited by residents of every state in the union and representatives of every country on the globe, yet it is as backwater and provincial as any small inland one-plant town.

This most uncosmopolitan capital is overshadowed by that giant of metropolises, New York, only minutes away by air, and by Baltimore, with its wide open and blatant vice much nearer. The foreign trade commissioners, the visiting bankers, and all the important public personages go to Manhattan, where the United Nations is cutting into Washington's diplomatic monopoly. The lowlier links lam the 36 miles to Baltimore to cut up.

Not that Washington has no vice and venery. It has more of it than the escape havens. But, as in all ingrown towns, the "respectables" must go away from home to prance and play. It is the story of the deacon from Dubuque all over again, and what happens to him in the Big Burg. Only here the deacon is a Congressman, or—

As we unfold the rates of crime, vice, sex irregularities, graft, cheap gambling, drunkenness, rowdyism and rackets, you will get, thrown on a large screen, a peep show of this stately concentration camp of cold monuments and hot mammas where there are four women for every three men. Murkier than the "smoke-filled room" so often used as a cliché to typify a corral of politicos, it is a vast bedroom with a jumbo bottle of bourbon beside the bed.

And yet its manners and morals are those of the barnyard and the railroad-junction town rather than the romantic intrigue of the salon and the scented boudoir.

Washington has a kind of glamor all its own. It is not the kind one finds in New York, or Paris, or even Atlantic City. The Washington feeling comes from being close to great events and to the memory of great people. It is, to a certain extent, similar to the public appeal of Hollywood's famed Forest Lawn

Cemetery, the place where the movie stars are interred. Forest Lawn there is a must for tourists. There is no sacred peace about this graveyard. Trippers photograph its ornate tombs and profane its dead. The tombs were purposely designed by hams who craved publicity even in death.

Washington does remind one of a well-kept cemetery. Its gleaming public buildings of white marble are like so many mausoleums. It is the nation's Forest Lawn, where is sunk its priceless heritage, killed by countless generations of getters and gimme-ers.

Washington is a reflection of Los Angeles—a Los Angeles without palm trees. Where it doesn't look like a cemetery it resembles a movie set. It has a feel of unreality. This is a designed city, the only important one in America, and its streets are so straight, its architecture is so conforming, and its sidewalks are so neat and clean, it might have been set up in *papier-mâché* only today.

And it's a dead heat which—Washington or Los Angeles—has more yahoos from more dull places. New York gets its share, but its tourists include many from fairly alive communities; the plowboys hail from New England or other points not very far away. But the barbarians who inundate Washington and Los Angeles would be conspicuous if they visited Little Rock. Heaven knows where they come from. Their clothes, make-ups, manners and expressions are of the cow-pasture.

We were sitting in the Senators' Reception Room in the Capitol, waiting for one solon to come off the floor. This rococo room is open to the public. While we sat there, we idly contemplated the sight-seers who gaped at the mid-Victorian gold and mosaic with which it is embellished. One coatless yokel, with two dirty-nosed youngsters in tow and a dreary wife toting a wailing babe bringing up the rear, figured we knew something because we were wearing ties and sitting down.

"What room is this?" he humbly asked.   ·

"This is the President's private office," we replied. "No visitors allowed."

You should have seen them scram!

The number of transients who enter and leave Washington annually is in excess of 45 million. Most of them are peasants who shudder when they ride in an elevator and gape at an escalator. The sessions of Congress find them in the galleries of the noisy House and the sedate Senate. The men are negligee with firemen's suspenders, the women often suckle babes at their breasts while some Demosthenes below debates a bill vital to the world.

But the residents of the Washington area are, on the whole, remarkably well-dressed—not only the natives in Washington but the government employes drawn from every corner of the map. It is surprising how quickly they shed their corn-fed looks and begin to look like Easterners and try to act like them.

One wonders where the hoards of ill-dressed, low-mannered visitors eat and sleep.

Tourists may wander coatless through the White House and in the legislative office buildings, but all of the better restaurants and hotels require men to wear coats and ties at all times. This, of course, is universal in New York, but in Chicago, horny-handed, wilted hoi polloi are seen in lobbies of such swell hotels as the Ambassador and Drake in shirt-sleeves.

Washingtonians are completely white-collar. Its private business is merchandising. The service trades, such as feeding and sleeping visitors, form its chief non-governmental activity. Before the New Deal put a premium on alphabet soup, federal employes got miserly wages. Washington was a poor city. Now some secretaries make as much as $8,000 a year and Senators' assistants drag down $10,000. We talked to one babe, some kind of an expert in the Treasury, who draws $15,000 a year on a fee basis. In her spare time she checks hats in a joint which sells liquor after hours.

The average family income in Washington is the highest in any big city in the land, despite its disproportionate Negro population. Colored folk work for Uncle Sam at salaries equal to whites', in many cases get preferential treatment, and others draw liberal relief checks. Another reason for high family income is that in so many families husband and wife work for the government, and many who are grounded there also hold outside jobs, after hours. This practice is permitted in many departments. Even members of the Metropolitan Police are allowed to accept outside employment after their eight-hour day. Many drive taxies or are chauffeurs.

The per capita income in Washington is $1820, compared with the national average of $1330. Even rich New York is second to Washington with $1758.

Washingtonians file more income-tax returns per capita than do any other Americans. More than two-thirds of the homes in the District are worth more than $12,000. The city has the highest retail sales per capita on earth. Government employes are paid regularly by a boss who never goes broke—though that isn't the fault of the politicians.

Added wealth streams constantly into the city, from the cornucopias of lobbyists with no-limit expense accounts, tourists and representatives of foreign governments who let loose a few francs, shillings or lire before tapping our tills.

Here we have a city which, if mental cripples who believe in planned economies were correct, should be a happy place, free of crime and vice. Washington is rich and almost everyone in it is insured against want for life. Yet it has that apex rate of crime. The waterfront of Marseilles, the alleys of Singapore's Chinatown, the sailor's deadfalls of Port Said have nothing on it. Washington makes even Chicago look good. And that's been going on since Abigail Adams hung the family wash in the backyard of the then unfinished White House—and shuddered lest the President's drawers be stolen.

In the early years of the Republic, grifters and grafters, highwaymen and conmen, pimps and prostitutes flocked into the city. Instead of being a community where women greatly outnumbered men, as they do today, early Washington contained almost entirely males. The first Congressmen and early officeholders were easy pickings for the fancy girls and their fancy men, who arrived a jump ahead of the lobbyists. Lonesome men whiled their time at cards and dice, and ever since then Washington has been a gamblers' garden.

Foreigners and many American political philosophers say one great fault of our American system is our form of municipal government. They point out the astounding crime, legal laxity and municipal deviltry in this country where we elect our local governments directly and give them great power, whereas most foreign countries are ruled from above, with cities and provinces allowed minimum authority.

Well, Washington is ruled from above. It has no votes, no county chairmen, no campaign funds to be raised, no favors to be returned. It is policed by a constabulary appointed directly by the United States government and paid from the public treasury of the United States. Its judges are appointed by the President with the consent of the Senate, and all but municipal court judges serve for life. Its District Attorney is chosen by the President, as are its city commissioners, and through them all public District officials.

There is no chance for a neighborhood gang boss to establish himself through floaters and colonized flotsam. Yet there are neighborhood bosses. There is influence. Judges and police are bought. Washington has the blackest record of any city in the country on the F.B.I. ledger of reported crimes. Black is the color of its crime, too, as will be shown. The proportion of Negro crime to white is almost eight to one.

Another reason for Washington's defiance of the law which is made in Washington is that, except for ogling tourists, everyone who comes comes to get. To get jobs, contracts, favors, pardons, commissions, and sometimes social preferment. This acquisitive horde is not interested in the city. Toward local public affairs there is lethargy of mind, spirit and body, nothing conducive to enterprise or local pride.

This potpourri of human beings on the make remained within bounds until the first World War. There was room for all. As every schoolboy knows, the original grant of land from the states of Maryland and Virginia for the national capital was a square, ten miles wide. This proved too big and the Virginia part was receded more than a hundred years ago. The remaining area, all in Maryland, was ample for the needs of the city until overnight, in 1917, it changed from a country town to a madhouse in which all the residents are inmates. There was some respite during the 1920's, but since the coming of the New Deal, Washington burst its pants and overflowed back into Virginia and across into Maryland.

As with other large cities, the 1950 census returns found the rate of growth of Washington suburbs far outstripping the parent. At this writing there are about 800,000 people in the city limits and 750,000 in the satellite suburbs of Virginia and Maryland. The percentage of Negroes is higher than it is in Mississippi.

Seniority rules in the Congress, which permit one-party Southern Senators and Representatives to control more than their share of committees, account for continuance of its Dixie slant. So Washingtonians talk like Southerners. Even the Oregonians and down-Easters fall into the liquid drawl after a few years in the capital. With the dulcet Dixie dialect comes the Southern attitude toward the Negro. Fiery FEPCers from New

York, after a couple of years' indoctrination, wink in private over the "tolerance" they sell in public. As Negroes move in the whites flee out.

As residents of Virginia and Maryland, these automatically gain the votes they surrendered or never had. Though still employed in Washington, they lose all interest in its municipal affairs. They live, vote, pay taxes, send their children to school and join churches beyond the borders.

And, as the Negro immigrates and propagates, Washington's chance of ever getting the vote dwindles. Even Northern congressmen, with huge Negro voting constituencies at home, won't burn their hands with such legislation. They declare for the principles of home rule, sign petitions to withdraw bottled-up home-rule bills from committees, then secretly withdraw their names.

As these pages unfold you will get a picture of how more than 1,500,000 people live. Few would stand for some of Washington's nauseating conditions in their own towns. Yet they take them here complacently. Congressmen, the lords of the city, shrug at what would throw them out of office if the good burghers in Beloit or Boonetown suspected—and cared.

Washington has a heritage of "everybody's business is nobody's business." But the stimulation which sparks its evils is different, though the result is the same.

Of old, Congress didn't worry about local crime because all the people could do about it was write letters to the papers. But now, since crime is nationally syndicated, some legislators actively protect Washington crime, because it means more funds back in their bailiwicks from the branches of the swelling Syndicate of silk-lined racketeers who are allied with Washington's criminals.

So this is the nation's capital: with its panderers and prostitutes; gamblers and gunmen; conmen and Congressmen; lawmakers and law-breakers; fairies and Fair Dealers.

It is a city of moods, even drearier when Congress is away campaigning or vacationing; yet it turns electric when something big is about to happen.

It is a city of the wistful little people with adding-machine minds.

Over all, a feeling of fear pervades it. People become conditioned to talking in whispers. Senators will walk you to the middle of the room, then mumble, even when what they have to say is inconsequential. The main indoor sport is conspiracy.

We give you Washington: not the city of statesmen, but the stateless city.

2. "GORGEOUS" GEORGETOWN

WE SHALL begin this catalog of places with Georgetown, by far the oldest in the city.

Not all who reside in Georgetown are rich, red or queer, nor do all Washington millionaires, Commies and/or fags dwell in Georgetown.

But if you know anyone who fulfills at least two of the foregoing three qualifications don't take odds he doesn't prance behind Early American shutters in a reconditioned stable or slave-pen in this unique city within a city.

Georgetown was a thriving Colonial village when the rest of the District was swampland. It was included in the District of Columbia from the time of the original grant, but Georgetown remained an independent municipality until 1895.

If you like that kind of stuff, Georgetown, which lies in the extreme NW section of the city, has a charm all its own.

Some people like the smell of dead fish in Provincetown. Others like to climb up four flights of stairs to ratty garrets in Greenwich Village. Georgetown is quaint that way, too. Now all this is to be preserved for posterity forever, through an act of Congress setting up a commission to keep it looking the way it is under penalty of the law for modernizing anything in the community without the permission of some bureaucrat.

Until twenty years ago, Georgetown was just another rundown backwash in a great city. Most of its residents were Negroes. Most of its real estate wasn't even good enough for Southern Negroes, and don't forget that a Southern Negro is forced to live almost anywhere. New Dealers and the bright young braintrusters from Harvard reversed what seems to be a foreordained rule in every city in the country. In other words, the whites drove the Negroes out—as many as they could—and took over for themselves what was practically a blighted area.

This is how it came about: When Washington was suddenly flooded with a horde of crackpots from the campuses, Communists, ballet-dancers and economic planners, there was no place for them to live. They abhorred the modern service apartments. These people were "intellectual." The women wore flat-heeled shoes and batik blouses, and went in for New Thought. The men, if you could call some of them that, wore their hair longer than we do, read advanced literature, and talked about the joys of collectivism, though all of them were so individual they couldn't bear to live in skyscrapers.

Most of these people had dough. The others got good government jobs, became "contact men" or spoke at meetings and wrote for publications sponsored by rich left-wingers to provide automobiles and other luxuries for the needier pinks.

Washington had nothing like New York's Greenwich Village, but in the early days of the New Deal Mrs. Roosevelt herself, during one of the fleeting moments she was in Washington, "discovered" Georgetown and conceived it as a genteel bohemian community where her sandal-shod friends could find congenial company. She wouldn't allow the WPA to alter anything though sewage comes up from the river. Georgetown is overrun with rats, which frequently chew up Negro infants.

Ancient wooden houses, much the worse for the wear of centuries, which could have been bought lot-and-all for $2,500 in the '20s, skyrocketed as it became "smart" for society to move to Georgetown. Some properties are now worth twenty times what they brought twenty years ago, though terrible odors emanate from a nearby slaughter house.

Following the discovery of Georgetown, the truly gentle Negroes who had lived there, some for a hundred years or more, were driven out. Few owned their homes. Into rickety structures which had once housed as many as ten Negro families—seventy-five people—moved one millionaire left-wing carpetbagger and his wife. With improvements, naturally. Equality is okay to talk about. Hundreds of thousands of dollars were spent on some of these homes, modernizing, beautifying, disinfecting and furnishing them. Now they have house-and-garden tours for visiting Kiwanians.

Not all the Negroes could be ousted. Even today, Georgetown has a considerable colored population, though it is the only part of Washington where there are fewer Negroes than there were twenty years ago. Those who remain live in shanties so undesirable that no rich white fairies can be found who want to turn them into something gay. In fact, there's a saying in Georgetown now that you're not "smart" unless darkies live next door to you.

The sight-seeing buses point out historic Prospect House, now used by the government for visiting notables, but they don't show you the tumble-down Negro shacks behind it.

One of Georgetown's most distinguished residents is Dean Acheson. Emmitt Warring, king of Washington's gamblers, about whom more will be found in succeeding chapters, is in business nearby.

Warring is the kingfish of Georgetown. He controls its local police precinct as well as its local crime. As will be shown, he has direct affiliations with the national underworld syndicate.

Eleanor Roosevelt gave Georgetown that first big impetus after her son, Jimmy, who didn't "got it" in California, moved across the street from the old Imperial Russian Embassy, in the 3200 block of Q Street. It looked like good business to build up the area.

Soon the section filled up with all manner of strange people. Many of these were buddies of the First Lady. We have seen a letter she wrote to one Ben Grey, in which she pats such types on the head.

One of the queerest sights visible anywhere is the one from a window on the second floor of Dean Acheson's quaint home at 2805 P Street. It faces the 28th Street side over a back yard. The Secretary's personal lavatory faces that way. His mind apparently weighted by cosmos-shaking affairs of state, the Secretary forgets to draw down the shade.

It is on the second floor, and Acheson doesn't know he can be seen. This is to tip him off to what the whole neighborhood knows, first-hand and not confidential.

In the next block lives Justice Frankfurter. He and Acheson, fresh air fiends, walk to town every morning.

Another neighbor is Myrna Loy, out of films while on a special mission for the State Department. She is developing a "new type propaganda campaign." Well, she played enough spy roles in the movies.

Georgetown is also the home of Georgetown University, oldest and largest Catholic school in the country. The broad acres of its beautiful campus were undoubtedly originally responsible for preserving the historic buildings of the community from the onward rush of modernity which swept over the rest of Washington.

But also in Georgetown is the Hideaway Club. It is known in local parlance as a bottle club. A bottle club is a resort which gets around the law which provides that all liquor dispensaries shall close at 2 A.M. Despite a murder at the Hideaway and a recent Congressional investigation of such enterprises and a flurry of activity by the United States Attorney, there are still at least 500 of these unlicensed places, some say more, in the District, a subject which will be covered in detail hereinafter.

The area's favorite gathering place is Martin's Bar on Wisconsin Avenue where New Deal and Fair Deal policy is made. It was the hang-out of Tommy the Cork and Harry Hopkins, who changed the world over bottles while Georgetown students roistered around them.

Georgetown is relatively free of street-walkers who plague every other section. That is because there are no hotels and few transients. But what it lacks in ambulent magdalens is more than made up for by homosexuals of both indeterminate sexes. It seems that nonconformity in politics is often the handmaiden of the same proclivities in sex. Among the thousands known in the capital, a goodly proportion live in the storied ancient dwellings of the area. The fun that goes on in some is beyond words and was even worse when the staffs of the embassies of some of the Iron Curtain countries still found it feasible to travel about in society.

Some Washington policemen will tell you with a shrug of despair of the times the patrol wagons pulled up at particular homes as a result of complaints from neighbors, only to find the prancing participants in the unspeakable parties were Administration untouchables or diplomats sacred from interference.

Which, when you consider that Emmitt Warring also seems to be immune, makes Georgetown seem like a wonderful place to live in—nobody ever gets pinched there.

3. NW COULD MEAN NOWHERE

THE FIRST question asked by members of the new Seventh Congress, after taking the oath in the draughty and unfinished Capitol in 1801, was "where is a saloon with dames?" or the early 19th century equivalent thereof.

The chief usher escorted them to the steps on the Hill, which overlooked what there then was of the young city, a collection of boxes resembling nothing so much as a rude Oklahoma oil-boom town on a rainy day, and pointed northwest. "There," he replied. Ever since that historic moment, anything that matters and much that doesn't is in that part of the city known by its postal address as "NW."

"North West" is the only section of Washington which counts. It is the capital of the capital. NW is the works.

When Major Pierre L'Enfant accepted the commission to plan the capital, he went Caesar's Gaul one better and divided it into four parts. These he laid out like spokes around a wheel, with the hub "The Hill," on which he built the Capitol. He named each section after compounded cardinal points of the compass, NW, SW, NE and SE. The others you can throw into the garbage-can—NW is the city.

Other municipalities have distinctive sectors. In Washington everything, the rialto, marts of commerce, homes of the wealthy, are piled into this one corner, where they rub shoulders with the lowly, the dirty and the wicked, not to overlook Washington's No. 1 problem, the colored.

Washington's Main Drag is F St. if you could call it such. The crossing at 14th Street is its Times Square, its State and Madison—an insult to both. Most of the 1,500,000 who live in the District and environs, plus a half-million tourists, pass it daily.

Here are the movie palaces, but its sole legit theatre is almost a mile away. Its best-known restaurants are around the corner. Any night, Saturday included, the heart of America's heart is dark and quiet.

Washington's Main Stem is somewhat more somnolent than

those of most villages. Don't get us wrong—things do happen after dark. But—those who do them don't want them seen.

When one seeks the reason for the empty dreariness of Washington at night, where trees swaying in the wind often are the only living things, he is told what seems the obvious— Washington is a town of early-to-bedders who do not go in for night life. That is not true. Washington has hundreds of sneak-ins that remain open all night. Your hardy reporters almost collapsed before they could complete this assignment—to visit every place openly or surreptitiously breaking the law. Almost all are in NW, which should have made it easier.

After-dark Washington is the way it is because it has the smalltown mentality. People do their sinning in homes and hotels or in pseudo-private "clubs."

Now let's get on with NW.

Most Congressmen live there. That's a break for all except cab-drivers. Hack rates are regulated by zones. Passengers pay the same fee regardless of where they ride to in a zone, with a surcharge for each extra zone the cab enters. The Congressmen, who make all the District's laws, talked the Public Utilities Commission into gerrymandering the zone map in such a way it ended up allowing them and you and us to go almost anywhere from the Capitol into NW for a minimum fee. No one wants to go elsewhere, so it's a fine deal for all but the cab-jockies.

All the big hotels are in NW. That includes everything from popular-priced tourist fall-ins near the station to the luxury hostelries like the Mayflower, Statler, Carlton and the residential ones in the outskirts, such as the Shoreham and Wardman Park. And the assignation hotels are downtown, smack in the middle of everything, very snug.

Perhaps the most famous hotel is the Willard, at F and 14th Streets. They call it the New Willard now, though the new section was built during Teddy Roosevelt's first administration. For almost a century, VIP's from all over the world stayed here. Julia Ward Howe wrote the "Battle Hymn of the Republic" in one of its rooms. Now its cocktail bar is a hangout for lonesome government girls and other fancy-free women, best time after 5 P.M.

The new and modern Ambassador Hotel is at 14th and K, one of the many holdings of Morris Cafritz, husband of Washington's "first" hostess since the elevation to the Diplo-

matic Corps of Mme. Mesta. The High Hat Cocktail Lounge in
the Ambassador is a gay drinking spot, much patronized by the
lonesome of either sex because of its informality. When we
asked a cab-driver where we could meet a "friend" he directed
us to the Ambassador. We sat there five minutes, not long
enough to attract a waiter's eye. But the eyes of two blonde
things, young and not bad-looking, were quicker. One asked us
to buy her a drink. We did.

Before long we were old friends. They told us they'd spend
the evening with us for $20 each. We said we had to catch a
train. They thought we meant the price was too high and reduced it to $10—"if we had a place to take them."

We returned to the Ambassador half a dozen times, and all
except once we were approached. That time it was too late,
about 1 A.M., and all the volunteers had already booked themselves. We also saw other stags talk to girls with whom they
hadn't come in, but with whom they left.

Another cash-and-carry supermarket is the gracious old Pea-
cock Alley of the Willard Hotel, a broad indoor parade where
once world statesmen sat and sized up famed society beauties.

These hotels are not unique. All of Washington's respectable
inns and cocktail bars are plagued with loose ladies; there's
nothing much can be done about it, because the muddled situation of District law and law enforcement makes it impossible
for the managements to bounce that sort of undesirables—if they
are so regarded. The cops would refuse to eject them for fear
of suits; the hotels and saloon-keepers are subject to the same
liability. We saw hookers, or busy beavers that looked remarkably like them, speak to strangers in the cocktail lounges of the
Statler and Carlton, and we were approached by one in the
former place.

The hotel situation is never static. Comes war or emergency
and the town is always short on rooms. In times of depression
or recession there are too many rooms. When your authors
began their regular trips to the city in search of material for
this book, Washington had not started to take on its Sino-
Korean war dress. We and our money were welcomed with
open arms. We spent lavishly throughout the summer at the
Carlton, a haunt of New Deal and Labor aristocracy, where
John L. Lewis and White House assistant David K. Niles maintain luxurious suites.

As the summer wore on, Washington filled up with hoards

of businessmen, manufacturers' agents, lawyers, fixers and other finaglers. They had unlimited expense accounts. Remembering what happened in Washington during the years of World War II, some leased permanent suites. Others slipped large and welcome tips to room clerks and executives. Then reservations at the Carlton for mere confidential reporters were bitched up. They were unceremoniously moved from room to room, given second-class accommodations, notified they must get out; so better spenders could get in—and our bills had been running to $100 a day.

The Shoreham asked permanent guests to leave. Included were many Congressmen who had been living there for years. Some had voted against rent control in the District. But now they were Displaced Persons.

It was no secret that among the permanents who were in danger of being forced to go house-hunting were several statuesque blondes whose rents were being paid by high officials, diplomats and senators. The swank Shoreham, one of the most beautiful hotels anywhere, has figured prominently in police court and divorce court news more than once.

Washingtonians smile when they wonder if the Shoreham's managing director, Harry Bralove, asked his pretty ex-wife to find other lodgings, too. There was a lot of gossip when she and Bralove were divorced. Once, when unable to meet an overdue $900 alimony bill, he convinced the court he no longer had an interest in the hotel, merely worked for it. Meanwhile he and his former spouse renewed their sentiments, but figured they'd be happier as friends than as man and wife. So the former Mrs. Bralove moved into the Shoreham.

A very pleasant exception to the general rule about kicking the guests around is the Mayflower Hotel, after three decades, still the choice of Washington's smart set. In the wing devoted to private apartments are housed some of the most prominent people in the nation and they haven't been moved to enable the management to snag profiteer revenue.

What there is of show business is in NW. That is little. Yet it was not always so. In the early days Washington was a hell of a show town. There was gaiety then. Long before the streets were paved, dignitaries attended the theatres and dined sumptuously at famed eating spots.

The theatre figures prominently in Washington's history. The martyred Lincoln was slain in Ford's Theatre, now a museum. President Wilson was an incurable vaudeville fan with the real habit, attending the same theatre every week on the same night. He used to slip out of the White House to Keith's, a block away, where the management held a seat in the back row, where he tried to be unobserved. Washington had top vaudeville before the demise of that medium. Today Keith's is a grind movie house. The only thing resembling variety is at Loew's Capitol, where four or five modest acts are sandwiched in between runs of a picture.

Washington's sole remaining legit theatre was the National. Once Washington was a hot road show town. Many New York hits-to-be had their tryouts there. Successes played week stands after leaving Broadway. Washington had minor population but supported many houses. Its residents were avid show-goers. The National gave up the ghost and turned into a movie house because of the race problem. Few Washington theatres permit colored patronage, though Negro theatres allow whites.

The National was restricted against colored attendance in its lease. A couple of years ago, a race-conscious Actor's Equity Association, steamed up by Eleanor Roosevelt and her "we're-all-brothers" group resolved not to permit its members to appear in any theatre in Washington while racial discrimination was enforced. Equity did not issue the same edict against theatres in the rest of the South, all of which are so restricted. The operators of the National were bound by the terms of their lease and could not change their policy. Rather than risk a long, costly fight, they converted the house into a cinema. Meanwhile, for two years, the capital of the world's most literate nation was barren of all living drama.

Within the last few months, the owners of the Gayety Burlesque, on 9th Street, which is Washington's Skid Row, converted it into a legit house. The Gayety had offered pretty low entertainment, because practically anything is permitted. But trade wasn't too good. The cagey operators, not hampered by contractual restrictions, switched. To accent the fact that they were going all out on this new line of race tolerance, they booked as their first attraction a show with a mixed cast, "The Barrier" starring Lawrence Tibbett and Muriel Rahn, who is a Negro. Its theme was miscegenation in the Deep South.

The opening in the old home of burlesque, surrounded by shooting galleries, tattoo artists and cheap sex movies for "adults only," was attended by the top layer of Washington New Deal and left-wing weepers and critics for the Negro press and the *Daily Worker*. The show was panned by the other reviewers. It closed prematurely, after five days. Producer Michael Meyerberg said, "We shouldn't have opened in Washington."

After that, the theatre limped along, sometimes lighted, sometimes dark. The Negroes showed no zeal to patronize it. The whites passed it up. Now the Theatre Guild is sending shows there, subsidized by highbrow subscribers.

Many who want to see good drama go to New York. There's usually a Broadway hit playing in Baltimore.

During the summer, attempts are made to present road shows of New York companies on The Water Barge, in the Potomac, and in some neighborhood playhouses. Regardless of the success of some individual play, Washington can be written off as a theatre town.

Despite all the hardships, there are always optimists, especially when they can get their names in the papers. One of these is Congressman Klein, of New York, a screaming New Dealer, who represents one of Gotham's most poverty-stricken neighborhoods. Klein is trying to get the government to spend $5,000,000 for a national theatre. Naturally it is to be named the Franklin D. Roosevelt Memorial Theatre. Some of his constituents need shoes, but F.D.R. needs another monument. His bill forbids barring any person from appearing in it or attending it because of race, creed, color, religion or national origin. It would be conducted by the Secretary of the Interior, who at this writing is that well-known showman, Oscar L. Chapman, of Denver, Colorado, who is a co-founder of the Spanish-American League to Combat Exploitation of Mexican Workers in the United States, an arty cause, no doubt.

For most of the area's 1,500,000 permanents and 500,000 transients, movies offer the big night out. How much longer, in the face of TV competition, remains to be seen. At the present time, attendance runs 100,000 a day. Most film houses in white neighborhoods are restricted to whites. Negroes have their own. One of the most famous is the Howard, in the NW colored section, which often augments its shows with top-flight Negro stage shows. At such times the place is apt to draw more white customers than black. Washington has its hep-cats. Many of the younger social and diplomatic sets get a bang out of hot licks. These people who willingly sit next to dark folks in the

Howard refuse to permit them in their own theatres or restaurants. That's typical Washington thinking.

The high-class shopping street—the Fifth Avenue—is Connecticut Avenue, running from Lafayette Square, past the
Mayflower Hotel, and out into Cleveland Park, past residential
hotels and swank apartments.

There are plenty of first-grade shops here, with chic imports,
expensive antiques and other gewgaws to lure the feminine
dollar. Despite the great wealth of the District and the presence
of an international set, all is not pheasant for these merchants.
New York and the magnet of its style-conscious stores is too
near. Even Baltimore gets some of the trade which can't find
enough smart things at home. But a curious reverse process has
been taking place in recent years. Whereas many Washingtonians travel to New York to shop and to dine, a couple of
Washington's best-known institutions have been reaching out
and taking over some of the same places in New York which
Washingtonians travel 225 miles to patronize.

Garfinckel's is Washington's high-fashion department store.
A couple of years ago, its proprietors bought out the ancient
and aristocratic New York men's furnishing house, Brooks
Brothers. Within a few months, the Garfinckel octopus reached
out and gobbled up one of New York's oldest and best-known
Fifth Avenue stores, de Pinna.

While this was going on, a couple of smart Swedes, who had
made a tremendous success at Olmsted's Restaurant, a popular
eatery with fine food in the NW business section, bought New
York's oldest and most famous restaurant, Luchow's, on 14th
Street, one of the last places left in the country where dining
is still a fine art.

Reference to the appendix will show many other Washington eating places, some good, some bad and not all recommended, but most of them are in NW.

One of the best-known and best is Harvey's, on Connecticut
Avenue, near the Mayflower. This is J. Edgar Hoover's nightly
eating place when he is in Washington. Like most Washington
restaurants, Harvey's has been in business long. It specializes in
sea food. The room does a sell-out business and it's almost impossible to get a table at the height of the dining hour. Service
by ancient Negro waiters is slow. Best time to eat is after 9,
because most Washingtonians dine early; 6 o'clock is the stand-

ard time. Many start at 5. Those are the homely habits. Some restaurants close at 8, and a few at 7.

Julius Lully, who owns Harvey's, is the butt of J. Edgar's robust sense of humor. Once Hoover had a batch of wanted-fugitive-identification "fliers" made up showing Lully in his World War I private's uniform. He had them nailed up on posts for miles around Lully's country place. When the hick sheriff locked up the restaurateur, who sputtered and gave Hoover as a reference, J. Edgar said he had never heard of him.

On another occasion Hoover sent a letter, purporting to be from Oscar of the Waldorf, threatening to sue Harvey's for appropriating his salad dressing. Lully hired a lawyer and told him to offer the Waldorf $2,500, but J. Edgar advised him it wouldn't be enough.

The Occidental is hoary with age and legend. Pictures of presidents, cabinet officers and generals cover the walls. This was our favorite, but the Occidental has succumbed to the new boom. An officious head waiter, with a typical Prussian attitude toward customers, lined us up like prisoners of war, then heaped contemptuous abuse when we dared question his excellency about the possible chances of being seated and served. Washingtonians take it. They are used to being kicked around. Senators or cabinet officers they may be, but at heart most are grass-rooters overawed by the big city. We didn't take it. We walked out. We are used to consideration and hospitality, spoiled by the good manners of heartless Manhattan.

When Major L'Enfant plotted the city, he provided that the streets should run in three directions, north and south, east and west, and diagonal. Where the diagonal avenues, which are named after states, cross the rectangular streets, generally numbered or alphabetically lettered, there are wide circles or broad squares. One of those is Lafayette Park, known to all Americans because it is the square in front of the White House. Here, less than a hundred yards from the President's front door, is one of the most sordid spots in the world. At night, under the heroic equestrian statue of Andrew Jackson and in the shadow of the foliage of overhanging trees, there is a constant and continuous soprano symphony of homosexual twittering.

The President knows about it; he reads the papers. The police superintendent knows about it. Congress, which governs the District, knows about it. Recently, the secretary of a Senator was arrested there, charged with indescribable misbehavior. He was acquitted by a jury. There are few convictions.

Lafayette Park is one of the showplaces of NW. Another is Thomas Circle. Years ago, the circle and all the streets leading into it were lined with mansions. Now you can pull up in your car in front of a newsdealer there, at any hour, day or night, and place a bet on a horse, buy a deck of junk or get a girl—$10 asking price, $5 if you put up a struggle.

Another NW cynosure was Dupont Circle. It was social. There were the homes of such as Princess Eleanor Patterson. Now they've been razed or cut up because of taxes, death benefits, estate distributions and the high cost of maintenance. Those that still stand have been turned into embassies, headquarters of national organizations, and rooming-houses in between. One triangular corner was torn down to make way for the Dupont Plaza, a glassy and glossy apartment hotel, swell for lobbyists, flashy girls and 5-percenters. What happened to Dupont Circle hit all the way out the length of 16th Street, which runs off from the White House, and Massachusetts Avenue. These two long, broad avenues run through all NW. They are the "Ambassadors' Rows."

Of the sixty embassies, legations and chancelleries, almost all are on one or the other. Both have a liberal sprinkling of organization headquarters, such as unions, trade associations and eleemosynary institutions, with the ever-present furnished-room coops and apartment hotels.

The complexion of NW is changing, growing darker. The area always had a large Negro section. There are no racial zoning laws. Restrictive covenants cannot be enforced. There are no longer any racial boundary lines and some people think that is dandy. They have been in the driver's seat since 1933.

You will find colored people living within a half a block of an embassy or around the corner from a new luxury apartment house. There is no reason why this should not be so, but the property-owners and the white residents do not agree. As the process continues, NW grows less swank and less desirable, while many of its rich residents move into Maryland suburbs such as Chevy Chase and across the river into Virginia.

The Negroes and other specific phenomena of NW will be considered in specialized chapters.

4. NOT-SO-TENDER TENDERLOIN

THE DISTRICT'S "red-light" region may be the largest on earth. That is because almost all of it is such, neither restricted by law, custom nor local habit to a particular part of town. But, more than any other, NW is the Tenderloin, in some ways more blatantly open than ever was New York's infamous Satan's Circus or Chicago's 22nd Street.

Of all places, you would think Washington would be the last location a practical, professional prostitute would pick to pitch her camp. With so many more women than men, so many dames lonesome and far from home, on the eager upbeat for a meal, a drink or even a kind word, you'd figure mathematically, psychologically and pathologically that this would be a ghost town for the trollops.

Part of such traffic is always supported by tourists and strays. Washington has a large and constant visitation of these, but many other places have more and have virtually expunged street-walkers and entirely eradicated the sweatshops where such operators do homework. Yet in Washington they flourish, though they are supposedly verboten, and the Weary Winnies parade the pavements. It made a couple of graying Chicago boys homesick for their childhood.

Lorelles—as the Parisians call them—are in the Washington tradition, claim the capital by long-established squatters' rights, almost by right of discovery.

The same stagecoaches which carried the first Congressmen to Washington 150 years ago brought also the first whores. They and their descendants have been here ever since, an integral, important segment of the population.

For the first 113 years they were protected by law. Segregation in the District was expunged by act of Congress in 1913, in the first year of the presidency of the school-teacher from Princeton.

In the early days of the Republic, whoring flourished as an essential and honorable trade. Transportation facilities were so primitive, many Congressmen and officials from backwoods sections had trouble getting to Washington themselves and would have found it impossible to transport their women. Trollops became an adjunct to legislation. Without them, it is doubtful whether a quorum could have been maintained for transaction of public business, which might not have been a bad idea sometimes.

The last compound of the trade was in what is now the Federal Triangle, between Pennsylvania Avenue and the Mall, from 10th to 15th Streets. The Willard Hotel, the Treasury and the White House are nearby—which made it convenient for all concerned.

In the Civil War, General Joe Hooker's division was encamped in Washington to protect the President. It was bivouacked in what later became the official restricted district. One story, accounting for the term "hooker," now world-wide, ascribes its origin to the habitat of local prostitutes, who gathered near the camp to pick up soldiers and remained after the soldiers left. When local blades went out for a night of hell-raising they said, "Let's go over to Hooker's."

Another version ascribes the origin of the word to the Hook, in Baltimore, the town's sailor section, where tarts picked up sea-faring men.

In the absence of a determination by H. L. Mencken, we will remain neutral as to the competing claims of the two neighboring cities, except to say that the residents of either ought to know what they're talking about, because there are so many hookers in both.

Leaving out all occasionals in Washington who do it for fun or because of temporary monetary embarrassment, and counting only pros—those who have no other form of livelihood, some say there are at least ten thousand floozies actively in full-time business at this moment. We were solicited by half that number.

Most of these girls work as loners on the streets or in the cocktail lounges and bring their earnings back to their pimps. Some function through call services, via a headquarters phone-number, a cocktail lounge bartender, or a switchboard operator in a cheap hotel.

Many are tough and predatory. A 20-year old youth was stabbed and slashed after he turned down a street-corner proposition at Third and E. He fled when the woman drew a knife, but two colored men caught up to him and gave him the business.

Until recently, Washington was loaded with whore-houses,

was in fact the last large city where this ancient and storied institution existed.

That's because it was necessary to take care of the transients and the male government employes and officials away from their wives. The war and the post-war housing shortage virtually put the final kibosh on such dives here as it had done a few years earlier in other towns. Property became so valuable, landlords could do better by running it legitimately.

We spoke to a police captain who told us that obstacles were no longer placed in the way of the vice squad when it came to raiding these premises; but it is impossible to keep the girls off the streets and out of the hotel lobbies and cocktail lounges where they had transferred their business addresses.

Under the law of Washington, as well as all other municipalities, vice-squad detectives are forbidden to partake personally of forbidden wares while on raids. If they do, they have no case, for a prosecution then becomes "entrapment" and they are agents provocateurs.

During a recent raid, an operational plan was drawn up in advance. One of the cops, the handsomest, made the pick-up, and his confederates were supposed to crash in five minutes after he entered the room, which would give both time to disrobe, and that is enough evidence to make a collar.

But the raiders were late. The honest, hardworking cop went through the motions of undressing. Finally he had to get in bed with the wench; 15, 20, 30 minutes passed, and still no raiding party. He couldn't stall her off any more.

By the time the doors were busted in, the evidence was null and void.

The figures in this chapter refer solely to white tarts. The black sisters are mentioned in another one.

Health records indicate that 50 percent of Washington's white street-walkers are infected with venereal disease. With the colored ones, it goes up to 99 percent.

Many of the white women who solicit on the streets are young; it takes some time for these girls, fresh off the farms, to get the nerve to hustle in high-class hotels. Police have arrested girls 14, 15 and 16 hawking their bodies on the public highways. Many of these children, who should be home doing their schoolwork, left the hills when they were 12, after first having been raped by a local lout, usually a relative.

This story is not apocryphal. A very young street-walker was formally charged by the arresting officer with "practicing prostitution."

"That's not so, your honor," she piped up. "I don't practice any more. I know how now."

The going rate for whores, the pick-up kind, is $20 and down. Pretty fair ones will take $10, and many will come along for $5. These prices are low compared with the current tariffs in other large cities, the reason being the extraordinary amateur competition.

Many of the girls roll their customers, mugg them or use knockout drops and then go through their pockets. But Washington's prostitutes are not so hard-hearted as the street sirens in New York, where it is commonplace for one to be taken to a hotel-room and wake up doped and robbed, but never loved.

Many Washington nymphs conscientiously give value received.

In other cities the cops take stern measures against the untrustworthy whores. It is considered the lowest form of larceny to take advantage of a man with his pants down. New York police recently sent a young married woman to the penitentiary for five years for just such an outrage, but in Washington the appointed judges, many unrealistic and some downright dishonest, condone and encourage such unethical practices.

David L. Miller, 43, a resident of the Soldiers' Home, picked up Alma Lee Dugent and took her to a 16th Street, NW, room. He said the 33-year-old woman robbed him of $2 in bills and a $30 wrist watch while he lay asleep. The woman pleaded guilty of petty theft.

"This man is as guilty as the woman," thundered the judge. He ordered Miller to pay half of Mrs. Dugent's $25 fine.

At this writing there are few really big madames operating in Washington. One of the last big operators was Carmen Beach, deported to Spain. But Nancy Pressler, who figured prominently in the conviction of Charles "Lucky" Luciano, international Mafia overlord now in Italy, when she turned state's evidence against him in New York, is in business in the capital.

Though many of the girls work as independent contractors, except for the inevitable pimp, they are loosely organized for emergency purposes in the event of arrest, through bail-bond brokers and lawyers who specialize in underworld cases. The law staff of Charles Ford is frequently in court defending intercepted prostitutes, who usually get off with a small fine or a warning.

Many singed doves get their weekly check-ups from a physician in the 1700 block of K Street, who charges them $5 a visit. They learn about him through their community of interests.

We have studied commercial vice in most large cities. It is as a rule confined by public tolerance to certain streets or sections. When we wrote about New York and Chicago we were able to name these thoroughfares and state exactly what kind of merchandise was for sale in each. That is not so in Washington, where the city seems to be one huge red-light range, with tramps falling over themselves trying to grab unattached men.

We made a contact on the southeast corner of 14th and New York Avenue, NW, in front of the cigar store, with a young pedestrian who told us her name was Sue. She came originally from Florida and had been hustling in Washington for four years. We asked how to get in touch with her again and she said, "Just call the Astoria Hotel and ask the operator for Sue." When we inquired her last name she said she was the only Sue there. The Astoria is a cheap hotel on 14th Street.

About two weeks later we were walking through the plush lobby of the new Statler Hotel and saw Sue ensconced in one of the comfortable armchairs. We stopped to watch. The slender blonde leaned over to a gent in another chair and asked for a light. In a couple of minutes they struck up a deal and walked into the elevator together. When she came down half an hour later we asked her how much she got.

"Ten bucks," she exclaimed, "and the tight-wad stiffed me out of luck money."

When we first came to Washington to work on this book almost everyone we spoke to, except cops who knew better, said we wouldn't find any professional whores, because why should anyone pay when so many government girls are easy?

We took some of these friends—government officials, members of Congress, newspapermen and others, on our tours. And this is what we showed them:

We were solicited by two girls at Jack's Grill, 3rd and G Sts. Three broads came up to us at 4th and G NW and asked us if we wanted company. We also saw girls bracing strange men at the Purity Lunch and Grill, 3rd and G NW, and at Mitchell Grill on the same corner. Mitchell's is the hangout for precinct cops who saved its license after charges.

A white prostitute tried to date us at the Mai Fong restaurant, in Chinatown, and two other girls spoke to us at the China Clipper on 14th.

We could have made pick-ups—$10 asked, $5 bid—at the corner of 14th and R. We were approached by girls at the Casablanca Tavern, 421 11th St., NW, and the Covered Wagon, 14th and Rhode Island. The manager of an all-night diner back of the Statler offered to get us a bed companion for $15 if we bought a bottle of Seagrams for $8.50—cheap when you consider it was after hours and he didn't have a license.

Few if any restaurants and bars employ B-girls. These are women who in Chicago circulate from table to table and hustle drinks on commission. They are illegal in the District, though quite common in Maryland, near the border and in Baltimore.

The femmes fatale who frequent Washington joints usually do so in free-handed reciprocity. The management steers lonesome men to the gals who hang around regularly. They, in turn, bring their customers in for drinks or tell them that's where they can find them. A saloon which gets a reputation as the hangout for the best-looking dames finds its gross up.

When a girl closes a pitch, she usually has a place to take the guy, if he can't or won't bring her to his own room. Most Washington hotels, including the largest, are very broadminded about this, and if you don't make noise they don't make trouble. But this situation is changing as the hotels are getting more crowded and more independent.

Few small hotels, even if so inclined, properly police their guests. Some of the girls take their clients to the New Colonial and the Fox.

A former madame named Jackie is now running a rooming-house at 703 Mt. Vernon, where some of the girls steer their customers. You can usually find seven or eight girls hanging around Ivy House Inn, on New York Avenue.

Among the most active hookers are Kay Saunders and Peggy Proctor, both 29, who were once arrested while entertaining 15 male customers. At this writing they are still in business on the second floor of a house in the 2300 block, Lincoln Road, NE.

One of Washington's most famous characters is a toothless old hag known only as Diane. She hangs around 14th and Florida. Diane reminds old New Yorkers of the fabulous

Broadway Rose, who used to panhandle in front of Lindy's until she was carted to the bug house.

But, unlike Rose, Diane is an out-and-out hustler. Once upon a time, they say, she was a good-looker. But her main trouble seemed to be that she liked her work too much to commercialize it.

We spoke to a man in his late 30's who remembered her when he was a school boy. He said the kids used to pick her up because she would take "small change." Now some of her old customers, matured and prosperous men of the world, occasionally drive by her corner to stake her to a hand-out.

All she can get now are colored men, "winos" and dregs. But she refuses to retire.

We picked up a girl by the name of Doris who had just been discharged from the Federal Hospital for narcotic addicts in Lexington, Kentucky. The story she told us illustrates how girls are recruited for prostitution in the District.

Doris said she lived in a small town in West Virginia. She and a girl high-school mate occasionally did a little free-lance whoring on Saturday nights, on call of a bell-boy in the local hotel. Once he sent them to a room occupied by two men. One, whose name was Grigsby, tried to sell the girls on coming to Washington. He said he'd put them in a swell house. The teen-agers were afraid of the big city. Grigsby told them the landlady of the house was in the next room and called her in. She was a motherly sort. They consented to come with her.

They found themselves in the house of a madame named Billie Cooper, on 7th St., in the 1000 block. Doris told us she was an instantaneous success in the Cooper menage. She was only 17, fresh, buxom and bucolic. Madame Cooper's clients were charmed. After she'd been in the house a few weeks, the madame asked Doris if she'd like to get a "kick." She produced a hypodermic needle and gave the child a shot in the arm. Doris liked the sensation, wanted more. This went on for several weeks, Doris said, and every day Billie Cooper increased the frequency of the shots.

One day Doris woke up, nauseated and ill.

Billie Cooper exclaimed, "You're hooked!"

She informed Doris she had become a dope fiend, that henceforth Doris must pay for the shots.

The girl went into debt, though she was taking in up to $50 a day and, no matter how much she made, the dope always cost more. She knew no one else who sold it. She was truly hooked, which was Billie Cooper's original purpose, to keep the young girl in her joint and take her money away from her.

Billie Cooper's clientele was mostly Chinese. When U. S. narcotics agents raided her establishment at 5 A.M., gaining entrance with a ladder borrowed from a fire-house, so two T-men would get into Billie's bedroom before she had a chance to flush the narcotics down the drain, they found several Chinese customers in the place. While the search was still on, 15 more came to the door and were admitted; of these two were officials of the Chinese embassy.

In the trial it developed that Billie Cooper, who was sentenced for violation of the narcotics laws, was charging Doris $7 a deck for heroin, which she bought at half that price from Chinese peddlers. The F.B.I. proceeded against Grigsby for white slavery violation and he, too, was convicted.

Doris swore to us that she was off the stuff now. She said she was living with a Chinaman who worked in a gambling house in Chinatown.

The glamorous brothels are no more. Not since the notorious Hopkins Institute was closed by the F.B.I. some years ago has there been anything operating on a lavish scale. Now there are some so-called masseurs who use that classification as a blind, but nothing on the grand scale.

When F.B.I. men raided the Hopkins Institute, an innocuous-looking massage parlor in the 2700 block on Connecticut Ave., they uncovered one of the most sensational call-houses ever in Washington. Not only was the clientele accommodated at the so-called Institute, but a phone call could arrange a date on short notice almost anywhere in the District. The establishment kept a detailed and up-to-date written record on each patron, fees paid, dates of service, and eccentricities. Girls there said this list contained entries that could flabbergast some very prominent persons, in and out of Washington.

The proprietor of the Hopkins Institute was one George Francis Whitehead, who lived in New York and seldom visited the place. Profits were sent to him weekly by the "resident manager," Diane Carter, who was vice-president in charge of the operation. The Institute was established originally by someone else and was bought by Whitehead in 1941. He ran it for several months, then engaged Diane Carter to manage it at a salary out of earnings. Her principal duties entailed accepting calls, arranging to send girls to answer the calls, and to have girls available on the premises.

Whitehead left Washington in 1941, after the girls began to complain that his presence was hurting business because of his excessive drinking, untidy habits and uncouth deportment. He did not live up to the dignity and spirit of an Institute. The girls threatened to strike.

The record system was originated by the first operator and passed on to Whitehead. In addition to other entries, initials of each girl filling an assignment and the amount of the fee were noted. For the fees a code was used, to conceal the fact that some paid more than others. The word "FITZGERALD" was the key to the code. Each letter stood for a digit, i.e., F was 1, I was 2, T was 3, etc. Thus the symbol "FD" beside the name of a customer meant $10; "TD" meant $30, etc. This method was used also to bamboozle Whitehead, if he checked on his share of the proceeds.

The U.S. Commissioner issued warrants for the arrests of Whitehead, Diane Carter and 13 girls involved, on charges of violations of the White Slave Traffic Act. Whitehead was arrested in New York and extradited. Two indictments were returned against Whitehead, Diane and nine others. Whitehead pleaded guilty to both and was sentenced to one to four years on the Act and to eighteen months on conspiracy. But he was adjudged insane and committed to a mental institution.

Diane Carter pleaded guilty to both indictments and was sentenced to three to nine months on each, the sentences to run concurrently. Seven other defendants were found guilty.

The Circuit Court of Appeals reversed the convictions of the seven, held the violations were of legislation of the District of Columbia and not of the White Slave Traffic Act.

But the racket was broken. The place never reopened. The F.B.I. seized the files and never revealed a name, but hundreds of men still tremble when they remember the Hopkins Institute. Some still attempt pressure to try to get their names blacked out. They have no success with the F.B.I.

5. HOBOES WITH NO HORIZON

THE PRIDE of the bum, even when he has abandoned the virile vitality to hold out his paw as a panhandler, is a terminal twinkle of consciousness that he is only resting between Election Days, when he is a man. These derelicts have swung cities and states. But in Washington even that last link to a reason for being is lost.

No Hinky Dink, no Pendergast caters to him, gives him free beer and rot-gut or a kip in the flop on the joint. No eager dirty duke stretches forth to greet the floater and the repeater. He can do nothing for anyone.

So he is just a shade lower, lousier and grizzlier than the ones at whom you shudder as you pass them in your own town. Agglomerations of beachcombers vary little, even with differences of climate. Every city has its Skid Row. But Washington has three of them. Like everything else here, they are departmentalized. No alphabetical designations have yet been allocated to them, but don't despair.

One is for the general riffraff; the second is for old-timers; the third is exclusively for sailors.

But first let us tell you about 9th Street—NW, natch—and specifically where it crosses Pennsylvania Ave.

Stand on one side of the avenue and you are in the shadow of the great marble structure which houses the forces of law and order. This is the Department of Justice Building, and the corner we're standing on is the entrance to the F.B.I.

Cross Pennsylvania Avenue and walk into 9th Street, and you are an intruder in the most publicized Skid Row of the three—they call it the Bowery here, to distinguish it from the others. As such thoroughfares go, this is pretty classy-looking. It is wide. All Washington streets are kept clean, so neither rubbish nor drunks litter the pavements—anyway not by day. By nightfall, topers rendered hors de combat on smoke and cheap wine pile up in the doorways.

This part of 9th Street is packed solid with "play lands," featuring pin-ball machines, peep show movies and souvenir stands which sell composition statuettes of the White House and Washington Monument, and embroidered pillows tastefully lettered with "Love to Mom from the Nation's Capital."

But this human dump lacks romance and legend. No songs are written about it. There are no grisly tall tales, such as are told about the Barbary Coast, Basin Street and Chicago, much near the Loop and most of the old Levee. This is merely a street of convenience, moved up from around the corner when Pennsylvania Avenue itself was flophouse lane and Al Jolson and Bill Robinson performed on the sidewalk for pennies.

There's no law agin' stripping or peeling in Washington, but it doesn't pay off well enough to build a permanent industry around it. The old Gayety Theatre, which ran pretty high-class traveling burleycue, is now, probably only temporarily, a legit house. Meanwhile, the burlesque fans buy their titillation in the cheap movie houses adjoining the Gayety. Sometimes they amplify their celluloid bills with "living dolls," at other times the customers have to get their kicks out of sex movies advertised "For Adults Only." An ad before us, of the Leader Theatre, says, "Burlesque's brightest stars on screen." The day's program provided snake-charming Zorita in "I Married a Savage"; body-peeling Ann Corio in "Call of the Jungle"; and Maggie Hart, the stripper, in "Lure of the Isles," plus "two more thrills."

In and in front of cheap saloons, cocktail lounges and lunch rooms, are tarts, reefer-peddlers and novelty salesmen whose chief stock in trade is "sanitary rubber goods." Pistols are on sale at $20. The local law isn't tough on gun-toters.

Though Washington's legal liquor closing on week-days is 2 A.M., this street, like all in the city, is deserted early. Long before midnight its habitués have already made sleeping arrangements or are snoring in the alleys, cheap overnight lodgings or hallways, paralyzed by alky or cheap domestic red wine.

Crossing 9th Street here, is D Street, known as Pawnbroker's Row. But get this—hockshops are against the law.

When you see a shop with a sign reading "Pawnbroker's Exchange," don't believe it. The window looks like any "Uncle's" anywhere in the world, with a profusion of new and used articles ranging from mink coats to tin watches. But that's the build-up. These exchanges are only second-hand stores which buy and sell uncalled for articles pledged in other jurisdictions, where the three balls of the De Medicis are legal.

The temporarily embarrassed visitor, in need of cash quickly, often gets rooked in one of these pseudo-hock shops. Take the case of the stranger who runs short of petty cash until he can wire home. Suppose he has a $200 watch which he wants to put up for security. Needing only perhaps $25, that's all he asks for, figuring when he redeems it in a few days he will pay only that, plus accrued interest. Yet when he asks the pawnbroker's exchange man for $25, he is actually selling the $200 watch for that.

Some of the more legitimate shops get around the law by guaranteeing to sell the article back to the owner at a specified rate after a specified number of days. What usually happens to the unsophisticated is that they have lost their security for a fraction of its value, because it has already been sold.

Little effort is made to police the Bowery stretches of 9th St. The armed forces maintain a few MPs, but practically anything goes, short of mayhem, and even that is not uncommon.

The tomatoes who solicit the young and lonesome men in uniform in this neighborhood are pretty low. The five bucks they ask, plus three dollars for a room in a handy flea-bag, should be reported to the Better Business Bureau, considering the quality of the merchandise and the strong possibilities of picking up souvenirs of the sort they don't display on counters.

Interspersed between the shooting galleries, theatres and hamburger hideaways are the usual bargain men's clothing stores, army and navy outfitters, etc. One of the clothing stores, visible from the windows of the Department of Justice, was built by money inherited from a gangster who isn't around to enjoy it, due to a sit-down strike in an electric chair.

This street is a little too fast, flighty and noisy for the old-time bums and stiffs. It is for younger men. The perennials, who know every flop-house and smoke-joint in the country, and travel from town to town with the seasons and the harvests, prefer the Skid Row at 3rd and G Streets, NW and vicinity, around the corner from Chinatown. Come to think of it, Skid Rows all over the continent are around the corner from Chinatown.

We call this Mission Row, because it's where the mission stiffs hang out. These are the hoboes, bums and tramps who get their morning's coffee and their night's sleep on the benches of a gospel shop nearby on H Street, in return for listening to a "Come to the Lord" sermon. Mission Row is the best-looking

Skid Row in the country. The streets are broad, with grass and trees, and most of the set-back buildings are reconverted residences with stoops and a surviving air of charm. We have been assured it is refreshing to wake up in the gutter here with a smoke hangover.

You find no brassy newcomers in these quarters. Young tramps abhor missions. They prefer 9th Street, with its zip and excitement. The mission stiff, almost an extinct species, is on in years and no longer troubled by dames. His animal needs are taken care of by a bowl of soup and as much red-eye as he can drink. If only one of the two is available, the former can be dispensed with. Some of these mission-moochers are junkies. But dope, like everything else, is suffering from inflation, and the wherewithal is forbidding.

The Greek colony, large for the size of the town, runs into this Bowery. Many Hellenes are gamblers. Hecht's Hotel, at 6th and G, where girls take their men, was owned by a Greek arrested last month in New York on narcotics charges. The Hellenic Social Club, next door, is a gambling house.

There's one Skid Row no visitors and few Washingtonians ever see. That's Sailors' Row. Unlike the other two, which are in NW, this is in SE—8th Street, down near the Navy Yard. After Chicago we thought nothing could make us blink. But some of the dives on 8th Street made it. At the northern approach of this stretch of howling hell are a couple of Filipino joints where bus-boys, house-boys and valets pick up white whores. Eighth Street runs into Sailors' Row proper, a line of groggeries and lunch-rooms that hit bottom.

The undermanned Washington cops can do little to keep it orderly. The Navy's shore patrol takes over most of the policing. We saw Navy paddy-wagons in front of Guy's, the Ship's Cafe and the Penguin. But the SP's seldom make a pinch unless there are fights. We visited four or five of the bars—not alone, because hereabouts, even in the shadow of the Capitol's dome, outsiders who travel in parties of less than four are crazy.

We saw hustlers working in the Band Box, the Ship's Cafe, Guy's and the Penguin. These were the frowsiest broads we have ever seen, dilapidated, toothless, drunk, swinging the shabby badge of their shoddy trade, long-looped handbags.

The worst and the cheapest were in the Ship's Cafe, where two girls—call them that in charity—offered themselves to us at $3. The going price in the other places was $5. They circulated along the bar and from booth to booth and from table to table. They do not work in these saloons as B girls or house prostitutes. They use them as points of contact with their trade, apparently with connivance of the management for the business they bring in. In these Sailors' Row joints we saw many amateurs, typical sailor-crazy bobby-soxers, servant girls and Victory girls. These may ask for money but can be talked out of it. There are many cheap hotels and rooming-houses close by. But the dark streets or alleys are free and busy.

6. GREEN PASTURES

*A*GONIZED ORATORY through the decades has been banging against the walls of the Capitol, demanding that Washingtonians be given the precious privilege of the vote. It is as futile as spitting against the wind.

And we will tell you why there will be no vote—Confidential.

If Washington got home rule, its first mayor would be a gentleman affectionately known to his constituency as Puddin' Head Jones. And Mr. Jones is a Negro.

We will tell you what no one else has dared to publish—there are more Negroes than whites in Washington. We will prove it by incontrovertible figures.

There is an amazing underground proclivity in all big cities, south, north and everywhere, to fake the facts on Negro population. For some distorted reason, both races conspire in this foolish flummery.

Census figures are off the beam. They always lag in summing up minority races. Most of the migrant census-takers assume that they should help to make the picture as light as possible. If a Negro is not unmistakably black, he is encouraged, if he does not think of it himself, to be listed as a Cuban, a Puerto Rican, a West Indian, a South American, Filipino, Indian, Mexican or even Eskimo; the blood of all these is sprinkled through many generations of admixture.

There is no way of calculating how many light-skinned citizens can and do "pass." Some Negroes sleep in shifts in crowded premises, so that a count in the regular course would register

about one-third of the true total. Many are house servants and
these do not go into the tally where they are employed, nor are
they home during the hours when enumerators call.

More Negroes than whites are police characters, as will be
demonstrated. And as a rule members of the race are wary and
suspicious of questioners from "the law." Many census-takers
deliberately duck more than superficial duties in predominantly dark districts, because they are confused and afraid after
getting hostile receptions and responses.

But in Washington there is one indisputable check.

The District of Columbia has a single Jim Crow law, segre-
gating Negroes and whites—in schools. When pupils are en-
rolled they must reveal their true race. There can be no tam-
pering with these statistics.

And in the winter of 1950–51 there were registered the following in all public schools through all grades from elementary
to teachers' college:

Negroes, 47,807; whites, 46,080.

Broken down, these figures are even more definitive. There
are more Negroes than is evidenced by the bare totals. Negroes,
because of their economic outlook, do not keep their children
in school as long as do whites. That is sharply proven by the
enrollment in the senior high schools:

Negroes, 4,787; whites, 7,176.

But there are 10,146 colored children in junior high schools
compared to 9,270 whites.

The attendance at parochial and private schools is minor.
Washington has the largest per capita Negro Catholic population in the United States.

Even an excess of 10 per cent of whites in the grand total and
allowing for unmarried government workers would still indicate
a Negro majority over all, because of the earlier departure from
school of Negro children, as shown above.

This reveals a startling metamorphosis in a ten-year period.
In 1940 the school record showed 66,000 whites and 36,000
Negroes. Thus there has since been a decline of 20,000 white
children and a rise of 12,000 Negro children. The over-all decline is due to removal of white families to suburbs.

Negroes lived in Washington before the first President chose
the rolling land along the Potomac to bear his name. Slavery was
legal in the capital until the emancipation. The population of
Washington about doubled between 1860 and 1870. Much of

this influx represented slaves who escaped from plantations and got through the Union lines during the Civil War. But the big swell came when thousands of ex-slaves, free and foot-loose for the first time in their lives, left the destroyed and deserted Dixie farms and headed for Washington, which was not only near Virginia and Maryland and the Carolinas, but which exercised a fascination for them because they felt safer near their savior and their demigod, Abraham Lincoln.

Until the middle 70's, Washingtonians of all colors had home rule, elected their own officials under a territorial form of government similar to that now practiced in Alaska and Hawaii, where mayors, legislators, judges and other lower-level officials are elected. They sent a delegate to Congress.

Long before LaGuardia, Marcantonio, Ed Flynn and Ed Kelly found the formula of organizing Negroes into blocs which could be voted en masse to perpetuate control of left-wing and criminal political groups, that was old stuff in D.C., where it was invented by one "Boss" Shepherd in Washington, the first large city in the country where Negroes were allowed to vote, and where there were enough of them to throw any weight as citizens.

Washington had been a sewer of iniquity during the Civil War; when Shepherd took over control it turned infinitely worse. The stench asphyxiated the members of Congress, who were exposed to it so intimately, and they exercised a forgotten constitutional prerogative, "to exclusively govern the District." The polling booths made swell bonfires.

As will be seen, however, under the unique voteless system, the Negroes now exercise far more power, and Puddin' Head Jones is by common consent the "mayor" of Washington's Black Belt. As we progress you will be let in on how that could come about.

Despite the high enrollment of Negro children in public schools where they enjoy facilities for education equal to white children, Negroes continue to have an illiteracy far above the full population. In 1942, illiteracy in the District was only 1 percent for all races, whereas the Negro group showed 4 percent. Weighing these figures against the proportions of population in 1942 would seem to indicate that the Negroes were about 15 times as illiterate as whites.

Much later figures are available, however. Only 4 percent of Washington's white youths who took the Army's mental tests in

1950 failed, but nearly 29 percent of the prospective colored recruits were turned back.

New York's Harlem is self-contained. Though Chicago's Bronzeville has gone over its borders and set up tributary colonies in other sections of the city, it is still the center of Negro life there and contains most of its colored population.

But Washington's Black Belt is no belt at all. It is sprawled all over, infiltrating every mile and almost every block in sections which for 150 years were lily white.

In New York, when you refer to Harlem, everyone knows what part of town you're talking about. Similarly, Bronzeville and Central Avenue have definite meanings in Chicago and Los Angeles. In Washington, you have no way of indicating Darktown, because the Negro section has no generic name and it isn't a section. It is all of Washington.

What is occurring in Washington is happening on a lesser scale in large northern population centers, except probably Manhattan, where Harlem is geographically restrained by Columbia University and Central Park, though Puerto Ricans are generously overflowing its borders on both sides.

In Chicago, instead of being bound in black ghettos, Negroes have preempted many sections, including former residences of millionaires. They live along wide and vernal boulevards in once splendid apartments and luxurious private homes with greeneries, and in palaces of packers and pioneer pirates.

This process is being repeated in Los Angeles, San Francisco, Detroit and especially Philadelphia.

The South, with its restrictive practices against Negroes and its underpayment of them, is gradually being denuded of its cheap labor, which is drawn North.

The recent census showed the population of most metropolitan cities remained stable. But their suburbs, beyond city limits, increased in many from 50 to 100 percent or more. This growth of Suburbia was made by whites who left as Negroes came. That kept city populations in status quo.

The words used to paint the picture in Chicago may be repeated in Washington, but with emphasis and re-emphasis. Here they took mile after mile of fine old dwellings on wide, tree-lined streets. And they also overran the slums. But Washington, despite the anguished yelps of the do-gooders, long was and now is practically slum-free.

Some rookery regions are on F St. and New Jersey Ave. near

the Union Station and Capitol. But there are poor whites living in hovels equally depressed. On the other hand, 95 per cent of the Negroes live in lodgings as good as and better than most white residents'. Negroes have taken over most of the desirable blocks near the government offices and downtown.

We have before us an article on "The Negro in Washington," in a recent issue of *Holiday* magazine, a slick-paper, 50-cent pleader for leftist causes, published, curiously enough, by the staid, rich and conservative house of Curtis, owners of the *Saturday Evening Post*. This effusion is illustrated with four pages purporting to show the Negro's treatment in Democracy's capital, which the editors call a "democratic contradiction." There are photographs of Negro children at play in cluttered backyards which are called typical of the city's overcrowded Negro slums. Another picture shows a Negro woman in an alley dwelling; another is captioned, "Capitol Dome presents a contrast of obvious irony to the Negro slums which it overshadows. Overcrowding, dirt and disease are all prevalent."

Your authors traveled up and down 1,000 miles of streets and boulevards, 404 of alleys, not once but a dozen times. They saw the slums illustrated in *Holiday* magazine, but they saw few others, because there are few others. At the most, 20,000, of a total of 400,000 Negroes, live in these "slums," which, even at their worst, are turreted castles compared to the degraded dwellings in which Negroes and myriad whites are forced to live in New York.

Holiday did not print one picture showing the thousands of fine homes and small apartment buildings in which most of Washington's Negroes live.

Cup your ear and we'll let you into a little secret about these "slums." Whether you read *Holiday* or not, you've seen the pictures, because they are the ones which are always used by Reds and Pinks to point up to the world how gruesomely America treats its dark step-children. The reason you've seen these pictures—always with the Capitol dome in the background—is that there are no others available.

Eleanor Roosevelt was one of the chief propagandists who exploited this "blot" on Washington. This particular slum, always photographed, always on every sight-seeing itinerary, is only a couple of blocks long and is surrounded on all sides by presentable Negro homes. But this slum is permitted to remain behind the Capitol only so the lefties will have something to breast-beat over. It remained there during the Roosevelt administration, when public housing and public building projects were reshaping the face of Washington, only because an official who was in Mrs. Roosevelt's confidence ordered it undisturbed—for propaganda purposes.

The headquarters of the National Association for the Advancement of Colored People is in a ramshackle old house near the New Jersey Avenue slums. These are the specious ones referred to elsewhere, which are kept untouched and maintained to impress visitors with the shocking degradation forced on Negroes in view of the Capitol dome.

The N.A.A.C.P. is rich and could locate in one of the prosperous, more imposing Negro sections. But that would wipe out the psychological advantage of bringing its visitors through the stage-managed slave-quarters area.

Under Negro occupancy, some of the best dwellings in Washington, once residences of ambassadors, cabinet officers and the hated capitalists, now look like the slums the Fair Dealers decry.

In Washington, a Southern town with a Southern mentality, Negroes are not popular, are not accepted as brothers except by a nagging and noisy minority. The Negro is not Jim Crowed in street cars. There is no law against a Negro's attending a theatre with whites, eating in the same restaurant or sleeping in the same hotel. But the law has upheld proprietors who refuse to serve a Negro, though United States Supreme Court decisions have gone otherwise elsewhere.

Yet there is considerable intermixture between the races. It is not uncommon to see white girls with colored men, especially jazz band musicians, who seem to exert a magnetic appeal for Caucasian women all over the country. Many Negro madames and pimps employ white girls for their colored trade. In some New Deal left-wing circles it is considered chi chi to meet socially and even sexually with Negroes, though, because of accepted restrictions against Negroes in the better spots, these contacts are not evident in the better public gathering places.

White people frequent colored night spots. Most of the reputed 480 Negro after-hour bottle-clubs cater also to whites, though no white club admits Negroes except possibly a prominent entertainer or band leader.

It is not uncommon to find white women living with colored men. Practically no instance has come up in recent years of white men consorting with colored women, except temporary pick-ups or in brothels.

A raid on the Logan Hotel, at 13th Street and Rhode Island Avenue, disclosed a white girl living with a Negro. She was the daughter of a Texas physician.

Police answered a trouble call at 17th and Q Streets and found a white girl, employed by the Social Security Administration, visiting with a colored janitor. He confessed that six other white girls from the same U. S. agency visited him regularly for intercourse, one each night—and paid him for it.

Another white girl employed by the Government was arrested at her home in Alexandria, after having received marijuana from a colored musician named Brisco. Brisco, well-known in Washington, mailed the marijuana from New York. According to U.S. Narcotics Agents, two white Washington girls under 18 admitted smoking marijuana with him and said they had unnatural sex relations with him—they were afraid of pregnancy.

Due to determined efforts of local reformers, Jim Crow seems to be on the way out in Washington, as it is everywhere and should be. Until 1949, the city's six public swimming pools were restricted, to either whites or Negroes. In 1948, the last year of such rules, the total number of swimmers was 415,000, of which only 69,000 were Negroes. Two pools were set aside for colored and four for white. In 1949, when there were no racial bars, total attendance dropped off to 332,000. One pool, Anacostia, was shut down for most of the summer after disturbances started when colored swimmers first attempted to use the pool. McKinley's white patrons stopped using it completely.

It was hoped that whites would have learned tolerance by 1950, and toward the end of the season many of the loudest crack-pots brayed about the success of the new policy. In the fall of 1950, Eleanor Roosevelt, in her syndicated column, mumbled about how all friction was ended and the millennium had arrived. As usual she was wrong. Official figures released a few days later showed attendance had skidded another 33 percent, down to a total of 220,000, of which—and get this—only one-third were Negroes. In other words, whites had almost stopped using the pools; on the other hand, there were barely more Negro patrons than when the pools were restricted. Agitation was heard from tax-payers to shut the pools, now run at a heavy loss to the city.

Only in public schools does legal Jim Crowism hold out. Recently a performance of a tableau representing the Sesquicentennial of the founding of the city was banned from the stage of a high school auditorium because it had a mixed cast. The school board said: "Congress makes the law and we enforce it." There is a technical question about whether a colored member of the board may visit white schools, and vice versa.

Adopting tactics employed by the National Association for the Advancement of Colored People elsewhere, Washington Negroes and whites who are trying to break down racial restrictions often picket restaurants and other facilities which refuse to serve Negroes, and sometimes stage sitdown strikes within them. After such an experiment in the John R. Thompson chain, the demonstrators for racial equality were arrested for disorderly conduct and sentenced by a judge who at this writing has not been overruled.

But the lot of Negroes is enviable compared to that of their brethren elsewhere. We called Chicago's Bronzeville Black Paradise. But that was before we saw Washington's Negro Heaven.

The life of the Washington Negro is made pleasant by the force of many circumstances. The odds are he is employed by the government, which has raised salaries. If he doesn't work for the government, he serves government workers. He shares in the highest per capita earnings, yet the cost of living in Washington is not so high as in New York and many other large cities. All streets, in white sections or colored, are broad and tree-lined.

No Negro is ever fired from a government job if it can possibly be helped. When necessary to cut down a staff, the whites go first, reversing the process of private business.

If they can't do their work, whites are hired to do it over for them. An instance, typical of thousands, occurred in the Bureau of the Census, where five Negro women were so inefficient that their department head requested permission to discharge them. His immediate superior almost had a stroke.

"If Eleanor hears about this," he gasped, "there'll be hell to pay."

Eleanor no longer lives in the White House. But she is still a potent force in Washington, where her kitchen cabinet continues to rule the nation that President Truman thinks he rules.

The upshot of the matter was that the section head was told to keep the five colored women and to hire five white girls to do the work over for them, on the night shift.

The same sort of favoritism is shown Negro job-holders and applicants throughout the whole governmental set-up in the District. When a white man wants to become a cop he takes a stiff civil service test and is subject to a searching investigation. Most of the Negroes who have been getting on the force recently did it on political pull.

Kid-glove handling of Negroes is the rule in every phase of Washington life, in addition to favoritism in appointments to the public payroll.

Apparently no effort is made by the police and other public authorities to enforce the liquor laws in the dark sections. The local Alcoholic Beverage Control code provides that no one may be served while standing. Bar customers must be seated on stools, and even then may be served only beer and wines. Hard liquor may be consumed only at tables. This is strictly enforced in resorts catering to whites. But almost all colored saloons sell liquor openly over the bar, where drinkers stand—as long as they can stand. Few attempts are made to restrict gambling or policy-slip sales in the colored sections.

Almost 500 Negro after-hour clubs are running, most of them not even bothering to get club charters. Thousands of Negro flats are operated as blind pigs, where liquor, mostly gin, is sold openly to all comers at all hours. None has a license, naturally.

Occasionally hokum raids are made and sometimes the defendants are fined $25. Next day they are in business as usual. Honest policemen are afraid to make too many pinches in Negro neighborhoods for fear the pinkos will list them as "nigger-haters" and send their names up above—maybe even to the White House. One cop whose name we will not mention told us that one night after he pulled in a colored after-hour spot, word came directly from the White House to the 13th precinct station, in which the arrest had been made, to lay off. F.D.R. was President then.

Despite the maudlin tears of reformers about the horrible conditions existing in Washington's "Negro Ghetto," there are probably more new Cadillac convertibles being driven from its doors than from any others. Sleek, new, expensive convertibles of the flashier brands have become the sine qua non of Negro policy-peddlers and reefer-pushers here, as well as in all other major American cities. Respectable people are returning to the old-fashioned closed models for fear their bankers will wonder what they've been up to.

Yet, despite the flashy visible prosperity of Washington's Negroes, a disproportionate number are on public relief. Many draw dole and social security checks under one name while gainfully employed at one or two jobs under other names. This racket, invented for the residents of New York's Harlem and Little Puerto Rico, has been brought to its full flower in Washington.

The humanitarians and the New Dealers, worrying about colored votes in the northern states, help to put butterfat in the colored man's milk in the capital. If the colored man works it right, he can get a relief check the first day he lands in Washington.

This story wasn't published, but the federal agents who made the pinch and compiled the record had carried it on their chests so long, they ached to unburden it where it wouldn't come back and bite them. When they broke in on a Negro whom they suspected of selling narcotics, he indignantly asserted, "You can't arrest me. I am a friend of Mrs. Roosevelt."

To prove it, he brought out a couple of letters from the First Lady, one of which was addressed "Dear Jim," or "Joe," stating she was sorry to hear that his relief check had not arrived on time, and she would see that he was not pushed around in the future—he shouldn't worry. The boys arrested him and got a conviction.

Mrs. Roosevelt, while in the White House and out, sincerely sought to improve the position of Negroes everywhere. But sometimes her efforts went to such extremes she hurt the cause. Once she made a reservation for a small banquet party of sixty at the swank Hay-Adams House, across the street from the White House. When the managers discovered it was to be an interracial affair they cancelled it. On September 14, 1950, Mrs. Roosevelt tried to register three Negroes in her party into the Willard Hotel. She was staying elsewhere, with friends. The Willard refused.

White property-owners tremble at the financial danger that would result should Negroes crash white residential areas.

But entry is made through a tactic known as "block-busting," developed by the National Association for the Advancement of

Colored People and utilized by it and by white real estate agents out to make a buck.

Government agents first heard about it when they arrested a Negro woman on narcotics charges and asked her for her occupation. She replied with dignity, "I'm a block-buster." She explained to the mystified T-Men that she was employed by a real estate shark and her duties were as follows:

When her employers had scouted an all-white neighborhood they thought ripe for plucking, they would find a white property-owner who, for a bonus, was willing to sell his property to a Negro. If the place was worth $25,000 he would be bribed with as much as another $25,000 to sell out. There are few neighborhoods where not one greedy white man could be found after a searching survey by private detectives.

After the block-buster—in her own name—made the purchase, she and her large Negro family moved in. Immediately, all other property in the neighborhood sank in value and most of it was thrown on the market. The far-sighted realtors then bought it up at greatly reduced values. Then they resold it or rented it to Negroes at inflated prices, and started another Negro island in the city.

When this was accomplished, the block-buster moved on to another base and repeated the process.

You can sense a neighborhood in the process of being block-busted by "For Sale" signs on porches or lawns, oddities in this otherwise overpopulated, under-housed metropolis.

In cities where Negroes and whites live in separate and distinct sections, opportunities for racial strife and violence are rare. In Washington, where they live side by side all over, use the same street cars and buses, patronize the same stores and constantly brush shoulders on the streets, there is friction which sometimes flares high and hot. Some of their leaders advise Negroes to be assertive, aggressive, to demonstrate their equality. They pick fights and needle Caucasians, most of whom are afraid to make complaints, because when they get into court the federally appointed Yankee judge, whose robe was bestowed upon him by a "civic rights" President, in many instances finds for the Negro and castigates the white complainants, especially policemen.

Among Negroes on the national political level who most zealously fight to assert prerogatives of their race in the capital are:

Congressman William Dawson, vice chairman of the Democratic National Committee, chairman of the mighty House Committee on Executive Expenditures. He represents Chicago's vile Bronzeville and is a patronage-dispenser for the malodorous Cook County Democratic Central Committee. He is extremely friendly with big shots of the infamous Mafia, which controls all crime and corruption in the United States. Before a Congressional Committee, Dawson was charged with being the defender of the rackets. The charge was made by the late Bill Drury, former Chicago police captain, who was slain by assassins who ambushed him in an alley after Drury tried to reach the Kefauver Committee in an effort to put the full inside story of the underworld on the record.

Congressman Adam Clayton Powell, Democrat from New York's Harlem, who usually voted hand-in-glove with Marcantonio. He is supported in every election by the successors of "Dutch" Schultz, whose policy-slip and murder ring had its headquarters in what is now Powell's district. He is married to Hazel Scott, Negro pianist, who has been frequently cited by Congressional and Legislative committees as indicating pro-Russian proclivities. She has denied it. He and his wife live in a swank Long Island home, far from his bailiwick, and ride in a chauffeur-driven $6,000 limousine.

William Hastie, former governor of the Virgin Islands, now the first Negro on the exalted bench of the United States Circuit Court of Appeals. In volume 17 of the published records of the Special Committee on Un-American Activities of the House of Representatives, Judge Hastie was cited as belonging to at least five Communist-front organizations. He was, however, subsequently appointed to the Federal bench by President Truman.

Wherever Negroes live, they have their own snobberies, castes and social strata. Rich ones and light ones are contemptuous of the poor and the black, and toward them they more often use the tabooed word "nigger" than do most whites. And they add one extra prejudice, not found among whites—resentment of the native-born Negro for the recent comer from the Southern plantations.

7. MIGHTY LIKE A ROSE

THERE IS a daily in Washington (as there are others in principal cities) which never identifies a Negro as such unless he wins a Nobel prize or is selected the rookie of the year.

We protest. News cannot be honestly reported by arbitrarily slurring facts. Of almost all other non-whites, many are marked by recognizable names. Most Negroes have Anglo-Saxon names, many of them adopted centuries ago from their slave-owners. For instance, Thompson's Ebenezer evolved into Ebenezer Thompson.

That same newspaper does not bar true and fair reports of misdeeds by people named O'Rourke or Ginsberg or Dinkel-spiel or Stanislawsky or Protopulus or Garcia or Potapinsky or Napolitano. Concealment of the identity as Negro distorts the truth, for the natural assumption then is that the miscreants are white and we have an unjustified libel on the Caucasian population.

The most rabid Negro papers publish the crimes of their own people and then editorialize on the cruel inequalities which help to cause them. That is the proper use of freedom of the press. Arbitrary withholding of vital facts is an imperti-nence and a misuse of the common franchise.

Fancy if you can what this chapter could not tell were we to suppress racial references.

Of every four felonies and other breaches of the law in the grades where a defendant has the right of trial by jury more than three are committed by Negroes. That is not confidential, but official. Arrests for Part One felonies—the more serious—in 1949 were as follows:

Colored males,	7,715.
Colored females,	1,085.
Total colored,	8,800.
White male,	2,396.
White female,	309.
Total white,	2,705.

Here is a breakdown on some:

Murder, colored 40; white 8.
Manslaughter, colored 6; white 1.
Rape, colored 140; white 23.
Aggravated assault, colored 2,651; white 381.
Burglary, colored 2,322; white 640.

Negrophiles and impractical activists for brotherhood of all God's children campaign to force newspapers to omit racial identification of the lawless and hide it with white lies. That is the foggy, unrealistic policy of visionaries, sparked by the cold, hard practicality of Reds.

Arrests for Part Two felonies (less serious) and important misdemeanors showed an even higher incidence of Negro crime.

Estimating the Negro population at 50 percent, this means half the people commit 85 percent of all the crimes. As will be shown in a later chapter, a large quota of the white crimes can be charged to transients.

The data on crimes by whites are incontrovertible. Those by Negroes in Washington, as well as in all other northern cities, do not give the full picture. Most police officers prefer not to arrest blacks, especially if there is no white complainant. They have nothing to gain by such a pinch; they merely invite an uproar for "persecuting the gentle Negro."

Many colored law breakers are never arrested; many who are are not booked, the officers often preferring to mete out summary punishment on the back stairs, which they know is a better deterrent than the inevitable discharge or suspended sentence by a timid, "seen" or left-wing judge.

If you doubt that, the following is from the record of a Congressional hearing and there are plenty of other stories like it:

Private Hamilton was assigned with Detective Sergeant Clyde Rouse for midnight cruising. They observed a stolen car parked on Q Street NW, with two occupants.

Rouse and Hamilton walked up to the car. Rouse went to the left and Hamilton to the right. Rouse recognized the driver as Charles W. Scott, colored, 24, of 476 O Street NW, wanted for questioning in connection with stolen auto hold-ups.

Rouse opened the door and tried to seize Scott, but only succeeded in shoving the gear shift lever out of gear. Rouse was on his knees on the front seat, practically on top of the other occupant of the car, a woman, who proved to be Marian Holston, 20, colored, of 16 Q Street NW, who had been picked up by Scott.

Rouse made a desperate effort to reach the key to cut off the motor but the woman fought him, kicking, scratching, and biting. The Negro driver of the stolen car shoved the gear lever in and with the accelerator down to the floor board, rocketed the car into high speed. Hamilton, his head and shoulders through the window, holding on to the wheel, attempted to steer. It was impossible for either officer to jump or let go. The stolen car finally collided with a barricade, ran over the sidewalk.

With Rouse still fighting to gain control, and Hamilton still struggling, the car, without headlights and at a terrific speed collided with a tractor trailer truck. The stolen auto was completely demolished.

Private Hamilton was killed.

Scott had a record which showed he had been committed eight times as a juvenile delinquent on charges of larceny, and in 1943 was sentenced to from two to five years for auto stealing. Thereafter he was involved in six charges of robbery.

But the U.S. Attorney's office refused to prosecute the Negroes and the police were advised that if they insisted on going through with charges before a judge, the DA's office would nolle prosse the case, because they did not believe "a conviction could be obtained" against colored people who had so unfortunately become involved in the killing of a policeman. But when a policeman kills a Negro in the line of duty, the politically chosen District Attorney is frequently highpressured by the N.A.A.C.P. into bringing murder charges.

We have pointed to the misguided tendency to minimize the size and extent of the Negro population. If more than half of Washington's population is not black, the per capita crime rate is even more appalling.

Like white crime, Negro crime is organized and syndicated. This does not mean every rapist, hold-up man and car-thief takes orders from above. But it means that when he gets in trouble he does seek certain directed sources for bail-bonds, lawyers and fixers.

Policy-sellers, bookmakers' runners, reefer peddlers and junk salesmen are employed by an organization which protects them also.

The process, as it works here, will be described in detail in the chapters devoted to crime and law enforcement, as it is part of the general picture of organized evil.

In Washington, as in other cities, Negro crime on the consumer and go-between levels is operated and controlled by Negroes. They report to, kick back to, and make their fixes at upper levels with, white criminals. The topmost control rests in the hands of the international Syndicate, the Mafia, the Unione Siciliano. The Washington Negro crime-ring has more autonomy than usual, because there are few Sicilians and even fewer interested in crude crime. The national Syndicate prefers not to show its bloody hands openly in the capital, but lurks in the background—in New York, principally.

The most powerful Washington Negro is the aforementioned Puddin' Head Jones. Jim Yellow Roberts is the boss of dope and reefers. He makes his buys in wholesale lots in New York, Philadelphia and Baltimore, direct from the importers. While temporarily embarrassed by a jail sentence, Roberts continued to run the Negro dope trade.

"Whitey" Simpkins is king of the Black Belt's numbers racket. Johnny W. Carter, who owns the Club Bali, a black-and-tan resort, is one of the gamblers' chiefs. Their payoff is a percentage which eventually reaches the Syndicate through channels which will be set forth in detail in the chapter devoted to dope and gambling in Washington.

One of Washington's most important Negro underworld figures is Lamarr (Polly) Brown who has been implicated in every form of illegality from operating after-hour clubs to the sale of narcotics. Odessa Madre, known as the "Queen of the Fences," is just what her honorific implies.

Following the white pattern, the largest, gayest and most colorful Negro section is also laid out in NW. This part of town abounds with colored flats where a white man may take a white or colored woman. These holes sell gin without licenses, provide bedroom accommodations for those who want them, and girls for those who don't have them.

Many Negro cab-drivers pimp for white girls, first getting acquainted with them when they pick them up as passengers. They set them up in apartments, most of which are in NW, and sell their services to white or colored men. These cabbies also handle reefers and after-hour liquor.

If you rode with us in Washington, through the NW colored section, these are some of the things we could have shown you:

First, we parked our car at the corner of 10th and B Sts., in front of the Lincoln Barbeque. We waited five minutes, a colored man came out of the restaurant and took our order for bootleg liquor. It happened after two, when the bars were closed. His prices were moderate, no more than 50 cents to a dollar above the established tariff. But the stuff was moonshine and cut.

Let's go to 1919 14th Street NW. This house was formerly the Star Dust Club, an after-hour drinking and gambling place. Now it's a shoeshine parlor. It's owned by William J. "Foots" Edwards, a notorious Negro gambler. If you want a game, you can find stud in the basement.

The dark corner of 5th and K looks quiet and serene. The colored damsels who parade past here singly and by twos are not. Stop your car at the corner and they will come over and solicit you. Business all night. If you're a Negro you'll know where to take them. If you are a white man they'll go along in your car to an alley or steer you to a buggy rooming-house. Another corner frequented by dusky hustlers in search of white trade is 9th and Rhode Island.

At about this time, we'll run through the 7th Street district, which is the Broadway of the NW Negro section, with the chief shops, restaurants, night clubs and theatres. You can make pickups anywhere around 7th, Georgia and Florida Avenues, but these streets are brightly lighted, so most white men who want to change their luck play the darker streets. And there it is not unusual to see white girls brace black men.

In addition to sex on sale at the corner of 7th and Florida, you can buy reefers or policy slips.

U Street, from 7th to 15th, is another bright light belt in the colored section. The Dunbar Hotel and the Whitelaw are the swank Negro inns. The Dunbar was once the aristocratic white Courtland Hotel. In its basement is the 20-11 Club, one of the Nation's best-known colored cabarets, which caters to the cream of the colony and is patronized also by white novelty-seekers. Rich and visiting Negro celebrities check in at the Dunbar. So do Feds and cops, who have occasionally made pinches there for narcotics and morals violations. In the 20-11 Club you can pick up girls of any race.

On the corner of 7th and T are three hot spots—the Off Beat Club, for musicians, the Club Harlem, and the Seventh and T Club. We saw them serve drinks after hours and cater to fairies of all shades, female white thrill-chasers and Negro reefer addicts.

Washington, like Chicago, is a city of alleys in every block of residential property and many business squares, bisected by the rear passages. As in Chicago, they are conducive to crime, afford dark, narrow lanes for rape, assault, robbery and the pleasanter crimes of crap shooting and soliciting.

In some Negro sections where housing is at a premium, they live in shacks in the alleys. These are some of the slums already referred to—not many, but picturesque and odoriferous. One of the best-known is an alley oddly named Temperance Court. If white people lived there it would be fashionable at premium rents; it is similar to the aristocratic Washington Mews in New York's Greenwich Village. But it is inhabited by some of the lowest members of the Negro race in Washington—and that means low.

Temperance Court is between 12th and 13th, T and U Streets, near the 13th precinct station. More dope peddlers and ginmill operators are annually arrested in this block than on any other street of comparable size anywhere in the world. You can buy anything you want there—girls, bootleg whiskey, cocaine and marijuana, stolen property, guns and knives, articles of perversion and sadism. Anything but a virgin past the age of puberty.

A notorious dope peddler operated there until recently and may still be there when this comes out. He is John Frye. He has so many children, some sleep on the roof, four on a bed, and there is always a new baby in the carriage. Narcotics agents said he hid junk in the baby's diaper. A competitor in the same block was Wilbur Kenny, known to the cokies merely as "Y."

Another byway in the NW Negro section, which is unpublicized in the slick magazines, is Goat Alley, off 7th Street, near M. This is terribly tough, with reefer peddlers, two-dollar wenches, a mugging a minute and murders common. Close by the Negro sections of crime and perversion is Ledroit Park, once surrounded by the mansions of aristocracy. This is back of Griffith Stadium, which, like Comiskey Park, home of the

Chicago White Sox, is engulfed in a sable sea. Baseball lovers must travel through miles of dangerous streets to the stadium.

Nearby is Freedman's Hospital, the world's leading institution of its kind for colored people, one of the outstanding institutions in the world. Its internes are Howard University medical graduates, and among these are great doctors. They get plenty of practice. The worst Negro assault cases go to Freedman's. On Friday and Saturday nights the floors of its emergency wards look like slaughterhouses. Knifings are frequent; shootings run second. Even on weekdays the place teems with police interviewing victims.

Garfield Hospital, also near a large Negro community, is the second in assault cases.

One of the largest Negro islands in NE has as its center Central Avenue—same name as Los Angeles' Harlem, though purely coincidental.

Gamblers in the NE section get action above the colored poolroom at 507 8th Street and E.

SW's colored section is one of the largest in Washington and perhaps the oldest. It begins within a thrown stone's distance of the Capitol and runs through to the Army War College. If you've read about this neighborhood in some pinkish publication before seeing it for yourself you will be looking for something awful. But you will drive through miles of wide avenues with deep lawns. They're littered with rubbish and junk, of course. This homey residential section is reminiscent of God-fearing, law-abiding middle-class sections in typical Southern towns.

But what goes on inside these cozy habitations is not sleepy. The streets, so quiet by day, take on a sinister aspect at night. This whole section is known as Bloodfield. It's worth a white man's or woman's life to walk there unaccompanied. Even respectable Negroes are not safe.

Young colored hoodlums of both sexes, adept at mugging and knifing, prey on strangers. The white man who comes here for pastime will find his luck all bad. The best he can hope for is a beating and maiming. But white women who are known to be Negro lovers are given safe conduct by the men, though they are attacked often by Negro women who resent the intrusion. These streets are barely patrolled by police.

The main shopping and drinking boulevards of the SW Negro section are 4th and 7th Streets. Around here the Negroes moved into and drove out what there was of a Jewish ghetto. The street where Al Jolson lived as a child and where his father practiced as a cantor is now all Negro.

The SW dope peddlers and whores make their hangout on 6½th Street. The chief madames are "Mamma Liz" and "Big Tit" Flossie.

We have indicated that many white women—especially government workers—are receptive to sexual attentions of Negro men. But the comparative ease with which a black man can get a white girl, even a so-called respectable one, does not seem to deter colored men from committing rape on women of their own race and whites.

As these lines were being written, all Washington was shocked and alerted when a 22-year-old South American girl, visiting with a diplomatic family, was stalked, attacked and ravished in a park near Arlington Cemetery by a Negro, who, Tarzan-like, leaped from a clump of trees entirely naked.

The popular form of Negro attack is mugging, a process in which the assailant comes up behind a man or woman and throws his arm around the victim's throat, closing it sharply with the elbow out, and jabbing a knee into the small of the back.

But in Washington colored people call it "yoking," derivation of the word unknown. It includes all forms of street assault. One process consists of sneaking up behind a lone pas-er-by, usually one who apparently has been drinking, and tapping him on the shoulder. As he turns around, he is hit square on the jaw with a stiff arm, then kicked in the groin when he falls. Most victims are robbed. But many young and exuberant Negroes get up yoking parties just for the joy and excitement.

Three young colored boxers, aged 14, 16, and 17, terrorized Washington a few months ago, committing at least 19 yoke robberies, netting more than $2,000. The 17-year-old was a semifinalist in the 160-pound class in last year's Golden Gloves tournament. The youngest boxed at a boys' club. The 16-year-old was a quarter finalist in the 135-pound class. These activities are said to breed good citizens.

The three bet among themselves which would land the first punch on the victim and whether it would be a knockout.

Police arrest hundreds of Negro yokers every year, most of them in their teens. Thousands of yokings go unsolved. The yokers are usually highly organized into juvenile gangs which fight also with home-made pistols, sawed-off shotguns and switch-blade knives.

Many of these young Negro gangs terrorize students, white and black, in public schools, offering to sell them "protection" and punishing them when they don't pay up.

Startled public officials first heard about these gangs some months ago after incidents at Banneker High. An 18-year-old colored boy was held for the grand jury on a charge of robbing a 15-year-old Banneker schoolboy of a wrist watch on the school playground. He threatened to whip the younger boy if he talked. School officials were awakened to the fact that all the schools in the city had this problem. According to the assistant superintendent of schools G. C. Wilkenson, "the gangs are made up of boys who aren't in school and who aren't working—mostly from 16 to 21 years old."

Officials try to minimize the situation, but there is a wave of terror in every public elementary and high school. Young Negro gangsters lurk about the schools, sell reefers, molest girls, and commit mayhem on children who won't pony up. Boys and girls thus forced to pay tribute are told to steal from their parents or do a little shoplifting if they have no other means of procuring the extortion money. Youngsters are put on heroin and morphine by the youthful gangsters, and soon enter a life of serious crime.

Other yokers use a tactic borrowed from the dacoits, a murderous religious gang of India, throwing a cord over the victim's head from behind and garroting him.

Some of these colored juvenile mobs have been in existence for 15 or 20 years. When boys and girls outgrow them and become adult criminals on their own, they are replaced by new children on the way up. Among the older and better-organized kid mobs are the Fastest Runners, the Forty Thieves, the Purple Cross Gang and the Protective Association.

The Fastest Runners is composed of younger boys who fight with switch-blade knives. When they grow up they graduate into adult gangs. All these organizations have female auxiliaries, membership in which requires the young colored girls to solicit on the streets and turn the proceeds over to the boys. Girls as young as 11 participate and at 12 are "debs," with full standing.

Among offenses which are practically Negro monopolies in Washington are the following:

Numbers and policy slips. Almost all numbers sellers, even in white neighborhoods and in government office buildings, are colored men and women. In other cities Sicilians, Puerto Ricans, Filipinos and Mexicans get in on this activity, but there are no sizeable groups of such in Washington. The modus operandi of numbers selling will be described in the chapter on gambling.

Sale of reefers. Almost all marijuana retailers are colored, which also is unique to Washington.

Theft and conversion of government checks at the lower level. The men, because so many are janitors and elevator boys, have entree to apartment buildings and tenement houses and access to mail-boxes. These thieves strike at the middle or at the end of the month, when checks are sent out by the Treasury for G.I. remunerations, Social Security benefits, pensions, army subsistence and similar regular allotments. Those who do the manual stealing seldom attempt to cash the checks, which are turned over to fences, often white, including storekeepers and sometimes bankers.

Another Negro industry is *the sale of bootleg booze.* The rings operate in many fashions. On some streets you find peddlers who sidle up beside you, or come up to your car when you stop for traffic lights. Many shoeshine "parlors" are moonshine dispensaries. Groceries and poolrooms also sell, usually gin, but sometimes what is supposed to be bourbon—corn for the Southern taste. The gin is mixed with cider to dilute the taste of raw kerosene and the combination has a wallop.

That good old Negro money-raising institution, known as "the rent party" elsewhere, has a specific, generic name in Washington, where it's called a "chitlin party." Chitlins, hogs' innards, are a delicacy in some blacker parts of the South and are used here as a decoy to attract guests to the homey brawls which are a regular part of Blacktown's social life. In New York's Harlem and Chicago's Bronzeville the paying guest at a rent party gets nothing in exchange for his contribution except the right to bring his woman, drink his gin, and get into the fracas.

We met a white fellow who has run Washington's chitlin industry up into a million-dollar-a-year class. He gets the stuff from the butchers for nothing. They're almost willing to pay him to cart it away. Then he packages it in 10-gallon jars which he sells for $2.50, or two bits a gallon. That means the capital's Negroes consume 4,000,000 gallons a year.

These chapters were, of course, not in print when a young man known as "The Sniper" was, for a few days, the most famous person in Washington. If he were around now, our critics might have said we incited him. The Sniper—a young white man—was a congenital Negro-hater. He boiled up into an insane rage every time he saw a sable woman or man. He hid in various sections and hit bullseyes from roofs, behind trees and through open windows.

Before he was caught there was a wave of terror. For days Negroes remained indoors. Crime sagged, because even the worst elements were afraid to leave their homes.

Police Lieutenant Barrett, now Major and Superintendent of the Metropolitan Force, got him after he had killed a half-dozen men and wounded scores.

While the Sniper was in jail on suspicion, he met a drug addict, one Richard Harlowe, and confided in him where he had hidden his gun, in Baltimore. Barrett recovered it and came back to find his bird had escaped. He was recaptured in Georgetown. Barrett's fame helped him to become the chief. His friends say it had nothing to do with the fact that he was related to Major Edward Kelley, a previous chief.

8. CHINATOWN CHIPPIES

SAM WONG, an owner of the China Clipper, Quonsett Inn, the Dragon and other popular restaurants, was indicted on a $250,000 tax fraud. The government charged he gave most of it to two blondes—sisters—who lived with him. The case was tried in Baltimore. (Note: Though Washington is the nation's capital, it is merely part of the Maryland Internal Revenue collection district.)

When the case was called, the courtroom filled with poker-faced orientals. The government called some, the defense called others, including Wong, whom it put on the stand.

But not one Chinese witness testified coherently. They gave their names, addresses, and so on, muttered and mumbled irrelevant replies. Even the defendant remained mute after being put on the stand by his own attorney.

The lawyers had read *Chicago Confidential*, in which these reporters revealed that Chinese will have no truck with American courts or American law. So they gave a copy to the court and D.A., hoping the judge and jury would realize the impossible position in which the defense legal battery was placed. It did no good. Wong got a year. The blondes weren't Chinese—and they convicted him.

Some go to Chinatown for chop suey and chow mein. We will write about those who seek other delicacies.

Washington's Chinatown is neither as large as Frisco's, as colorful as New York's, nor as odoriferous as Boston's. You will see no ancient, pajama-clad women on its streets, and only a few young slant-eyed Sadies.

Chinatown is a mere three or four blocks on H Street, beginning in a block about 8th and extending barely to 5th. It's almost all neon-lighted restaurants, with the shops of a few wholesale merchants and traders sandwiched in between. H is a typical wide Washington street with set-back buildings. If it weren't for the garish Chinese characters on the illuminated signs and windows, and the pale yellow-faced men with sad old almond eyes sprawling on the stoops, you'd think you were anywhere but in a Chinatown.

As in all Chinese quarters, various locations and various businesses are divided between the tongs. Only two operate in the East, though there are scores in California.

The On Leongs are dominant here, though not in the nation, through an alliance with the Hip Sings, cemented many years ago, when they drove the competing organizations back to the West Coast. Then they turned on their ally. After a series of bloody wars, they established themselves as the top dogs, with the Hip Sings the poor cousins.

The tongs are, primarily, trade and benevolent associations. Their membership is comprised of certain families or immigrants from certain villages in Canton. When the authorities clamped down on tong wars in the 1930's, the tongs began to enforce their decrees and decisions by peaceful means, which include trade and social boycott.

According to members of the Chinese colony in Washington, there are only 500 of them, but these figures are far out of line with our count of at least 7,500. There are hundreds of Chinese restaurants and laundries in the town. Chinese always underestimate their population, as do Negroes. But with them there are more concrete reasons. Three-fourths are entered illegally, through many subterfuges, such as forged birth and marriage certificates, as well as actual body-smuggling over the Mexican and Canadian borders and from the West Indies. The price of entering a Chinese now is $5,000, as against a modest $1,000 twenty years ago. The fee is paid the smugglers by the Chinaman's tong or family society, for whom he then works to pay it off. Nowadays most of this illegal entry is by air.

Chinese are cagey at census time, because if the rolls show anywhere near as many in the country as there are, the difference in numbers between those here and the ones on record would be so startling, it would cause an investigation and wholesale deportation. Another reason is that they are on a gentlemen's agreement quota basis with agents of the Federal Bureau of Immigration and Naturalization. When an agent runs across a group of illegally-entered Chinese, he gets practical about the whole matter.

If he turned them all up at once, he'd get a pat on the back from his superior, then have to go on a new job next week. But if he reports only one every two weeks, he doesn't have to do another lick of work for months. So the agent makes a deal with the head of the tong, who delivers the unfortunate Chinese at set intervals, and thus everyone is happy: the government because it gets the Chinese, the agent because he can loaf, and the wealthy Chinese laundry and restaurant owners, who are not suddenly faced with labor shortages.

Washington's Chinatown is important beyond its numerical strength because it acts as a lobby for Chinese all over the country, regardless of tong affiliation, and for Chinese merchants and enterprises all over the world. There are not enough Chinese voters in the country to enable them to influence elec· tions, but they make up for lack of numbers by intelligence, ingenuity, wealth and Oriental cunning developed by centuries of intrigue with no qualms of honor owed the white man.

Communists never overlook a trick. They quickly took advantage of the Chinaman's unique possibilities. Many Chinese are vulnerable because they have relatives in the old country. Thus they are subject to pressure. Many are technical lawbreakers or illegal entrants, so the Reds, with their influence in high places, can threaten effectively. Chinese societies make swell "drops" for the transmission of messages and intelligence, and are being used, an angle not yet brought out publicly.

They'll tell you it isn't so, but some of the recent tong fighting is a war between Nationalists and Communists.

Chinatown, only a few blocks from the White House, the Capitol and the center of the business and commercial life, is a focal point for all, whites as well as Orientals, visitors and natives. In this town, where almost everything shutters by midnight, the Chinese propensity for staying up all night and sleeping most of the day has brought about several phenomena. Unless you are welcome at a bottle club, there is no late place to go to in Washington except Chinatown. Most of the restaurants there are open all night, selling food. More than a few serve liquor after 2 A.M., if they know you, in a tea-pot.

There is hectic activity all evening. Most of the white bag-swinging street-hustlers work the neighborhood. Any cab-driver will direct you there if you ask him, "Where can I get a girl?" These self-sellers usually ask $20, but will take what they can get. They go on duty at around 8, and by 10 most have made arrangements. From 10 to about 1 or 2, the restaurants are taken over by respectable people, mostly young couples who stop in for a bite of exotic food after the movies. After 1, when the tarts have completed their rounds, they come back again for more trade. At this time the drunks who have been ejected from the cocktail lounges and night clubs are transported wholesale by cab to Chinatown. Many of the drivers have deals with certain girls and some of these girls have deals with the Chinese restaurants they habitually visit.

Many of the hookers hang out at the Mai Fong.

We could find no Chinese whores in Washington. The proportion of Chinese women to men is one to ten. Any Oriental girl, no matter how homely, can make an attractive marriage. Many Chinese men are married to white women. There are no Chinese waitresses in the Chinese restaurants, except an occasional relative of the owner; they are whites. Few are for sale, but many will help get you one who is.

When the tramps finish their second round with the guys they have picked up at 2, they come back to Chinatown at 5 or 6 in the morning, by which time the waiters, chefs and bartenders, all Chinese, are locking up for the night and ready for a bit of shacking up themselves. Many of the prostitutes live with Chinese men from the restaurants and the gambling joints. These are useful to the Chinese colony, which entertains influential white people lavishly. Many members of Congress, high government officials and influential lobbyists are feted at private parties, where they are served exotic twenty-course meals of raw octopus and lambs' eyes, washed down by shark's fin soup. Police Chief Barrett, always accompanied by his aide-de-camp, a lieutenant, is frequently entertained in these private rooms.

Amiable blondes are supplied by the hosts if wanted, and rooms are available down the block, at the Eastern House, a cheap Chinese and white hotel, where federal agents frequently pick up dope-peddlers.

Selling narcotics is another large Chinese industry. Unlike other cities, it is not confined to selling to Chinese. In all other Eastern cities, opium, the favorite Chinese dream-smoke, is peddled by members of the On Leong Tong, who have the cream of everything, won through violence and chicanery.

In other cities, Hip Singers must content themselves with the sale of white stuff—heroin, morphine and cocaine—which is seldom used by Chinese. In Washington, Chinese are among the main retail dope purveyors for the white trade as well as their own people. There are few Puerto Rican and Italian drug passers available. So both tongs sell everything. Junkies cruise Chinatown at all hours of the day and night in search of dope, and can make a buy without any trouble. If anyone stands on a corner and looks sad for more than five minutes, he will be approached by a peddler.

The net result is that, with narcotics as with girls, the Chinese find a potent weapon with which to further the interests of their fellow Orientals all over the country. More than one high government official is on dope, which he procures from Chinese dealers, who in turn have him at their mercy because they control the source and because they have the power of blackmail.

The Chinese import some, obtain the rest from the central Mafia sources in New York, Philadelphia and Baltimore, or directly from abroad, as will be described later. They frequently cooperate with the Mafia in smuggling narcotics and other contraband. It is a matter of record that many Chinese secret societies have worked with their ancient Sicilian counterpart, the Mafia, over the centuries. Both Cantonese and Sicilians are widely dispersed over the world, but each faction is bound together by a common language and secret societies. Chinese societies are remarkable transmission belts. And among Chinese are many natural-born gangsters—sly rather than bold in white men's countries.

Dope can be hidden in rice, vegetables and even wet-wash. The Chinese societies also provide the Mafia with facilities for transporting contraband money from country to country or from town to town.

There's hardly a location in Chinatown without some form of gambling going on, quite often open to the street. Almost every restaurant has a game in the rear. Many stores are blinds for the huge wagering that goes on behind. If you came in and asked to buy some article you saw in the window, you'd be laughed at; they are usually dummy props. Huge sums are won and lost in these games, and bankrolls of a hundred or two hundred thousand dollars on the table are not unknown. This is always syndicate money. Sometimes as many as 500 or 1,000 partners all over the country are in the play. These games go on 24 hours a day, without pause. Each syndicate's players are chosen for their ability as gamblers. They play in teams with others who relieve them.

We saw open gambling in the Fong Wah Co., in Eng Hon, in the On Leong building, and at numbers 601, 603, 606, 607, 608 H Street, in Chinatown.

The police know all about this gambling, but take no action unless white men put in a beef. They explain you can't make a pinch stick on Chinese: the games they play are not understandable to whites, and it is almost impossible to make an identification of an Oriental, or to get one to testify, for or against.

When the Chinese hook a fat white sucker, the game moves every hour to a different location.

Sixth Street, at H, is the dividing line between Hip Sing and On Leong territory, with the Hip Sings below 6th, the less desirable part of town. The division of businesses gives all restaurants to On Leongs and the laundries to Hip Sings, therefore all chop suey parlors in Chinatown are above 6th Street.

Kwon Seto is the local On Leong boss and one of the most powerful men in Washington. George Moy, secretary of the On Leongs, is the "mayor" of Chinatown. A man named Yee is the real boss. Moy owns the Joy Inn, where an investigator for a crime committee was steered by a District official, then "mickeyed."

9. THE OVERFLOW

OF EVERY 100 residents of the metropolitan district, 45 live in the suburbs—over the line in Maryland and across the Potomac in Virginia. The take from these sections, in legitimate taxes and the proceeds of vice and crime, is so attractive that the city fathers of Washington have their greedy eyes on annexing this adjoining land onto the voteless District.

Almost everywhere else, unincorporated territory across city lines is a world apart. These county sections usually look different, smell different and are different from the city. They are bad or good, where people go to get away from the law, or go to get away from the lawlessness of the big city.

The border of D.C. is arbitrary. As the population of the capital grew, it spread. For all practical purposes, nearby Maryland and Virginia are as much a part of the city as any part of the city itself. Most of the residents of the suburbs work in the capital.

The entire area is really one municipality, though those living in Virginia and Maryland can vote.

There are no caste or social lines between the District and the suburbs. Society people may live in Washington, Virginia or Maryland. Residences of high government officials are spread over the three. The big wheels of the underworld are likewise scattered. The same overlords control the rackets in the entire metropolitan district.

The state lines provide gangsters with yet another safeguard. Extradition warrants are required to move them from one area to another. For some specific crimes, the authorities are hampered by the fact that no extradition is authorized. Smart lawyers take advantage of these false barriers. For instance, each day's collection of lottery money in the District is moved into Maryland. Conversely, much of Maryland's bookmaking take is deposited in District banks. That is all done on legal advice.

Technically, police officers in hot pursuit may cross state lines to make arrests, even for traffic violations. But few crimes are committed in the presence of a cop, and almost never any involving the upper echelons of crime. The satellite regions are remarkably free of Negroes, who prefer the city which they have all but taken over. That's why the suburbs grew in size to such extent that Silver Spring, Maryland, adjacent to the District, of which outsiders seldom hear or read, is now the second largest city in the state.

The suburbs run the scale from swank sections where only those of great wealth reside to dingy squatters' rows where moonshining, murder and mayhem are daily dillies. Most of the ritzier suburbs are on the Virginia side. Chain Bridge Way, Warrenton and Middleburg are peopled by the horsey set, where there are great estates lived in by possessors of ancient, honorable family names, as well as by the newly-made aristocrats of the New Deal, union officers, left-wing lawyers, five-percenters and State Department aides. Chevy Chase, partly in the District, but mostly in Maryland, is tony, too. So is Bethesda, Maryland.

But the great mass of suburbanites in both states are middle-class government employes who commute to and from work, play bridge, go to the movies and propagate.

As will be seen here, you can find almost anything in the way of crime or vice in Washington, but what you miss can usually be met in some of the Maryland suburbs when the heat isn't on, especially in Prince Georges County, which, for its size, probably has more slot-machines, strip-teasers, resident hoodlums and general deviltry than any other place in the world—subject to a "clean-up" in progress at this writing.

A. Maryland

This is the Free State, where anything goes.

Chicago has Cicero, Washington has Prince Georges County.

The same cause which gives Washington the unenviable lead as the Number 1 law-breaker among cities—public apathy—is what usually makes Prince Georges County unique among county areas of the country. Washington does not have the vote, the residents of Prince Georges do have it. And they exercise it by usually voting Democratic and corrupt. Last November they kicked over the traces for the first time since 1864.

But the Republican county commission won't get far, even if it tries.

Without a dream of winning, the GOP nominated well-meaning nonentities without a policy, organization or knowledge of the local problems. Their victory was as surprising to themselves as to these reporters.

The facts for this chapter were gathered shortly before the November election. The new county government was sworn in on December 5. We returned to Prince Georges in early February for a recheck and found little changed. The new sheriff, Carlton Beall, made ten raids since New Year's Eve. But the strip-joints still ran, though not so blatantly. Instead of featuring the nudies in their ads, they gave them second billing and headlined the male M.C. instead. But the babes were just as bare.

The gambling was under wraps, too, but it still flourished. The big gamblers took the precaution of moving their books and their bank accounts back to the District, whence they had fled a decade ago.

The crime syndicate's technique was to keep moving across county lines from Anne Arundel to Howard to Prince Georges in the area near Laurel, where the three join.

The militant Republicans fired the Chief of Police and appealed to Senator Kefauver for aid. At this writing, the Senate Crime Investigating Committee tossed the hot potato right back into Maryland. One of Kefauver's four colleagues on the Committee is Senator Herbert O'Conor, Maryland Democrat, elected with the aid of the corrupt Democratic machine so soundly trounced last November.

The second act of the new Republican commission was to hire another Democrat to succeed the ousted Democratic Police Chief.

The Prince Georges border is a 15-minute drive from the heart of Washington. Depending on the road you take out of town, you soon reach Bladensburg or Colmar Manor. The latter is Rum Row, with several blocks of dirty drinking-joints where wind-broken broads solicit drinks, roll drunks and whore, often as a pastime when no dough is available.

If you go to Colmar Manor to spend money, Silver Spring in adjoining Montgomery County is the place where you can get money. This is no gag. The entire main street of Silver Spring and nearby Mount Rainier in Prince Georges is lined on both

sides from the District border for more than a quarter of a mile
with personal loan agencies. This is because D. C. law makes it
almost impossible for small loan firms, which lend you money
on your own signature or that of co-signers, to operate. It so
limits the interest rate as to make the business unprofitable,
fixing it at one percent a month. On the other hand, both
Maryland and Virginia are much more liberal with the loan
companies. The former allows three percent monthly and the
latter two-and-a-half. The Washington wage-earner, working for
the government or privately employed, does his borrowing
across the borderline. If he should default, the loans are col-
lectable in the District, though its courts are increasingly looking into the conditions under which the loan was originally
granted and refusing to issue judgments where they believe the
interest is usurious.

Most Washingtonians know Prince Georges County as a
place to go to have fun. This is not because Maryland's laws,
or even their enforcement, are more liberal than the District's.
With few exceptions, they are not.

The legal liquor closing on weekdays is 2 A.M. in both. No
hard liquor can be sold at all on Sundays. They cheat in Prince
Georges.

Prince Georges County is lined with dumps that specialize
in strip-teasers. There are also many fag-joints. Peeling isn't
against the law in Washington, either. It goes on in the 9th
Street burlesque houses when they operate, and at Kavakos',
near the navy yard. But Washingtonians prefer not to patronize the nuders near home. Their feeling of delicacy is overcome
when they drive five miles.

Washington's huge homosexual colony overflows up to the
Baltimore Highway and into a place called the Conga. Mike
Young's occasionally specializes in fairy shows, too.

Prince Georges is a long strip predominantly devoted to
gaiety, night life, gambling and whoring. At this writing, one
of its most famous places is in a barnlike structure called the
Crossroads. It has strippers and corny shows. Its huge bar is
loaded for a pick-up. In case you do, but are not prepared,
"sanitary rubber goods" are dispensed in slot-machines in the
men's rooms. The night we were there, we saw three fancy one-
armed bandits whirring and swallowing. These were manufactured by Bell, which means their take goes direct to Frank
Costello, instead of reaching him indirectly through other sub-

sidiary companies, which sell machines to local syndicates. The Crossroads is a hangout for hoodlums. We recognized some well-known police characters there.

One of its owners is local gambling overlord Snags Lewis, about whom more later. Last year there was a shooting in the room, but Prince Georges County Patrolman Burgess made no report because his father had a piece of the place. Burgess is now off the force.

The Dixie Pig is a few yards down the road from the Crossroads. This barbecue bazaar is a hangout for prostitutes and gamblers. It is owned by Earl Sheriff, who, strangely enough, was the sheriff of Prince Georges before he went to Lewisburg penitentiary on an income tax charge, after pleading nolo contendere to protect the top shots.

Sheriff, now out on parole, is still electioneering, fixing and collecting campaign funds for the local Democratic machine. He worked hard for defeated Senator Tydings.

While Sheriff was having his troubles, Ralph Brown, late chief of the Prince Georges County Police, settled with the government out of court. The Democratic leaders of Prince Georges who were unaware of the vice there, or blind, are Congressmen Lansdale G. Sasscer, T. Howard Duckett, and T. Hampton Magruder. The latter two are attorneys.

Prince Georges County has a police force of 41 men, plus its village and town cops. But the county never asks for State Troopers. That is not surprising, because while we were gathering information for this book the Prince Georges grand jury said there was no gambling in the county. We saw a lot of it with our own eyes. Maybe state cops could stumble on some of it. Maybe.

Clean-up or no, there usually are more floating crap-games, illegal bookies and after-hour spots in Prince Georges than there are in Reno, where all such things are legal. The Republicans may temporarily drive them under cover—or back to the District—but those boys never stop.

The local Democratic machine was so powerful that, in 1947, the United States Department of Justice had to intervene directly with Maryland's then Governor Lane to close down some joints. State troopers quickly shut all gambling houses—save one run by Mike Meyers, who was too cantankerous even for them. They finally drove him out by stationing police-cars around his joint every night, and taking the names of customers. After the heat was off, however, the county reopened wide.

The Prince Georges underworld was ruled until his death last year by Jimmy La Fontaine, who is known in gangland circles to have been a 20-percent partner with Frank Costello, the Mafia boss in New York, who handled the other 80 percent of the Prince Georges take. La Fontaine was a big financial backer of the local Democratic machine, though his own plush gambling casino across the street from the District line is now closed, pending probate of his multi-million-dollar estate by Attorney Charlie Ford, who gets the cream of all gambling, whoring and other organized criminal cases in the District of Columbia, Maryland and Virginia.

Now the underworld is run by lieutenants of those who operate as vice overlords in Washington. Among them are Monk Seal, the bookmaker, who also has a piece of the Crossroads, and the aforementioned Mike Meyers, who handles the dice end. Snags Lewis is the local representative of the nationwide horse wire service, owned by the heirs of the late Al Capone, and is Frank Costello's direct representative.

Policy-slip collections in the District are paid off to Pete Gianaris at night at the close of business. Gianaris is an interesting character who ran a $50,000 party in the ballroom of the Statler Hotel to celebrate the christening of his young son. This was cheap, considering that he imported such expensive Broadway stars as Buddy Lester to entertain the cream of local society. He is a beloved, big-hearted citizen.

The Costello interests were operating hundreds of slot-machines in Prince Georges. Some years ago, they were legalized by local option, but they remained contrary to state law, which was not enforced. Some locals, pushed out of the picture by Costello's strongarm boys, started a tax-payers' suit in the state courts and the Prince Georges local option law was thrown out. But some of the officials apparently haven't heard of the decision yet.

That is not so surprising, since the sheriff, who seldom finds time to enforce the state laws, is busy applying the lash and cat-o'-nine-tails. Archaic Maryland law provides for whipping some classes of prisoners, the sheriff acting in person.

Among other joints in the county is one called the Hilltop, in Hillside. It was formerly a barbecue pit, now is a snake pit—a noisy madhouse catering to school and college kids who want to see what the well-undressed peeler isn't wearing. The Quonset Inn, also in Prince Georges, is run by the Chinese syndicate of the District, which has established perfect harmony with the white bosses. You can see naked women at the Senate Inn, Waldrop's, and occasionally at La Conga.

Meanwhile, the temporary exodus of Prince Georges gamblers has stepped up wagering activities in other nearby Maryland counties. Montgomery, mainly residential, with swank Chevy Chase and hard-working middle-class Silver Spring, woke up to find its Elks' Club the victim of a police raid.

Then Sam Morgan, also of Silver Spring, described as one of the most important gamblers in the area, was locked up by State Troopers when they swooped down on "lay-off" establishments near Laurel Park and Ellicott City. These were nerve-centers for the transmission of contraband money in and out of the District. Morgan drew a suspended sentence. No one ever goes to jail.

The Baltimore Highway houses many tourist cabins, where pleasure-bound Washingtonians can drive and hire a room without baggage for $3, if not using it all night. A big turnover is the gravy for these guesthouses. A few cabin resorts are reserved for Negroes only.

The Negro population of this part of Maryland is comparatively small, most of its members doing menial or service labor for the white folk. However, the well-heeled boys of Washington's colored set like to drive up the road a bit with their dusky dames in their Cadillacs.

The nearest amusement park to the city of Washington is Glen Echo, about seven miles away, in Maryland. This is the typical smalltown Coney Island, with swimming-pools, crazy rides, dancehalls, hot dogs and the inevitable pick-ups. Many professionals work the park in the summer, but they are outnumbered by the forlorn femmes from Washington who come there in pairs or even larger parties, looking and hoping.

B. Virginia

The Virginia suburbs present a more respectable exterior, though under the surface there's plenty going on. The policy of the Old Dominion is policy.

Virginia's laws do not permit the sale of hard liquor for on-premises consumption. Only beer and wine may be drunk that way. Hard stuff must be bought at liquor stores and taken out. This isn't conducive to anything like gay night life. Virginians go into the District or up to Maryland if they want hi-jinks. Otherwise, most of their fun-making takes place at house parties. There are a few dives. But the after-hour "bottle-clubs" which plague Washington are to be found in Virginia too. One of these is the Commonwealth at South Pitt and Wolfe, in Alexandria.

The average resident of Virginia's suburbs is financially a step or two above his Maryland neighbors. There are more fine homes and estates on this side of the river. The Negro problem is not so incendiary, because this is Virginia, where Jim Crow is king by statute, and colored people live in restricted areas and behave, or else. This is one of the reasons why the Negroes floated into the District, where they changed places with the whites, who overflowed back into Virginia. Remarkable was Prince Georges 64-percent population increase in the decade; but Arlington County, Virginia, had 125 percent.

The absence of night life in the nearby Virginia suburbs has been noted. This minimizes prostitution. Gambling is an important industry, as it is all over the nation.

Virginia authorities are disturbed by an influx of book-makers and policy-sellers, white and black, from the District. Recently a Negro woman was arrested in Arlington with $3,000 in a paper bag, which was picked up that day in pennies, nickels, dimes and quarters—for numbers bets.

Sam Lano, who used to operate the Syndicate slot-machines in Prince Georges, is president of the Arlington Music Corporation, which flooded the county with pinball machines, many being used as gambling devices by local merchants. Lano came here from New York two years ago. Over a year ago he was convicted in Marlborough Circuit Court for having threatened a Prince Georges tavern-owner with prosecution on a bad check if he didn't keep Lano's machines in his place. He was sentenced to a year and his conviction was upheld by the Maryland Court of Appeals. So far, however, Lano hasn't served one day in the cooler, and no effort was made to detain him when he transferred his operations to Virginia. The police of Bangor, Me., are looking for him for the removal and concealment of mortgaged property.

Considerable moonshine liquor is available in the Virginia

suburbs. It comes from stills operated in the mountains in the western part of the state, and from Georgia.

On the whole, you might compare this area to the best of Westchester, or Chicago's North Shore outskirts, or Beverly Hills. That doesn't mean there isn't plenty of dirt. It does mean it has to be something special before it hits print.

Meanwhile, considerable friction is developing as well-heeled northerners flock in; a repetition of the carpetbag days.

10. UNCLE SAM: LANDLORD

THIS IS Washington's largest segment—the federal domain. More than 40 percent of the property in the District is owned by Uncle Sam. (Queen Wilhelmina of The Netherlands is said to be the largest private owner of real estate in the District. She owned the huge Westchester apartments, but sold the property recently to Hilton.)

Though not contiguous, it has an entity of its own. It is immune from local law. That is important, because some federal property oozes across District borders, such as the Pentagon and the National Airport, both on the Virginia side.

To complicate the confused problem of law enforcement, this federal potpourri has its own local police—not one force, but several. The Capitol Police have jurisdiction on the Capitol grounds and several blocks on either side, as far as the Washington Union station. The Terminal Police police that. The White House Police are the cops for the Executive Mansion and surrounding areas. They are under supervision of the Secret Service, a branch of the Treasury. The Capitol cops are under control of Congress itself. The terminal, owned by the railroads and the government, picks its own bulls.

The Park Police are part of the National Park Police, a division of the Department of the Interior. They are the law in the parks and squares, on the boulevards, and on the road in Virginia leading to the Pentagon and the Airport.

All other government buildings are policed by the Public Buildings Police, a Treasury unit. The National Airport, in Virginia, has exempt status. Its own cops not only patrol the

grounds, but the main road. The Pentagon, Arlington Cemetery and other military establishments in the vicinity are
under jurisdiction of the Armed Services Police.

Hundreds of thousands are employed in this federal domain.
Many more use its facilities or live in its lee. This makes the
task of policing almost too complex to be figured out by any
court.

Elsewhere, when there is a conflict of authority over the situs
of a crime, both jurisdictions fight for the right to arrest and
try the accused. In the District it works the other way around.
If it's a borderline case, both sides duck.

For instance, if you're pinched for anything on or along the
road leading to the National Airport there is a conflict between
the National Park Police, the Airport Police, the local Virginia
Police, municipal and county police, and possibly, the MP's.
No one wants any part of it. So there is merry law-breaking in
this federal domain.

At this writing, 27,000 people are employed in the Pentagon.
It is a city within a city. Like all cities, it has its peccadillos.
Many elevator operators are runners for bookies. Many colored
messengers, male and female, sell policy slips. Reefers can be
had. The cops—all kinds—don't know what to do about it. The
military police don't like to arrest civilians, even those employed by the Army. The Virginia police say they have no authority because it's federal property.

The same apathy that marks everything in Washington pervades the Pentagon and other federal buildings. A high Army
officer, highly placed because his brother is close to the President, is a homosexual. He had gathered 95 other officers of
similar inclinations to form what was known as the "Fairy
Brigade." Though scandalously abnormal acts have been committed within the Pentagon walls, no consequences ensued. No
one knew how to go about it. Instead, the suspected fairies
were transferred to distant posts—separately, of course—in the
hope that when they got into trouble in their new stations their
commanding officers would pick up the buck.

More recently a Signal Corps captain in the Pentagon was
apprehended lurking in the stair wells, where he exposed himself to young women. The Army took the easiest way—transferred him to Fort Monmouth, where he was eventually chased
out of the service.

The same situation applies in all government buildings in

the District and in the suburbs. No one wants to do anything about anything. There is scarcely a government installation anywhere in Washington where you can't place a bet or buy a numbers slip. When elevator jockeys aren't selling them, clerks and typists, white and dark, are. Dates and assignations are made on U. S. property by government girls looking for fun or extra earnings, and by come-getters who barge in and solicit men for dates after work—even sometimes for affairs right on overstuffed leather couches which we own, you too.

Any punitive action in these cases is not by police officers. When things get out of hand, department heads fire the culprits.

While the Kefauver Committee was investigating bookmaking, two elevator operators in the Senate Office Building, in which the hearings were conducted, were taking bets on horses with full knowledge of most Senators, many of whom were placing wagers.

That guy you see at the corner of 1st and B, outside the House Office Building, talking to a cop, is a bookmaker's runner. That's his station. That's where typists, messengers and other help in the House of Representatives lay it on the line.

Many have fallen into debt because of the convenience with which they can place bets all day. Hundreds are in the clutches of the loan-sharks in Maryland and the shylocks, who work their trade right in the government office buildings, exacting 100 percent interest for a one-month loan. Many are in arrears on their income taxes for this reason; those who owe more than what is withheld. This has posed a serious problem for the collecting authorities, who are balked by a quirk in the law which forbids them to garnishee tax delinquents among federal employes.

The indifference to rules that apply in private employment results in a sort of Alice in Wonderland atmosphere throughout the unwieldy federal domain.

Humorist George Dixon's story about the two crews hard at work in the Pentagon sums it up:

One crew puts up partitions. The other crew takes them down. The paths of the two crews seldom cross, though there have been embarrassing occasions when they arrived at the same office simultaneously on conflicting missions. But that was the fault of "inefficiency" higher up, not of the putters-up and the takers-down.

Retired brass which had come roaring back to the Pentagon found itself assigned to broom-closets because many mere swivel-chair warmers had commandeered enough office space for a bowling alley.

That's why the Pentagon has two crews, working independently, day and night. One makes offices bigger for new brass, the other makes them smaller for the old.

The confusion is proving hard on fixed Pentagon employes. They suffer severely from wet paint.

PART TWO

THE PEOPLE
(*Confidential!*)

11. THERE'S NOTHING LIKE A DAME

*W*OMEN are the same everywhere, except in Washington, where they not only are different, but there are more of them.

Females generally fall into two categories, good and bad— the good being so because they can't get the necessary masculine cooperation to be bad.

We have seen them all, all over the world, but nowhere else are they like they are in Washington. This town has 100,000 more nubile women than men. Forty-five percent of all its females earn their own livings. Most of them are government employes, and thus have better security than is provided by a husband. Many support husbands, or assist toward the expenses of the mutual establishment. Being self-supporting, they are, on the average, better dressed than you'll find them anywhere else. That is on the "average." There is little "high-fashion" except in diplomatic and social circles, because government salaries are average, not high.

Most Washington men are only fair wage earners, too, and that limits the loot. It is not so easy to promote a mink coat in Washington as it is in New York, though there are more minks per corpus in Washington than are won, wangled or plain bought in Philadelphia, Chicago or Boston.

Our capital is a femmocracy, a community in which the women not only outdo the men in numbers, but in importance. Males hold more exalted positions, but such work as is

74

accomplished could not go on without the efficient, well-trained and permanent secretarial corps, almost all female.

Everything in Washington is slanted toward dames. The accent in the stores is on things women do or buy for themselves, instead of on home-furnishing and children's clothes, which are the bedrocks of department store trade in other cities.

Elsewhere, femmes are divided into specific classes. They are wives, whores, glamor girls, home girls and office workers. Here none matches her opposite number as you know her. The females in the capital defy classification by other standards, and lap over into categories not laid out by economic divisions or natural vicissitudes of physical appeal. Prim, bespectacled bachelor-girl secretaries enlist as $10 call girls after hours or on Saturdays and Sundays—not for the money, but for adventure, substitution for romance. A friend of ours had to entertain visitors. He phoned for three call girls. When they arrived he saw to his horror one was his secretary.

Washington's biggest she-group is made up of G-girls, government girls, who will be taken apart in later paragraphs. Running a close second are O-girls, those who work for organizations, such as unions, charity groups, scientific societies, trade and mercantile bodies, and those who do the paper work for lobbies which maintain permanent offices here.

Washington proves that the emancipation of women is baloney. See what happens here. They have jobs and make as much as most men. They have the freedom to live alone and like it, but they don't. They have the opportunity to do vital work, to carve out careers in the civil service, as some do. But all, including most of the married ones, are desperately unhappy. They are caught in the unreality of this huge farce. It can't be a home, it can't be a place to live in and love, it's just a rat race running the same course every day.

Tens of thousands of young and ambitious girls flock into Washington from every state, territory and dependency, and from foreign nations. There are even two from Samoa, pretty Laida and Marion Kreuz, whose brother, Peter Coleman, is a policeman in the House Office Bldg., and a night law student. The mass migration is similar in number, but not in purpose, to that which occurs in New York and Hollywood and to a lesser degree in Chicago and San Francisco.

The girls that come from the farms, the inland cities and the tributary towns to the other great metropolises come with stardust in their eyes. Having discovered that what they have is too good for the local cow-manicurists, soda jerks and grease station monkeys, they assume it can be used to start them on the road to fame and fortune in the big city. Most fail to find the golden pot at the end of the rainbow or even get anywhere near it in New York and Hollywood. The disappointed fall by the wayside or return home and marry the mailman.

The psychological urge which uproots girls from their native environments to come to Washington is the same, but its manifestations are different. The youngster who pulls strings to get a government job may be, and quite often is, prettier than her neighbor who hitch-hiked to Broadway. But apparently she hasn't the same confidence in her charms as her brasher sister, so she goes to Washington instead.

The young ones who come to the capital to work for Uncle Sam are on the whole better educated than kids who want to make careers in show business. Most of them must have graduated from high school and business school to get a government job. There are some among the chorines who stuck a toe in a college, but all they need for success is to know the difference between the right and left leg, and remember when not to cross them.

Not all girls who come to Washington come to work for the government. Not all are high school graduates. Washington draws more street-walkers, who are strictly out for business, than any other town. They set out from the nearby hills of West Virginia, Maryland and the Carolinas, and they are purposeful as to their objectives. Many aren't bad-looking. So the question again arises, why didn't they go to New York or Hollywood and try for bigger stakes where flexible morals pay off better and the field for a killing is bigger?

The answer again is—no confidence. They don't feel important enough to make good in the big league. They are afraid of the megapolis on the Hudson. Washington has small-town ways and the whores are small-town girls. Street-walking requires no influential connections, deals, financial backlogs, tests, skills. They step off a bus and can be in business before they pass a crossing.

The general belief is that when girls leave home they dream of going on the stage. Washington proves that many leave home just to get away from Home.

They have one commodity they can sell. And they don't have to carry samples in a briefcase. And they must go on the road for customers—too many complications where they are well known, have families, church connections, lovers or husbands.

12. G-GIRLS

A. Government Girls

*A*BOUT 200,000 women work five days a week for Uncle Sam. They come from every corner of the nation. And no matter how long they remain here, few of them ever really live here. They sleep in various kinds of barracks, rooming-houses, rundown hotels, board with retired married ones, and in all constitute a class so large and so displaced that the city cannot absorb them as it does working-women in other communities.

They are not all physically repellant, nor do they behave generally like spinsters are supposed to. The deadly monotony of their routine tasks and their lonesome lives wears out their charm before it destroys their looks. They are a hard, efficient lot, doing men's work, thinking like men and sometimes driven to take the place of men—in the proscribed zones of desperate flings at love and sex. Lesbianism is scandalously rampant, frequently an acquired dislocation rather than a pathological aberration.

The existence of the average G-girl revolves between routine grind and physical frustration. She leaves her job at five. If she goes home, it is to her tiny room or apartment to heat her dinner out of tin cans and ponder whether to wash her panties or write letters home, or get drunk.

It isn't all wrapped up in the fact of the female overflow. Left-over women can learn to do with half their share of men. But strangely, where every guy ostensibly could take his pick and date alternately, it doesn't work that way. The Washington male clerks and middle-class bureau employes largely avoid their opposite numbers. They, too, are hall-room habitués, and they fraternize by some unwritten rule with other men, usually normal men. Propinquity does not work its magic here as the dominant factor in the mingling of the sexes.

Thousands of visitors and thousands of servicemen from nearby installations, most of them dame-hungry, don't have to hunt; they are hunted. Not only that, but often they are paid, and seldom are they allowed to pick up checks without a struggle.

One of the sights of Washington is the outpouring of the janes at five o'clock. Many of them dash for cocktail bars, where they compete with the harlots, who violently resent them and call them "scabs."

A favorite after-work guzzle-and-grab spot is the Cafe of All Nations, in the Mayfair House, at 13th and F. Wise men in the mood are there awaiting the stampede—not only for pleasure, but for the gigolo's mite. Men and women are paid the same for equal work. Therefore the income is high for females and low for males as such things are usually adjusted. We gave the place a play at the right time and sat at a table with a third man who had come with us. A waitress shuffled up to us, and in voice and manner characteristic of an old-timer doing a familiar task, said, "The young ladies at the next table would like to buy you a drink." We nodded, the potables were delivered, our hosts raised their glasses, and soon they joined us. We had another round, and when we insisted on taking the tab, not only for our drinks but theirs, too, they left us; they knew we weren't "regular."

A T-man in the course of a check turned up one instance where 12 G-girls had banded together and were keeping one man, in an apartment on Q Street.

Of course, among hundreds of thousands there are thousands not so situated. Many are beautiful, their intelligence is beyond the average, and even humdrum government work cannot make eunuchs of all men. Desirable girls quickly find that they get preferential receptions and promotions even in civil service examinations. There is a middle-aged woman with a superior position in the General Accounting Office, who has risen because she functions as the procurement officer for members of Congress and other dignitaries. The G-gals hear about her specialty, get in touch with her, and if they have appeal they find fun and get ahead. Outstanding ones are sometimes invited to entertain legation attachés or visiting celebrities.

Second-class lobbyists, who cannot finance dazzlers in the top echelons, have lists of typists and file-clerks and secretaries who are happy to be taken out, or taken in, and are not prissy over how an evening winds up.

Beyond these escapes from a circumscribed daily existence, there is nothing else. A couple of gals will walk the Mall on Sunday, hoping to get picked up; or they join a church, or go to one of the countless dances held during the winter season by state societies, where they find everyone else as desolate as they are; or they scrimp and save all week for a thrilling breakfast-lunch on Sunday at the Statler, where they find to their dismay everyone else in the room is a government girl, too, and stranded for company.

Many secretaries of Senators, Congressmen and executives are their office wives. All Congressmen's offices contain sofas paid for by the Treasury.

These females, when they arrive, usually have accents, idiosyncrasies and dress foibles peculiar to their regions of origin. They quickly fall into the common mold. This is not surprising to your authors, who for years have been writing about Broadway showgirls. Within six months after one leaves the farm to join the chorus, she has acquired a new veneer which covers all she brought with her. You can't, in any one chorus-line, classify the girls, except by their current hair shades. They are as uniform as if they wore uniforms.

The government is like a chorus; instead of 20 girls there are 200,000, and they all talk the same—mainly about favoritism shown to another by the immediate superior whom they accuse of sleeping with her. They dress the same—usually in suits. They eat the same—salads and dainty desserts. They live the same—in spick and span tiny rooms, with intimate wash hung on the line in the bathroom, which does triple duty as a kitchenette. They drink the same—martinis.

Their sex-lives are remarkably alike, too. Some are afraid they will. Others are afraid they won't. And it all boils down to the same sustained jitters, but in different wrappers.

The G-girl is in an unnatural vacuum. She has no time-limits; her sentence is for life, usually. She isn't home and she isn't away. Her marriage outlook is bleak. No family ties console her. She is more often wooed by women than by men.

She makes a mockery of the theory that a woman's first instinct is for security.

B. Girls with Glamor

Let it not be surmised that government-girls are all the girls. There are wives and fiancées, college co-eds, a sprinkling of debutantes and other daughters of the rare society clans, smart saleswomen, even a few presentable sob-sisters.

But the true glamorette, as she is known on Broadway and Fifth Avenue, Vine Street and Sunset Boulevard, and even in such remote oases of joy as Galveston, Texas, is virtually non-existent.

Chorines are but a memory of leg and lavender for the old inhabitants. Except for a rare transitory line in a night club, there is no such thing. Occasionally an imported single or sister-act plays the vaudeville house. Some of the painted peelers who work in the suburban dives sleep in Washington hotels. A movie celeb popping in for publicity, to attend a birthday ball or be photographed smiling down on Truman from the top of a piano, is an event. If there are any gorgeous, dangerous, slinky spies, we didn't find them. Judy Coplon, by the men who specialize in the field, was called exceptionally lush for that trade. So we stopped looking.

The indigenous flora shape up about as they do in Brooklyn, except that they are better dressed and have less sooty complexions. They do not come downtown in slacks. Sloppy galoshes are de trop. Most girls at 16 appear and behave grown up.

But few can enter the accepted avenues where beauty may command a respectable commercial return. In any ranking hierarchy of glamor the model comes first, having long since passed the chorus girl, because of the more stable rewards and higher standards brought about by the great advertising demands. Washington has little need for animated manikins. Some of the choicer shops employ them to demonstrate clothes. There is no extensive advertising field.

The most lucrative and the steadiest calls for models come from sources not seeking those who might be employed in industrial cities for modeling. They hook on as hostesses, guides, ushers, and to decorate the booths and exhibits at conventions and trade shows, which are numerous. Those who are engaged sporadically earn a minimum of five dollars an hour, plus indeterminate tips. Their morals vary with the personal equation.

The models who are willing to pose in the nude at stag-parties get fifty dollars an evening. These register with surreptitious characters of the middle-world between flesh-market procurers and shady promoters.

Among the better-known models' agencies are Models Bureau, in the Chastleton Hotel; Ralston, 711 14th Street, NW, and Phyllis Bell, 306 13th Street NW.

The girl who sets out to be a model in Washington is usually one of those rare creatures—the native. An out-of-towner with such ambitions would naturally head to New York.

(*Note:* Most model agencies are schools instead of employment agencies. They seek to sign job-seekers to contract to learn how to walk, instead of sending them out to work. Some, billing themselves as agencies, provide girls—but not for modeling.)

Another reason for the shortage of really high class cheesecake is that there is almost always a displacement movement in effect.

The trains and planes to Hollywood are loaded with lookers, sent there with entree obtained for them by such influential VIP's as cabinet officers, four-star generals, bureau heads, etc. When a prominent daddy gets fed up with his dame, he can't just brush her off; she might make trouble, and that might get into print.

So the procedure is to phone Hollywood, where a liaison contact is instructed to obtain a job at a studio for the chick. The big film companies employ scores of so-called "contract" gals at $150 a week or so, who do nothing but pose for publicity stills, date chosen visitors, like out-of-town exhibitors, and otherwise make themselves useful and amiable around the lots. One in a thousand rises and may become a star.

The movie industry is always skating on such thin ice, what with anti-trust laws, etc., that a request from Washington is a command. So it's a happy out all around. Mr. Big gets rid of his discarded girl, she goes willingly because no girl can turn down a film contract, and Hollywood stores up a favor for the next time it needs one.

Many girls with talent originated here but they scrammed as soon as they were old enough to know better. Among them were Helen Hayes, Kate Smith and Mary Eaton, all members of the St. Patrick's Players.

Washington has no clubs or theatres with lines of girls. The best a babe with light feet can do is get in as a teacher at a dance studio, quite a business in Washington. The local classi-fied phone directory has four pages of listings of dance instruc-tors. That's because dancing schools are a swell way for lone-some people to meet each other, and that's what Washington has plenty of. The local Arthur Murray licensee, across the street from the Mayflower Hotel, is the largest Arthur Murray studio in the world. At least 2,000 girls find full or part-time employment working as instructors in the dozens of studios. Many of these girls are little more than taxi-dancers.

Pretty, personable ones can make up to $100 a week with tips. Those who take dates after hours do even better.

The real Washington glamor girl is the kept woman. You'd be surprised how many there are. All the bigger hotels and the glossier apartment houses around Dupont Circle and out Con-necticut Avenue are loaded with them. They are the ones you most often see in mink coats, in expensive beauty parlors and fine shops. They are maintained mainly by important govern-ment officials, Senators, sports and millionaires from all over the country who make their headquarters in Washington. Many an executive who commutes to the capital keeps a cutie there full time.

All Washington giggled when it heard the story of the tall, stately blonde whose bills were paid by a Cuban sugar million-aire, and who fell in love with an assistant manager of the Shoreham Hotel, where she was living in high style. Her Latin lover found her in flagrante delicto with the hotel employe. The men squared off for a fist fight, but first locked the babe in a clothes closet. They blacked each other's eyes—but she frac-tured her ankle trying to kick the door down.

To add to the embarrassment of the unhappy Cuban, his wife had been spying on him and his love through high-powered binoculars from Rock Creek Park, across the street. She sued him for divorce in New York.

A genuine glamor-gal does pop up now and then. One was Evelyn Knight, the radio and record star, who warbled for $75 a week in Washington hotels until a couple of years ago, then clicked in Manhattan and is now dragging down thou-sands.

Bette Woodruff, another home-grown dish, seems to be on the upgrade. A dress model, Bette had a yen to sing. One day, on a dare, she phoned maestro Dick Williams to tell him she was available. He didn't know her from Eve, took her name to shut her up. Next day his vocalist got sick. He phoned Bette in a hurry. That was less than a year ago. Now she's thrushing regularly, and well.

But Jan Du Mond, a five-foot-three night club canary, pianist and composer, drives a cab by day.

"My little coupe broke down," she told a reporter. "I couldn't afford a new car. Becoming a taxi-driver provided me with transportation at night to get to my engagement—the company lets me take the car home."

Besides, she meets the most interesting people!

Sometimes a government gal switches to a glamor gal. One was Sandra Stahl, "Miss Washington," in last fall's Atlantic City beauty contest. Sandra was a secretary for Air Force Intelligence, but she has a face, a figure, a noodle and a voice. She was the dark horse when she sang before 3,000 people in Rock Creek Park, but 14 judges, including the Treasurer of the United States, sent her to Atlantic City.

Sandra comes from Long Beach, California. In our "New York, Confidential," we noted that many of Gotham's orchids on display come from Southern California. Maybe Sandra got on the wrong train.

13. COMPANY GIRLS

*T*HIS is a specialty known only to Washington.

With the procuring situation as it is, the business of getting girls for fun, friendship, or what have you in mind is so commercialized, it's incredible.

In our excursions into life in New York and Chicago, we found that girls you pay for an evening can be divided into two classes: party-girls and call-girls.

You summon the former, but they are not necessarily whores. You whistle for the others only when there's to be a party.

If this seems contradictory, it's because the dividing line is so tenuous, it usually isn't there. But for our purposes, we shall group them together and call both "C-girls," which stands for company girls, which is just what the womanless men who call them want them to be.

There are as many kinds of C-girls as there are kinds of women. They range from the lowest, who will come to your room for $5 for a quickie, to the most ultra, who expects $100, plus expenses, as a fee for her company for an evening, and nothing guaranteed. If it happens, it must be romanced or financed with honorarium.

The C-girls include the cheapest cocottes and some of the smartest, prettiest New York models. The only thing they have in common is you can phone them or someone who acts as an agent to make a deal, sight unseen, for their presence. The more they get the less they give. The true party-pretty undertakes only to appear for the evening, maybe entertain an important customer or that Congressman who's going to investigate you or that general who places the orders. The call-dames are cheaper and more reliable.

They are available from all hotel bell-boys. A friend who lives in Washington said they weren't necessary, for you can find a street-walker on any avenue or a hustler at almost any bar. We asked how about the transient, who doesn't know that, so doesn't know where to look, or is afraid. The bell-captain, who can get anything, including booze after hours, is the functionary out-of-towners over the age of puberty call. Using his services also means no raid from the hotel dick, who is an ally.

Lobbyists have lists of company-girls whose services they utilize as required. They exchange names with each other, so most of them have a master-list. In addition, there are agents, quite often apparently respectable, middle-aged women, who run "secretarial bureaus" that supply company-girls, often do contract businesses with large users, whom they bill by the year.

The secretarial bureau is important in the blind date business in Washington. Without much trouble, you can get the kind of girl you want by calling almost any of them. The procedure is this: You phone for a stenographer to be sent to your hotel room. She, however, is never the "date." After giving her a nominal amount of dictation, you remark you are alone and friendless. She tells you one of her girl friends is lonesome, too, and would consider a date. You wait in. She arrives.

A problem for those who must entertain men of class is the low quality of the female commodity obtainable except from specializing agencies. Government gals, many of whom are on call, are superior intellectually, have better manners, though the professional predators run prettier. With the short supply of charmers, those who maintain a superior standard import them. Many big lobbyists and others who entertain frequently have lists of New York models and showgirls who will come down to Washington for fun, expense money, and maybe a mink.

There is a middle-aged woman in New York, who gives her name as Mrs. Hansen, who makes regular monthly trips to such Eastern cities as Philadelphia, Baltimore and Washington, where she meets prominent businessmen and offers to introduce them, at a fee of $10 each, to any of a hundred Powers and Conover models whose photos she has in a scrapbook and whose names she has on a typewritten sheet. She guarantees to produce any girl thereon in Washington within 24 hours, the girls to receive $100 and expenses for each day's company.

But that is still run-of-the-mill. A babe named Teddie, with an apartment in the building on the southwest corner of 16th Street, in the 1600 block, handles knockouts, some married, for as much as $250 a night.

Virginia Wall, who lives at 2500 Q Street (phone Hudson 8783) at this writing, was chosen by those who know her as— "the most promising younger company-girl in Washington." She knows many other company girls.

Florence Bowers, a Southerner who lives at 1716 Newton St., phone Hobart 5634, is a well-known company girl who will get others when needed.

Elizabeth Morley, 2124 P St., phone Hobart 7421, will get company-girls.

Mary Lou Vane, 1205 Clifton St., NW, is a superior company girl.

Washington has its corned beef and cabbage, but don't say we don't bring out its caviar.

14. FOR IMMORAL PURPOSES

IT MAY startle you, though not necessarily stop you, to know what very few know—it is a felony to transport a female one step up or down or sideways in the District of Columbia with what grandma used to call "dishonorable intentions."

The Mann Act was invented by a Chicago blue-nosed representative named Mann, after a hophead parlor-whore in melodramatic mood threw a note out of the window of the late Harry Guzik's cathouse on which she had written "I am a white slave." A milkman found it and turned it in at the 22nd Street police station. A puritanical young prosecutor named Clifford Roe, instead of laughing, made it so scandalous that the term "white slave" became the common synonym for a prostitute. Mona Marshall, the girl, was no slave at all, and when she came out of her fog she proved it. Her case history showed that she had been seduced in Wisconsin and brought to Chicago and placed in the house, quite willingly, by a traveling man who thought it was wasteful to give it away.

That came out in testimony and Congressman Mann fathered the law making interstate transportation a penitentiary offense. Too many jokes about crossing state lines have gone into the legend since then for anyone not to understand the possible consequences of taking 'em in one state and making 'em in another. But what has been very sparsely advertised is a phrase in the Mann Act which states, "or on federal territory." Washington is federal territory.

So, if you meet one in the lobby and take her up in the elevator, you're a candidate for Atlanta.

This clause has been enforced with ultimate results. But for many years, by unwritten policy, the Department of Justice stopped paying attention to private, non-commercial infractions. But in no way has the letter been ameliorated, and at any time this statute could be applied, as the income tax evasion law was used to convict murderous gangsters, if an Attorney General so instructs. It can be used without even the technical provisions required to substantiate an attempted rape.

The language states, "for immoral purposes." Such purposes need not be successful. There is a mistaken notion that paying a female's fare has something to do with it. It has not, except as evidence of the intent, which is the res gestae.

Let it not be assumed that this is a major deterrent for the Washington wolf, before whom is spread a field alabaster with white lambs generously interlarded with black sheep. Yet the fine art of subtle, sophisticated flirtation, with skill, poise and aplomb, which has illuminated the finest works of the masters through the ages in every form of expression, seems extinct here.

Those in residence are boors; the transients are in a hurry; and the distaff defense being negligible, no true swordsman deigns to fence when he can hit a broad on the head with the handle.

Chief among Washington ladies' men is handsome Warren Magnuson, bachelor Senator from the state of Washington, where some of his I.W.W. constituents would probably kick over the traces if they saw the highfalutin' fillies he runs with in Washington. The Senator is a man among men, with the reputation of seldom wooing one girl at a time. He often entertains several in one evening in his Shoreham apartment. We know. They talk.

Not all wolves are single. We will not divulge names, or tell how they cover up. Your imagination will picture how easy it is in a town where so many are seeking favors, to get a stooge to come along as the cutie's alleged "date," while the principal apparently came along only for the ride.

Not all wolves, of course, are Senators or such with official immunity.

A simple way to get acquainted is to watch the papers for announcements of State Society dances. Most lonesome G-gals belong to these societies, composed of expatriates from their home states. Once every week, throughout the year, one of these groups throws a party or a dance. Admission is open to all. The Officers' Service Club dances are swell, too.

At this writing there are no public ballrooms of the type of Roseland in New York or the Aragon in Chicago, not because they're illegal, but because they have been unprofitable. In the summer this lack is filled by moonlight cruises of the Wilson Steamship Line on the river. The boats leave from the 7th

Street wharf nightly, at 8:30, and the charge, including dancing, is one buck. Plenty of unattached women go.

The Potomac is mighty important to wolves. Practically the last of the night-boats in the country plies from Washington to Old Point Comfort and Norfolk, Virginia, summer and winter.

In years gone by, the fabled Albany and Fall River boats to Boston could have told such stories.

Steamers of the Old Bay Line charge $4.67 each way, with staterooms at from $1.50 to $5.50.

Last fall, a couple of evangelists chartered a Wilson liner for an evening prayer service on the Potomac. Many pious people showed up, but so did a swarm of scarlet sisters.

With all the game flying low you'd scarcely think it worth while for entrepreneurs to promote stag-parties. Yet many hotel ballrooms are engaged for shows at which talent, imported from Baltimore, is seen and appropriately appreciated. These nude nymphs perform also at Waldrops on Rhode Island Avenue, across the Maryland line.

Lots of smooth, mysterious guys in Washington, not pimps, make livings introducing lonesome men to pretty babes. One, named Al Walters, ran a series of dances called the "UN Victory Girls." He was investigated by the Washington vice-squad, which found nothing illegal, though it did determine that his net income from promoting these get-togethers was $325 a week. Walters is still around town, always surrounded by eight or ten pretty bimbos, usually blonde, and he can get to the right people because he is a great introducer.

Young love gets a break in Washington, too, because the burg with its environs is small-town in construction, with front and back porches, lawns and alleys, and plenty of dark streets and nearby country nooks to drive to. Chief among the lovers' lanes are Hains Point and the Anacostia Flats, along the Anacostia River, where the Bonus Army of '32 made camp. Not all who court Eros in these secluded spots are juveniles. Many adults take their occasionals there, especially white men afraid or ashamed to check into free-for-all assignation houses.

We got the following story from a cop who worked the case. A blonde waitress at the Copacabana restaurant, a rendezvous for Latin-Americans, went with a stranger in his car to the Anacostia Flats. A woman's screams tore the night air. Startled householders in the vicinity, rape-conscious because of the front-page sex murder of a girl the day before, phoned police. The squad car cops sped to a surprised girl and an embarrassed gent. "I always scream at a time like that," she elucidated, with indignation.

WISDOM OF A WASHINGTON WOLF

When you see someone waiting for a bus or streetcar, it's considered polite to offer a lift in your car. Washington gallants are very polite, especially if the hitch-hiker is cute.

*   *   *

We noticed Washington wolves seldom ply their dates with flowers. This may be because the girls are so anxious they'd give the guy orchids. Or maybe because Washington is an Eastern city, and in the East—New York especially—few well-dressed women wear corsages.

*   *   *

Most G-gals start work early in the morning. The wise Washington lupo learns to date them for cocktails at five in the afternoon.

*   *   *

Some characters tap the female college alumnae lists for recent graduates resident in Washington, then pick names at random and phone with an invitation to a Yale or Princeton hop which never seems to come off.

*   *   *

HOTELS FOR WOMEN ONLY: Hattie M. Strong Hall, (YWCA) phone ME 2100, Meridian Hill, CO 1000; All States (cooperatively owned) NA 2483. (If the gal you're phoning isn't home, ask the switchboard operator if anyone else wants a date. She could know one.)

*   *   *

The abortion racket is wide open in Washington, with illegal practitioners protected from high-up. Prices run from $35 to $500 a job, depending on your color and your bank-book. The lowest charge is for Negroes. Unmarried G-gals can get by for $75. Married women with husbands who work are charged $100. Single ones in a jam who have rich or important paramours are nailed for as much as $500. (In New York $1,000 isn't unusual.)

15. GARDEN OF PANSIES

*I*F YOU'RE wondering where your wandering semi-boy is tonight, he's probably in Washington.

The good people shook their heads in disbelief with the revelation that more than 90 twisted twerps in trousers had been swished out of the State Department. Fly commentators seized on it for gags about fags, whimsy with overtones of Kinsey and the odor of lavender. We pursued the subject and we found that there are at least 6,000 homosexuals on the government payroll, most of them known, and these comprise only a fraction of the total of their kind in the city.

The only way to get authoritative data on fairies is from other fairies. They recognize each other by a fifth sense immediately, and they are intensely gregarious. One cannot snoop at every desk and count people who appear queer. Some are deceptive to the uninitiated. But they all know one another and they have a grapevine of intercommunication as swift and sure as that in a girls' boarding school. Since they have no use for women in the main, and are uneasy with masculine men, they have a fierce urge, even beyond the call of the physical, for each other's society. They have their own hangouts, visit one another, and cling together in a tight union of interests and behavior.

Not all are ashamed of the trick that nature played on them. They have their leaders, unabashed, who are proud queens and who revel in their realm. Your reporters, after years around show business, are familiar with those of their breed, unembarrassed in their presence. But, with the exception of crude male prostitutes whom they have encountered in police courts and on the sidewalks of New York's Lexington Avenue and in Harlem, they still had a whisper of an illusion left: they got the idea, because they had met so many with marked talent, that by a pathological compensation many of them possessed artistic traits.

In Washington they found this false. The exceptional ones do drift to Broadway and to Hollywood. But they are no more representative of their numbers than are the gifted men and women who find their places in the arts of the great mass of people from whom they become detached to follow the livelier professions.

Now we have found out where the dull, dumb deviates go. We had assumed that, as they grew up in small communities where they soon became obvious and odious, they took flight for the stage, the screen, interior decorating, exotic literature and other fields centered in the metropolitan market-places. That is not true. Only a few can and do enter the avenues where their talents make them equal, often superior.

So, what becomes of the marked twilight-sex, unwelcome at home, pariahs afar? We might ask what becomes of the club-footed or pock-marked girl similarly situated. She is in a panic about the present, still more so about the future, and she searches for security. Where can that be captured? Nowhere else as surely as in the civil service. There, in the mediocrity and virtual anonymity of commonplace tasks, the sexes—all four of them—are equal in the robot requirements and qualifications. There is no color line, no social selectivity; not even citizenship is always a prerequisite. Once the precious appointment is filed in a machine which knows no discrimination, there it stays for life.

Like immigrants from foreign lands, for these people are aliens in their own, they attract—more often send for and finance —those who speak their language and live their kind of lives. Congressman A. L. Miller, of Nebraska, a physician, author of the District's new bill to regulate the homos, enunciated with an oratorical flourish the deathless statement that, "birds of a feather flock together." William Jennings Bryan came from Nebraska, too.

The 6,000 who made the perennial payroll drew many more thousands who flunked it. Like pug-nosed, freckle-faced girls of no distinction, who become waitresses and car-hops, these inverts who are washed in with the tide and beached in the mud become clerks in shops, hairdressers, waiters, bartenders, most often in the places habitually patronized by those of their own stripe.

The Washington vice squad had listed 5,200 known deviates. Dr. Ben Karpman, psychiatrist at St. Elizabeth's Hospital, believes they are in the tens of thousands.

Their chief meeting place is in leafy Lafayette Square, across

Pennsylvania Avenue from the White House. They make love under the equestrian statue of rugged Andrew Jackson, who must be whirling on his heavenly horse every time he sees what is going on around his monument. Lafayette Square is no bohemian section, like Washington Square in New York. The three sides not surrounded by the White House have such buildings as the Cosmos Club, formerly the home of Dolly Madison; the national headquarters of the League for Political Education of the American Federation of Labor; the Hay-Adams House, one of Washington's finer hotels, and other dignified structures.

How the fairies happened to pick this place for their rendezvous, and how the cops let them get away with it, no one can trace.

The police keep making arrests, but it does not deter the homos from hanging out around the square. They make pickups there and quite often engage in immoral acts practically under the eyes of the sparrow cops.

They also foregather in Franklin Park, a few blocks away, in the center of the business district.

There is no geographic section where degenerates generally live. That is part of the general picture, everything, everywhere, in Washington.

Many rich fairies and lesbians live in expensive remodeled Georgetown homes, the nearest thing to a left-bank neighborhood. This is also a left-wing center.

Some parties which take place in Washington pervert sets are orgies beyond description and imagination. Every invention of Sacher-Masoch and the Marquis de Sade has been added to and improved upon, and is in daily use. Weekends find the pansies and lady-lovers on broad, baronial estates of wealthy perverts in nearby Virginia and Maryland. Many of the third sex journey regularly to New York, where they have friends in esoteric circles.

Washington has its transvestites, who get their thrills from appearing in the clothes of the opposite sex. Some of the ritzier dress shops on Connecticut Avenue couldn't exist if it weren't for the fairies who buy French imports. Many dress in drag on Thanksgiving Day and mingle in the holiday crowds with the costumed young folk.

While these lines were being typed, a member of the staff of Democratic Senator Edwin C. Johnson, of Colorado, who recently made front pages when he attacked the morals of the movie industry, was arrested by two vice squad officers in the men's room in Lafayette Square and charged with committing indecent acts. Booked in $500 bail, he pleaded not guilty. He and Senator Johnson, who appeared with him in the preliminary hearing before the United States Attorney, made no statements. He was later acquitted by a jury.

The same day, Assistant U. S. Attorney Warren Wilson asked for the night closing of public comfort stations, calling them breeding places of perversion. Commenting on the increase of such cases, Wilson said, "90 percent of these offenses are committed in men's rooms operated by the Federal government."

Wilson mentioned Lafayette Square, Stanton Park, Dupont Circle and Franklin Park. He recommended that all these comfort stations be closed as soon after 4 P.M. as policemen on the 4-12 shift could do so, and be kept closed until 8 A.M.

"These stations were constructed when there were no other facilities in downtown Washington," Wilson said. "Today, hundreds of restaurants are required to have toilet facilities by law. Many hotels have been constructed since the comfort stations.

"Public places are becoming cesspools of perversion."

Many cocktail lounges and restaurants cater to irregulars. Most of them are near the Mayflower Hotel. The most popular resort is the Jewel Box, near 16th and L, NW, formerly known as the Maystat. It is a cocktail lounge with entertainment by a piano-player, who sings semi-risqué lyrics.

The waiters are obviously fairies. Most customers seem to fit into the pattern. The night we went there, a police car, with siren screaming, pulled up. We figured it was a pinch. After the cop threw out two customers, a waiter told us everything was o.k.

"Those boys got fresh," he said. "They tried to flirt with those two women sitting there. We don't tolerate flirting—anyway not with women."

Then he minced off, hand on hip.

Fags also like a restaurant known as Mickey's, behind the Mayflower. They patronize the second floor of a place in the 1700 block of H Street. One night two Congressmen, a couple of army officers, and two young servicemen were mixing beer and gin there, and kissing each other. They also swish around the Sand Bar in Thomas Circle.

A favorite meeting-place for keeping appointments is the

lobby of the Franklin Park Hotel. The Riggs Turkish Bath, the only one in town, under Keith's Theatre, was closed up because these undesirables took it over. Its license has since been restored.

Black Washington has its share of deviates, too.

There is free crossing of racial lines among fairies and lesbians. We have seen aristocratic Southerners, on the bias, hunt down Negro men for dalliance. We bumped into a gal in show business, who we know is queer, sitting with two mannish-looking women at the Jewel Box. She invited us to a party in Black Town, an inter-racial, inter-middle-sex mélange, with long-haired, made-up Negro and white boys simpering while females of both races mingled in unmistakable exaltation.

During the summer, groups of colored fairies make up "yachting" parties and cruise the Potomac on the steamer Robert E. Lee. One Saturday night, last summer, over 100 cops were dispatched to the docks when the "Society of Female Impersonators" was to have a midnight sail. They found 1,700 Negro men, all dressed as women, on the boat, and as many more trying to get on. A riot was in the making, but the cops busted it up and kept it quiet when they hauled away two wagon-loads. The ship finally got off at 2 A.M.

Two weeks later, in another melee on the same boat, a colored man was fatally shot by a police detective after he jumped into the water. Another Negro, who pleaded guilty to having started the riot, was fined $200 for having endangered the lives of 600 persons. Some months later, Washingtonians were mystified by an ad in a daily paper which read as follows: "S.S. Mt. Vernon—moonlight cruise—8:30 P.M.—beer—stag or drag."

No one knows how many lesbians there are, because the female—or is it male—of the pervert species is seldom spoken about and is much less obvious. Psychiatrists and sociologists who have made a study of the problem in Washington think there are at least twice as many Sapphic lovers as fairies. A large incidence of lesbianism is concomitant with the shortage of men, where women work together, live together, play together, so love together.

Some display themselves, strut around in fairy joints; all queers are in rapport with all others. You will see them also in some of the late bottle-clubs, on the make for the same girls the he-wolves are chasing.

The mannish women used to hang out at the Show Boat

Bar, H and 13th, until the management drove them out. Now in David's Grill, formerly the Horseshoe, in back of the Mayflower Hotel, they outnumber the pansies who haunted the place. Many lesbians frequent Kavakos' Grill, in the SE section, though this is not any joint so specializing. The club, owned by Bill Kavakos, a rich Greek who likes to gamble, is near the Navy Yard. It caters to sailors and slummers.

A breakdown of occupations in one group of 543 perverts who were arrested showed some interesting sidelights. Among them was only one actor, but 92 students. There were 58 army personnel and 28 from the navy. Even the rugged Marines appeared. Among the deviates were one bartender, one barber and one baker. There were four attorneys, only two doctors and only one embalmer. This is the record:

Accountant	7	Minister	3
Actor	1	Musician	5
Airport employee	3	Navy:	
Army:		Commissioned	1
Commissioned	9	Noncommissioned	27
Noncommissioned	49	Page boy	1
Attorney	4	Pharmacist	4
Baker	1	Porter	6
Barber	1	Radio personnel	3
Bartender	1	Realtor	2
Businessman	7	Reporter	2
Butcher	1	Restaurant personnel	27
Cab driver	2	Salesman	10
Clerk	48	Sculptor	2
Diplomat	1	Servant	10
Doctor	2	Service-station operator	2
Embalmer	1	Skilled laborer	17
Embassy personnel	1	Stenographer and secretary	4
Government employee	57	Student	92
Guard	9	Teacher and Professor	12
Historian	1	Technician	8
Horse breeder	1	Unemployed	50
Interior decorator	3	Unskilled laborer	31
Jeweler	1	Writer	2
Laundryman	6		
Librarian	3	Total	543
Marines, U. S.	2		

With more than 6,000 fairies in government offices, you may be concerned about the security of the country. Fairies are no more disloyal than the normal. But homosexuals are vulnerable, they can be blackmailed or influenced by sex more deeply than conventional citizens; they are far more intense about their love-life.

Foreign chancelleries long ago learned that homos were of value in espionage work. The German Roehm, and later Goering, established divisions of such in the Foreign Office. That was aped by Soviet Russia, which has a flourishing desk now in Moscow. According to Congressman Miller, who made a comprehensive study of the subject, young students are indoctrinated and given a course in homosexuality, then taught to infiltrate in perverted circles in other countries. Congressman Miller said:

"These espionage agents have found it rather easy to send their homosexuals here and contact their kind in sensitive departments of our Government. Blackmail and many other schemes are used to gather secret information.

"The homosexual is often a man of considerable intellect and ability. It is found that the cycle of these individuals' homosexual desires follows the cycle closely patterned to the menstrual period of women. There may be three or four days in each month that the homosexual's instincts break down and drive the individual into abnormal fields of sexual practice. Under large doses of sedatives during this sensitive cycle, he may escape such acts.

"The problems of sexual maladjustments are urgent and still far from a solution. In the Army, several thousand were discharged. When caught in the act, they were generally discharged without honor, which means loss of citizenship. Many failed to survive rigors of warfare and intimate association with men. The majority were unable to conceal their tendencies and were eventually eliminated with disgrace.

"Never is the bond which unites two friends such that the acquisition of a new friend by one is regarded angrily by the other; but quite otherwise is the life among homosexuals. Here jealousy reigns supreme. Male homosexuals will not share their fairy with anybody.

"The sexual attraction exercised by a male on another may be apparent in many ways. The homosexual will become excited by the mere presence of some man in a public place. They often approach that man, though he is a stranger. A taxi-driver finds fares making indiscreet advances. The homosexual has no sensation in the presence of the most beautiful and seductive female. Her amorous advances may be repulsive."

Until the recent purges in the State Department, there was a gag around Washington you had to speak with a British accent, wear a homburg hat, or have a queer quirk if you wanted to get by the guards at the door.

One high State Department official was a notorious homo who preferred young Negro boys. He was detected in a Pullman car of the Southern Railroad—on the funeral train to bury Speaker Bankhead, father of Tallulah—making immoral advances to a porter. The story reached newspaper offices, but before it could be printed the State Department sent out an urgent appeal to editors to "kill," because it might imperil the war effort. When this official's misdeeds were placed before President Roosevelt, it was said he refused to replace him because they both "wore the same school tie." After resigning from the government, this official almost died of exposure when a Negro farm hand, jealous because of his attention to another, slugged him.

Aware of the seriousness of the problem, the State Department has a highly hush-hush Homosexual Bureau, manned by trained investigators and former counter-espionage agents, whose duties are to ferret out pansies in Foggy Bottom.

But the department cannot free itself of boondoggling tendencies, for at the same time it retains a personable and intelligent young lady to prepare a treatise on homosexualism, the purpose being to see if it's possible to cure or contain the deviates who remain on the roles. Her assignment requires her to visit faggot dives, observe the queers in action and ask them how they got that way.

The following will be denied, but whenever possible the YMCA is vetoing the use of its facilities, especially the swimming pool, to all State Department employees, just to be on the safe side.

A man of almost cabinet rank in the Defense Department is also a pervert, with bivalent tendencies, a two-way performer.

These are no isolated incidents. The government is honeycombed in high places with people you wouldn't let in your garbage-wagons.

David K. Eichler, a brilliant 37-year-old Harvard post-graduate who was a top policy-maker in the State Department as Deputy Secretary General of the Far Eastern Commission until a couple of months ago, was arrested by Park Police on the Ellipse, charged with committing an unspeakable act with a Negro man. He put up $25 "forfeit," a Washington variation of bail cash, about which more in another chapter. The next day, at the hearing, the colored man pleaded guilty, but when Eichler didn't appear the judge told the prisoner he might change his plea, inasmuch as his co-defendant wasn't there.

The black fairy said, "Never mind, judge. I had a good time."

Shortly after his arrest, Eichler went on a vacation trip to the South. After learning about the pinch, security officials instituted a search for him and summoned him back to Washington. Eichler admitted nothing, but resigned his $9,000-a-year job. He wasn't asked to stay.

On the other hand, the Grand Jury voted a no-bill when Eugene Desvernine, 34, acting officer-in-charge of Caribbean affairs in the State Department, was arrested for an alleged sex offense against a 13-year-old boy. Desvernine, suspended from the department after his arrest in East Potomac Park, has been restored to duty.

The original charges against fairies in the State Department listed only 91, but considerably more than a hundred have been discharged from it since. More are asked to withdraw. And there are believed to be hundreds not yet shown up.

Republicans who tried to get a special "pervert squad" formed were voted down on straight party lines by Democrats, who found themselves having to protect strange bed-fellows. When you read of a fag being fired or quitting, don't think Washington's homosexual population is reduced that much. It isn't. Odds are the discharged degenerate is shifted up on some other government payroll. At least eight were transferred from the State Department to Agriculture. Hundreds of others driven from one department minced into others.

At the end of 1950, State said they were all gone. But on the first day of 1951, the Washington papers carried this brief item under the heading: "Two Men Face Sex Charges."

"Alan A. Wakefield, 26, State Department employe, was released under $300 bond pending a hearing on a disorderly conduct charge. Vice Squad detectives arrested him in the men's room of a downtown hotel." He was since convicted of disorderly conduct.

Dr. Kinsey wasn't appalled by the 6,000 fags in government jobs. According to his calculations, 56,787 Federal workers are congenital homosexuals. He includes 21 Congressmen and says 192 others are bad behavior risks.

We still favor the two-party system.

16. THE LITTLE RED HERRINGS

THE DISTRICT headquarters of the Communist Party—
the local setup, not the Washington nest of the national outfit
—is only a block away from the doorway of the F.B.I., on 9th
near F Street. So close is the line of battle drawn.

This Union Square of the District of Columbia is, appropriately, on Skid Row. It is the apparatus that recruits government
employes. And sometimes 9th Street is more active and important than 16th Street—the White House. The District chairman
is Roy H. Wood.

This book does not bandy the right or wrong of Communism. It accepts and proclaims it all wrong. But it will stay
within its limitations of discussing Washington, the city. So it
will conduct you mostly through the muck where crawl the
punks in the ranks.

The State Department boys call foreign Reds "Agrarian
reformers." We call them cobras. The real story of the extent
of their infiltration into the government will never be told.
Hundreds of files have been impounded or destroyed, and their
subjects cleared.

The following tale is no exception. It is, rather, the rule. One
night a mysterious informant called on Constantine Brown,
brilliant and patriotic foreign news analyst of the *Washington
Star*, with a photostatic copy of an order from a Deputy Chief
of Staff, directing the Army to destroy the records on several
thousand subversives.

Brown hurried to the home of Senator Styles Bridges with
the evidence. By 9 A.M., Bridges had called the Military Affairs
Committee together. An hour later it met and phoned the
offices of the Secretary of War with an ultimatum not to destroy
any orders. When the officer who had issued the order met with
the committee, Bridges looked coldly at him and said, "I can
forgive an officer who makes a mistake or loses a battle, but an
officer who betrays the security of his country ought to be shot."

Meanwhile, a similar order was given the Navy, but was not

caught in time to head off the destruction of the records. F.D.R. was President at the time.

We are hopeful these things will come to an end, but do not expect too much. That is because we know the C.I.A.—Central Intelligence Agency—is loaded with Commies at the lower level, with some seeping right up into the upper brackets.

A bright spot, however, is the advancement to the position of ranking minority member of the House Un-American Activities Committee of Harold Velde, young ex-F.B.I. agent, now representing Abraham Lincoln's old Illinois district in Congress. Velde, at 40, has been a G-man, a county judge, and is in his second term in the House. His training under J. Edgar Hoover sets him up as a canny spy-catcher; his hatred of subversives, left or right, will make him a brake on Commie-coddling. His predecessor on the committee was California's new Senator Nixon, who nailed Alger Hiss, and in Congress, Senator Dirksen, who beat Scott Lucas. The Senate's own Red probing committee is also good news.

Your authors delved into how the rank-and-file protectors and comforters of Communists in Washington got that way. We know about the over-educated Harvard prodigies, recommended to key spots by Felix Frankfurter, but how does a $3,000-a-year file clerk in State, or Defense, meet Reds in the first place? By what means is he wooed and won to betray his country? Jim Walter of the *Times-Herald* exposed a lot. Here is more:

Red spies came here as soon as Lenin and Trotsky pulled their successful November coup in 1917. But not until the late Roosevelt handed diplomatic recognition to the enemies of civilization in 1933, did a sizeable apparatus begin to build openly in Washington. In the early years of the New Deal it became fashionable to be "liberal," to love all radicals, including revolutionaries.

The government was overloaded with Reds, pinks, fellow-travelers, social planners, do-gooders, proletarians, boondogglers and Socialists. The federal establishment is still up to its neck in conspirators and collaborationists, despite a few publicized firings.

Let's take the case of this humble clerk who is seduced by Reds. Seduced is just that. We covered the modus operandi used by the Pervert Sections of foreign chancelleries in the previous chapter. But not all government employes are homos or susceptible. The normal must be romanced with natural methods. Sex-starved government gals are enticed by smooth, suave, good-looking men. Meek male clerks, in soporific jobs at standardized sustenance-pay, are awakened with a sudden whiff of the esoteric when fast-working, trained good-lookers make a play for them. These happenings are not cribbed from E. Phillips Oppenheim novels. They are planned that way and they come off.

Wealthy left-wingers with mansions in Georgetown cooperate avidly. Humble government employes are invited to exotic, erotic parties. This sudden entrance into a world of wealth, taste, refinement, liquor and libido is irresistible to hoi polloi.

Smart Red undercover agents try to get a hold of some kind on their victims, something insidious. Soviet agents press a systematic campaign to bring women employes of the State Department under their control by enticing them into acts of adultery and abnormality. Parties are staged in rich surroundings with pornographic exhibitions, unlimited liquor and every form of dope—and a hidden, talking moving picture camera recording it all.

As many as 65 or 70 attend these aphrodisiac get-togethers, where many wear rich Oriental costumes and Arabian Nights music completes the intoxication of all the senses. Not only potential friends are thus won and hooked, but foes are silenced. One gossip writer—certainly not Winchell—a feared crusader, has within the last couple of years become a virtual transmission belt for the Communist line. He was called into a secret projection room and shown a devastating film of his behavior at a drunken, depraved orgy. We have seen "stills" from it.

This use of sex as a means of recruiting is a basic tactic. It has been developed to such an extent by the Reds, they now seek to convert children thereby. Herbert J. Benjamin, long a key figure in the Communist Party in the United States, was arrested recently by vice squad men for selling lewd pictures and literature to Washington children, and convicted of violation of the D.C. code.

Benjamin, a former secretary of the International Workers Order, long a contributor to party magazines and periodicals, was mentioned in a memo by Earl Browder, November 27, 1939, as an alternate to the tenth convention of a national Communist Party committee. Later he was the organization's national press director and was in charge of the St. Louis office of a

Communist political association. He and his wife lived in the Trenton Terrace apartments, on Mississippi Ave., SE, where other tenants were Rob Hall, Washington correspondent for the *Daily Worker*, and Joseph Forer, a veteran attorney for Reds. Benjamin's wife was manager of the apartment house.

The pinks are still working strenuously to grab off and bring up new followers from the incubator stage. As these lines were written, three names listed by the District Board of Education as speakers for its in-service-training program were found to be also in the House Committee on Un-American Activities' files as left-wingers—Dr. Paul B. Cornely, Freedmen's Hospital medical director; Dr. Alice V. Keliher, of New York University; and Dr. Dora B. Smith, of the University of Minnesota. Superintendent of Schools Corning said, "The names were identical with names in the House Un-American Committee records." Since then Red and Socialist-slanted text books have been found to be in use in Washington's schools.

Until two years ago, there was considerable radical financial interest in radio station WQQW. The stock has since been placed in a voting-trust with a good American as trustee. For years this station refused to sign off with "The Star-Spangled Banner."

The Dupont Theatre specializes in interracial and foreign films, most of them slanted left. Danny Weitzman, owner of the building, was active in the Wallace presidential campaign.

The Reds and bleeding hearts play up their "love" for Negroes at every opportunity. This often pays off big dividends because so many colored people are employed in government offices. A few Negroes are dumb enough to be misled by the Reds' baloney about the brotherhood of man. But to their eternal glory, the great mass of Negroes are among the most patriotic citizens in the country. A few malcontents, who have been taken in by the crocodile tears of the Eleanor Roosevelt brand of reformer, occasionally indirectly render aid and comfort to the enemy.

To show how much they love the Negro, the white Communist brethren hold their District powwows at Shilo Baptist Church, a Negro house of worship in the NW section.

It is a Communist strategy to line Negroes into the party through white gals who, to show their complete compliance and condition of servitude, are urged to give themselves to col-

THE LITTLE RED HERRINGS

ored men. Into this specialized service they seem to wade with more than token application.

Mrs. Louise Branston Berman, millionaire radical who declines to state if she's a Communist on grounds of self-incrimination, spends much of her time in Washington. She uses her great wealth to help the enrollment of left-wing recruits through social contacts. Louts who never dined above a cafeteria before are invited to sumptuous banquets in her homes in various parts of the country. Visiting Negro dignitaries who can't get accommodations in hotels are her house guests. Mrs. Branston will learn for the first time here that when she put up the Negro singer, Paul Robeson, government agents had "bugs" in every room of her house from the parlor to the boudoir—she ought to hear the recordings. We did. They're neither intellectual nor musical—but they are illuminating.

A principal Communist apparatus and recruiting ground for new Reds on the lower levels was the late but unlamented UNRRA.

The organization was rotten with traitors during the time Mayor LaGuardia was its director. Either he didn't know what was going on, because he attended meetings only a few times, or he didn't care.

When UNRRA was disbanded, its Red membership was moved almost en masse to the payroll of the United Nations secretariat. Many are now stationed in New York, where they are sabotaging U.N. work as far as they can. Others are attached to U.N. field offices in Washington.

If anyone doubts it was the policy of UNRRA to aid Communism and that this had the approval of the present administration, which is bent on fighting Communism, let him read the following excerpts from a memo which we filched from the UNRRA files. It is an inter-office communication, written in 1947, and addressed to Col. Katzin, a South African, then an important UNRRA man and now top aide to Trygve Lie.

It follows: (The italics are ours.)

"It should be made clear that *the administration, in pushing for distribution to Communist areas* and in requesting Edgerton to report on such distribution, has in mind *actual shipments into Communist areas* and not merely movements out of Shanghai with the expressed intention of making such shipments."

Another paragraph reads, "In reference to Shanghai 6404, it

is interesting to note the U.K. position that *the program should be cut proportionately if the (Chinese) Nationalist government does not meet its obligations for Communist area distribution."*

In other words, we strengthened the Chinese Reds so they could kill our boys three years later.

Another batch of Communists and Communist-lovers came into the U.N. through its International Child Fund. This department is loaded with ex-State Department employes fired on suspicion of subversive activities.

That is a common habit. If all the homos, spies and other undesirables fired for cause were traced, hundreds would be found snugly ensconced in other bureaus, ostensibly screened, actually given screens of protection and falsification by the radicals in high places.

We are not indicting Eleanor Roosevelt or Supreme Court Justice Frankfurter as Communists. Yet it is impossible to study the set-up of the District of Columbia white collar Communist underground without finding tie-lines from them to members of this group.

The man of mystery in Washington is wealthy, brilliant, daring Max Lowenthal. He wrote the unwieldy book purporting to pulverize the F.B.I. which sold only 6,ooo copies. Almost as many were given away. Yet no one knows much about him. He is a shadowy figure who thrives on obscurity, though he has filled public posts of importance. Until Congressman Dondero, of Michigan, investigated him, his name was obscure in Washington. Today not ten people in the government know more about him than the fact that he is frequently more powerful than the President and the Congress of the United States. This is some of what Congressman Dondero charged on the floor of the House of Representatives about Mr. Lowenthal whom he referred to as sinister and surreptitious:

Like the Communist Party, whose cause he has served so well, he operates on two levels. One is seemingly respectable; the other completely underground. He is native-born. His name does not appear in Who's Who. To secure even a sketch of his biography has been a task.

Born in Minneapolis in 1888, like many other parlor pinks, fellow-travelers, Communists and convicted perjurers, he attended Harvard Law School. In those days he came under the influence of another man who through the years has manipulated Charlie McCarthys in Government office. There is a striking kinship between the master, Justice Felix Frankfurter, and the pupil, Max Lowenthal.

He served as a secretary to Judge Julian M. Mack in New York, then infiltrated the respectable law firm of Cadwalader, Wickersham & Taft. After a few years he founded his own firm, Lowenthal, Szold & Brandwen.

Later he secured an appointment as Assistant Secretary of the President's Mediation Board in 1917; in 1918 he was in the War Department; in 1920 he was an Assistant Secretary to the President's Industrial Conference. He became executive secretary for the Wickersham Commission on Law Enforcement, but when he found he could not run it he resigned. He became research director of the Banking and Currency Commission, was on the staff of the Senate Committee on Interstate Commerce, also affiliated with the Board of Economic Welfare.

In Germany, known as general counsel to General Clay, he had as an assistant George Shaw Wheeler, the American traitor, Communist and renegade who shocked all America when he denounced the land of his birth and asked Communist-controlled Czechoslovakia for asylum.

Evidence of his unswerving loyalty to Soviet Russia is clear and unequivocal. There is an interesting sidelight. The California authorities raided the office of the Russian-American Industrial Corp., whose head, the late Sidney Hillman, had turned on Communism, but his general counsel still follows the party line.

He was a member of the left-wing National Lawyers Guild, a member of the National Committee of the International Juridical Association with Lee Pressman.

Carol Weiss King, who represented more Communists than any other lawyer, was a law clerk in Lowenthal's office.

Lowenthal, living in New York, spent much of his time in Washington; his influence is a menace to the best interests of America—so said Congressman Dondero.

Don't kid yourself. The Reds are not on the run in Washington. No Communist control law means anything if the administration doesn't want it enforced. The anemic Security Board appointed by the President to apply the McCarran Act, loaded down as it is with left-wing apologists, is the tip-off.

One day after Senator Tydings, who became an ex because he "white-washed" Owen Lattimore, returned to private life he joined the law firm of his father-in-law, Joseph E. "Mission

to Moscow" Davies. A senior partner in that firm is Seth Rich-
ardson, appointed by Truman to head the Security Board.

Meanwhile, the rapid expansion of Federal employment has
forced the government to forego the usual pre-job loyalty checks
of tens of thousands of new workers—hundreds of Communists
are going on the payroll and will be there for months, possibly
years, until their backgrounds are delved into.

With a green light, the F.B.I. could break the back of the
Communists' underground. But J. Edgar Hoover cannot make
policies. He is just a cop who has to follow orders. At this writing the orders have not come. The traitors in Washington are
safe. On the other hand, those who testify against Reds are frequently harassed by Justice Department lawyers.

If this weren't so ghastly serious, some phases of the great
Communist spy-hunt would be laughable. For instance, there's
the story of the prominent woman lawyer from New York, retained to represent a left-winger about to be questioned by a
Congressional committee. This Communist kept his full status
well hidden. He couldn't afford to hire a lawyer who handled
Communist cases. So this portly Portia was retained. She had
no known Red connections.

On her way to Washington she stopped in Baltimore, to con-
fer with a well-known Communist counsel there, to be briefed.
It began as a business confab. They arranged a follow-up rendezvous in Washington. The Baltimore attorney's wife suspected him, followed him to Washington and caught him in
the act with the lady lawyer from New York.

The wife sued for divorce. The co-respondent testified, admitted intercourse but denied adultery.

"I was raped," she cried.

Cross-examination:

Q.—Did you have intimate relations with the defendant?

A.—Yes.

Q.—Did you consent?

A.—Yes.

Q.—Then how do you make that out rape?

A.—I found out since that he is a damned Communist!

17. KICKING THE GONG AROUND

*I*T MAY be news that widespread addiction to narcotics is a comparatively recent American manifestation. Long after the turn of the century, a few trickles supplied pig-tailed Chinamen, despondent prostitutes, ex-cons who had picked up the habit in stir and a few rich fools who would try anything for a bang. Juvenile use was unheard of. Marijuana was unknown outside pad-parties in the Harlem jungles and among a thin fringe of Mexicans. The Harrison Narcotics Law, first federal recognition of the existence of such an evil, is only 35 years old.

We are solemnly convinced that the great growth of this plague in the past 20 years has been parallel to the spread of Communism in our country. And it has not been confined to our country.

Estimates by the Narcotic Control Section of the United Nations, that one of every ten people on earth uses habit-forming drugs in some manner or form, are borne out in this country, where the evil is prevalent in all sections. It is the greatest tangible menace facing us. And dope addiction, on the rise, can be traced definitely to Soviet Russia.

It has long been a tactic of nations bound on enslaving others to deaden the ambitions and energies of their victims with dope.

Examples of this stretch back to the dawn of written history. In the last century, British imperialists introduced the habit into China to control that nation. Nazi Germany flooded Poland and Czechoslovakia. Japan built huge narcotics factories in Manchuria to weaken the Chinese opposition. Russia is doing more of it now. Raw stuff pours in from Mediterranean ports. It originates in lands behind the Iron Curtain. Its importation into the United States serves Russia twofold—prostrates a prospective enemy and gets its hands on needed American exchange to be used for propaganda purposes and payment of undercover agents here. International bank drafts could be traced.

One courier can carry $1,000,000 worth of uncut dope on his person.

There are many points of community interest between the Reds and that other great international conspiracy, the Mafia, which controls the sale of drugs in America. The Commies will team up with anyone who will promote civil disorder or do their dirty work. The Mafia is interested in making a dishonest dollar and will work with any partner.

The center of the narcotics industry in the United States is in the district of former left-wing Congressman Vito Marcantonio, in East Harlem. During the days of his ascendency, American Labor Party district leaders were able to supply police protection through alliances with both Tammany Hall and anti-Tammany Mayor LaGuardia.

Generally untrumpeted was the fact that when the infamous Charles "Lucky" Luciano was ordered deported from Cuba, the titular head of the Cuban Communist Party offered him sanctuary and appeared as his counsel.

A study of the Congressional Record will show that most of the bills and measures designed to weaken the enforcement of the Narcotics Act have been introduced by left-wingers and fellow-travelers. Many pink lawyers represent the underworld combine.

One of the most startling tieups was seen in the recent flooding of this country with cocaine. The Bureau of Narcotics had all but eliminated this devastating drug. There had been none here for 20 years. Cocaine for American consumption comes from Peru, where the coca leaves grow. A couple of years ago an Agrarian Communist group called the Apristas took over that country briefly. Seventeen cocaine factories were constructed in Lima, eleven licensed by the local Red government, and the others ran with the knowledge and connivance of the authorities. Their entire produce was routed to the United States. Coincident with saturation of this country with cocaine, which sank in price to as low as $1.50 a capsule, America went through its greatest crime wave.

When Commissioner Harry J. Anslinger traced the source of the deadly narcotic to Peru, the New Deal State Department refused to intervene, as it was required to do by the international treaties which outlawed the traffic. The reason for this failure, amounting to criminal negligence, was that we could not interfere in Latin American affairs. The cash for the cocaine was being used to foster Communism in South America.

Last year the Reds were kicked out of Peru by what Washington pinkos still refer to as "the oligarchy," who immediately thereafter closed the coke factories. Since then, this traffic has almost dried up in the United States.

Likewise the administration has failed to inform the American public that the Permanent Central Opium Board in Geneva, Switzerland, has branded Soviet Russia and several Iron Curtain countries as palpable violators of international treaties and UN conventions regarding the control of narcotics.

You will probably learn here for the first time that the following governments, in addition to Russia, were named as treaty-violators for failure to meet their obligations: Red China, Czechoslovakia and Poland.

Among others who failed to co-operate were Nepal, Saudi Arabia, Oman and Liberia, the African Negro republic in which Negro slavery is still practiced.

Narcotic conditions in the capital are shameful. This is no fault of the U.S. Bureau of Narcotics, whose fighting chief, Commissioner Anslinger, is handcuffed by red tape, apathy and a penurious budget. The Bureau has a personnel of less than 180 for office and field work throughout the world. Its annual budget is less than $2,000,000. This is a drip in an ocean, yet Anslinger must cope with the deadliest evil known to man, backed by a huge and wealthy underworld organization controlling tens of thousands of peddlers, sluggers and killers, and owning billions of dollars.

That the unsung agents of this Treasury bureau have done as well as they have is a miracle. They could do better, especially in Washington, if they had the cooperation of the judiciary. They haven't.

You can buy reefers on any corner in Black Town or in front of any high school in the District. You can purchase hard stuff at dozens of corners, of which we can name many and will note some. This disgrace indicts judges in the courts of the District of Columbia. All are federal, not elected, but appointed by the President. This goes for the Municipal Court bench, which sits for six years, as well as the District Court, appointed for life.

Every judge appointed in the last 18 years was put on the bench during a Democratic administration. More than 95 per cent are Democrats. Few are Washingtonians. With few exceptions, these judges are divided into two classes: Those representing the big-city bosses and gangs, and radicals named to appease bigger and redder radicals. The former, obviously, are expected to be lenient to law-breakers protected by the organized underworld. The latter, mostly fuzzy-minded intellectuals, do not believe in punishment, especially when the evildoer is a Negro or of any minority race. They can't find wrong in any man. They believe criminals are mishandled wards of society.

The Washington field office of the Bureau of Narcotics—with only three or four agents—arrests dope peddlers as fast as they can be found and turns up enough evidence to secure convictions. But the courts almost uniformly issue suspended sentences or small fines.

The stench was so bad, dope peddlers were selling the contraband across the street from the White House, at the eastern end of Lafayette Square. The great brains regarded the venomous situation without qualms. What's a little dope among dopes?

In desperation, Anslinger removed every agent—including one of his best men, former agent-in-charge Roy Morrison—from the city of Washington. He felt it was needless to risk his men's lives to get evidence against junk peddlers who were sure to keep out of jail because of a fix or muddle-headedness. Thereafter, for a short time, no effort was made to enforce the narcotics laws in the District. Conditions got so bad, even the judges knew they must cooperate to avoid a national blow-up. After Anslinger restored the agents, the judges began meting out stiff sentences. But the heat soon came off and they are back at their old habits.

An example of what often happens when a dope peddler is arrested in the District is the case of William Potts, indicted on 14 counts arising from the sale and possession of heroin. On the day set for trial, an essential witness of the government could not be found. The court was so informed. The judge turned to the counsel for defense and asked if he was ready for the trial. Defense counsel was, but the U.S. Attorney said he was not, because of the witness's absence. Thereupon the court asked if the defendant would waive a jury trial. He did. Immediately and without the pretense of trial, the court ruled, "I find the defendant not guilty."

William P. Estoffery came into court with a record of ten specific narcotics convictions, but the United States District Court gave him eight months to three years, which meant he could be back on the street in three months. One of his previous convictions was for possession of counterfeit prescription blanks.

Here is another sample of the judicial road-blocks erected against enforcement officers who arrest dope peddlers in the capital:

Constitutional rights to privacy also give a defendant protection from illegal police raids on homes other than his own, the U.S. Court of Appeals for the District of Columbia ruled recently.

The court made the ruling in reversing the conviction of Jesse W. Jeffers, Jr., on narcotics dealing charges.

Jeffers, 27, Negro, was found guilty in Judge Alexander Holtzoff's court on testimony that police, without a search warrant, raided a room at the Dunbar Hotel and found 19 bottles of cocaine he allegedly had hidden there.

Jeffers lived elsewhere in the hotel, but the room was rented by relatives of his.

Setting a rare principle of law, the Appeals Court held evidence of the cocaine cache should have been excluded from the case because the police raid was illegal. It pointed out the Constitution's Fourth Amendment specifically bans illegal searches of a defendant's home, and said the principle should be enlarged to cover illegal raids on "premises that were not his."

Judge E. Barrett Prettyman, in a dissent from the majority opinion, said "I do not see how an individual's rights can be invaded by Government seizure of . . . unstamped narcotics, not on the individual's person or premises."

He emphasized the case "is important in the enforcement of the narcotics laws."

The curious part of the whole affair is that the defendant admitted the untaxed, unstamped dope was his. In fact, he demanded its return from the government.

In another of its feats of legal legerdemain, beyond the poor reasoning of a couple of reporters who didn't graduate from Harvard Law, the august court said to the defendant in effect: "Possession of dope is illegal, so you can't have it back, though you didn't commit any crime when you had it before."

Try and figure that one out.

Shortly thereafter the Appeals Court again overruled the same judge in another narcotics case and ordered a new trial for Clarence Butler on the grounds that Holtzoff's "facial expressions" were prejudicial.

An official memorandum of the United States Treasury Department sets out facts as follows:

Since early in 1946, the Bureau has experienced repeated delay in obtaining prosecution of its cases in the District of Columbia. In numerous trials where out-of-town agents were witnesses the Bureau had to bear the expense of bringing them to Washington for testimony. Repeatedly, after the agents arrived, the hearings were continued. The Bureau could not stand this gaff and had to "stop narcotic enforcement in the District of Columbia."

Dope cannot be manufactured locally. The Washington wholesalers must get their supplies from the international monopoly. The general practice in other cities is for the organization to deliver the wholesale lots to localities where they are to be consumed, but in the case of Washington the wholesale jobbers go to the distribution depots in other cities and pick up carload lots.

All narcotics in the United States are controlled at the top by a tight ring of evil men who, in turn, issue state and territorial rights to middlemen. Washington merchants are ordered to make their purchases in New York, Philadelphia and Baltimore, but mainly in New York.

Marijuana is brought up directly from Mexico, but much inferior quality reefer seed is planted on farms between Washington and Baltimore and in Virginia.

The local dope set-up is largely controlled by Negroes, though Chinese also are active in the trade and have become more so since the Communists took over China. The two tongs frequently import their own. At this writing Red China has 500 tons of opium for sale abroad. This is equal to the world requirements for medical and scientific needs for more than a year. Chiang Kai-shek prohibited the production in China in 1934. The Communists have revived Jehol and Manchurian opium cultivation, and are reopening Tientsin dens. The tongs have not been adhering of late to the agreement which limited them to noncompetitive sales. Both are selling *pin yen* (opium) and *bok for* (heroin). Police believe the recent but short-lived tong wars on the West Coast were attributable to breaches of the basic compromise, plus efforts of Chinese Communists to take over the tong dope distribution machinery.

Occasionally, when sources of supply are temporarily cut off, or when the Italians are able to offer a more favorable price, the Chinese syndicates send a man to buy directly from the Mafia. This dope is stored in a warehouse near 108th Street and 2nd Avenue, New York City, in Marcantonio's bailiwick.

Another difficulty in narcotics enforcement, not even whispered about in Washington, is the leakage from diplomatic sources. It is politic for the Bureau to deny this is so, because nothing can be done about it. But huge amounts of concentrated dope come in envoys' sealed pouches. There is, as everyone in Washington knows, a lively racket in the diplomatic corps in black market money. No easier method of acquiring dollars is possible than through sale of dope. Some of this contraband is used by members of the embassy staffs, themselves. In some Near Eastern and Oriental countries, a daily intake of narcotics is considered as normal as our use of coffee and tobacco. Many Latin Americans are slaves to marijuana, especially in the eating form, not otherwise available in the States. Some of this, which doesn't find its way into the channels of trade, is presented by the diplomats to their American friends.

This will be denied, too, but ranking members of the diplomatic corps who are narcotic addicts and who can't get the stuff from other sources have it provided for them by the protocol boys in the State Department, who withdraw it from official government sources.

We were offered reefers by peddlers in the alleys along 4th Street, SW; also at the corner of 7th and T and 7th and O, NW.

In an all-night diner at Vermont and L, frequented by musicians and hep kids, we were offered reefers also.

Hard stuff is obtainable with no trouble from street salesmen in Thomas Circle. In this neighborhood, which is bossed by Attilio Acalotti, you can place a bet on a horse, buy a numbers ticket or get a call girl. The service is performed for you by sidewalk newsboys and pimps on the steps of the National Christian Church.

In recent years, rich white racketeers have gone in for opium smoking themselves. They get it in Chinatown, where a few poppy parlors are in operation. As noted, members of the On Leong Tong deal mostly in opium and the members of Hip Sing in heroin.

Heroin is sold openly on the corner of 5th and H, in the Hip Sing section of Chinatown. To prove this, we became accessories to a violation of the law.

This is how simple the whole transaction was: We were

steered to a broken-down wreck named Joe, a well-known
dope addict. Despite his habit, Joe is an expert locksmith, a
genius at his trade. He can't work steadily, but so talented is
he, the police and other local law enforcement bodies and
private detective agencies frequently hire him to pick locks.
That's how he gets the money to support his habit. We gave
Joe $6 to buy a deck of heroin and left him on the corner
while we drove twenty feet up the block as Joe waited for his
contact, across the street from the Gospel Mission.

We walked back and passed Joe as he handed the $6 to a
young Chinese, who had appeared out of an area way. Joe said
the Chinaman's name was Benny Wong. This is one of the
commonest Chinese names, there may be 500 with it in
Washington. While Benny went to get the stuff, Joe sat down
on a stoop and fell asleep. He had been loading himself with
secanol, a synthetic, to keep his nerve steady until he got the
heroin, and he was in a pitiable condition. While Joe slum-
bered, two metropolitan cops walked by. They thought he was
drunk. One went to get the wagon while we talked the other
out of pinching our decoy. A few minutes after the cops left,
Benny returned with the heroin. That's all there was to it.

The "hooked" addict's cost of supporting his "yen" runs
from $35 a week up, though if one "has a monkey on his back,"
meaning the urge is desperate and irresistible, he will be
soaked from $50 to $100 a week. Those who can afford the best
stuff or who no longer get a bang out of cheap grades are bled
for as much as $500 a week.

When Hyman I. Fischbach, brilliant counsel of the Congressional committee investigating crime and law enforcement in
the District of Columbia, queried Assistant Commissioner Harney of the Narcotics Bureau, some startling facts about narcotic
addiction were brought out, yet missed by the press and the
public. These hitherto unpublished excerpts make interesting
reading.

MR. HARNEY. That also depends too on the cost of the drug
and the amount of his income. Addicts can get along—during
the war we had lots of them who had needle habits. Their intake was probably one-fourth grain or half a grain a day of actual narcotic. The addict might develop until he gets as high as
20, 30, or 40 grains a day, considered a lethal dose for a non-
initiated person. They build up resistance power. They get
hoggish.

CONGRESSMAN DAVIS. What is that term?

MR. HARNEY. Use a lot of the drug. In days when drugs were freely available that was one reason for institution of cocaine. A man would stupefy himself with narcotics and with cocaine he would get an extra thrill and get out of it and brighten up and keep from going to sleep. The addict may spend $5 or $10 a day in addition to other expenses, and not being able, or disposed to work, usually becomes a thief. He can be a prowler or he might be a pickpocket. Some addicts are very good burglars. He might be a stick-up-man, not often.

A woman will be a prostitute or shoplifter. A man might be a panderer. Many addicts buy in decks, 8 ounces or 2 or 3 ounces. The preaddict would use a few grains. It differs in different localities.

MR. DAVIS. Does the price differ?

MR. HARNEY. Expressed in terms of actual narcotic content for the preaddict it may be $2 or $3 a grain.

MR. FISCHBACH. Mr. Harney, is it your point that an individual otherwise law abiding necessarily turns to petty crime in order to support the addiction?

MR. HARNEY. I would not say necessarily, but it is often apparent. I want to emphasize that addiction, particularly in the past, has been much among the criminal element. A man was down in a dangerous environment before he became addicted; he had to get in that sort of association in contrast to the casual person who might become an addict from medical reasons, but the ordinary addict becomes so by association.

MR. FISCHBACH. Then your point is there is an epidemic effect to it?

MR. HARNEY. We have a rather unusual and alarming situation which developed since the war. It does not quite follow the pattern I set out. My theory used to be that most addicts were old enough to be associated with criminals and get into the underworld with addicts before they themselves became addicts. Today, in certain localities, we have young people, some minors, and the pattern seems to be experimentation in marijuana first. That loses its thrill and those persons become addicts to heroin. Sometimes cocaine comes into the picture.

MR. DAVIS. Is marijuana used as a starter and later other narcotics are used?

MR. HARNEY. I would not say always, but frequently. Young

people get into the marijuana atmosphere and you have a field for the cocaine and heroin addicts.

Mr. Davis. Are they induced to begin with marijuana by purveyors of heroin, cocaine, morphine, and other drugs, to lead them into addiction?

Mr. Harney. That pattern follows. Later dealers sell all three commodities. Youngsters come into the marijuana smoking atmosphere and soon there is no kick in it, and someone will tell them, "Try this."

Mr. Fischbach. Now who is that person?

Mr. Harney. The peddler, or a cocaine addict, or a heroin addict.

Mr. Fischbach. I would like to direct the attention of the committee to the case of Charles M. Roberts, alias Jim Yellow, and ask if that case presents some problems which your Bureau experienced in the District with regard to the enforcement of the narcotics law. Present the facts in the case of Jim Roberts, what kind of a person he was, how he lived, what quantity of drugs he had when taken into custody.

Mr. Harney. Jim Roberts had two convictions for violation of the Federal narcotics laws. He had convictions for other crimes, including charges of assault. We used an agent in an undercover capacity. Roberts lived in a luxuriously furnished apartment. Some of these figures I cite are on his own statement and probably you will allow for bragging, but he had a beautifully carved television set which he claimed cost him a couple thousand dollars, and he drove a new Cadillac. While the officers were in his presence money was handed to him in a paper grocery bag. Roberts referred to a hatchet and said he was waiting to christen it in blood. When the car was seized the hatchet was under the seat of the car. Roberts' style of living represents big-shot narcotic dealers. It makes a tremendous impression on others who might think of entering the racket.

*   *   *

In addition to users of standard narcotics, many in Washington go in for esoteric kicks. A growing fad in the Negro district is to inhale incense with marijuana added.

Barbiturates are sold without prescription, because the D.C. law has no teeth in it. Some become habituated to these drugs and, instead of being put to sleep by them, get all the wallop out of them that others get from opium. Many drug stores sell nembutals over the counter for 25 cents each. Nembutals are the prostitutes' favorite. Among initiates they are known as goof balls, or nemies. They grew popular during World War II, when there was a scarcity of narcotics. Most who prefer goof balls to marijuana usually end up on morphine, heroin or cocaine.

Evelyn Walsh McLean's daughter, who was married to Senator Reynolds, died from an overdose of goof balls.

As elsewhere, reefers are the real menace. This product of the hemp plant is easily available, can be grown anywhere, is cheap, and in some circles is in good repute. There is no such thing as an innocent reefer smoker. Sooner or later, anyone on "muggles" must become a lawbreaker to some degree. Peddlers put their heads together, know how badly any customer is hooked. Then they jack up prices to beyond what most people can pay honestly.

All weed-heads are cop-haters. Even in reasonably normal condition they carry a fierce resentment against conventional forces of society.

Reefer smoking is not habitual in the sense that the addict suffers "withdrawal" symptoms, as when he is taken off other stuff. But neither is cocaine habit-forming in that sense. Both work on the emotions. Their use causes a physiological change in the brain. The reefer smoker who gives the stuff up does not turn violently ill. But he doesn't give it up. He likes its effect and needs its lift to give him courage.

Sooner or later, all reefer smokers go on to cocaine, because the effect is the same as from reefers, a hundredfold. When the bang of the hemp wears off, cocaine is the only thing that can take its place. And because cocaine is so expensive, one must become a criminal to afford its use. And the cocaine gives one the courage to be a criminal.

The subject of tea-hounds brings us quite naturally to our next chapter, juvenile delinquency, in which stimulants are a large factor.

18. THE YOUNG IN HEART

*J*UVENILE delinquency as a topic has become a bromide. You'd think there was little left to add. But here we found not only more of it, but conditions behind it were frequently the exact opposite of those obtaining in other populous cities.

It is generally accepted as beyond dispute that youngsters go wrong because of poverty, congestion, lack of play-space, exposure to the tenement atmosphere, the saloon and miserable home life. But Washington, with its top average of prosperity, nothing that could rightfully be called slums, no tenements and no out-and-out saloons, has a more alarming per capita of teen-age lawbreakers than New York, Chicago, Detroit or Kansas City.

Remarkable, moreover, is the discovery that white youth is more delinquent proportionately to the total of all criminals of their race than Negro youth. Over all, however, more colored children break laws than whites. A study of records, talks with social workers and personal prying into many cases make it evident that more young people go wrong because of overprivilege than underprivilege.

Most kids who get into trouble are well fed, over the height and weight scientifically charted for their age, are well dressed, and have superior intelligence quotients. We checked on one, 15 years old, five feet nine inches tall, weighing 140 pounds, the son of a government official who earns $12,000 a year. He confessed to more than 100 larcenies, burglaries and purse-snatches, and he had escaped from two postal inspectors who arrested him for looting mail-boxes, searching for government checks on which he intended to forge endorsements. He and a 12-year-old accomplice had broken into 37 houses in the NW area in 20 months and had robbed scores of cars. He said:

"Everybody here is on the make. We want money, too."

Of 2,412 arrests of white males for Part 1 offenses, serious crimes including homicide, rape, robbery, burglary, larceny, auto-theft and aggravated assault, 564, almost 25 per cent, were committed by boys 15 and under; 1,897 of the 2,412, or 75 per cent, were committed by boys 20 or under.

The figures for Negroes are the reverse. There adults are in the preponderant majority. During the time when white males of all ages committed the 2,412 specific offenses for which they were arrested, 7,729 Negroes were apprehended. Of this large number, only 1,702 of the crimes were committed by Negro boys 15 and under; of these the number charged to males 20 years and under was 3,477, considerably less than half, whereas white juveniles rolled up 75 per cent of the total for their race.

Also a departure from the usual big-town findings is the sex proportion. Juvenile delinquency is almost a complete male monopoly, about the only one in the female-heavy District. Harlem and Bronzeville, Hell's Kitchen and the dregs of Brooklyn have their "debs," the feminine auxiliaries of the boys' gangs of muggers, street-fighters and thieves. The girls constitute a good one-third of the problem children, engaged in picking pockets, shoplifting and prostitution. But in Washington, in the period when the 2,412 serious crimes were charged to white males, only 309 were committed by females, and of these only 19 were under the age of 15; 96 were 20 and under. Negro females of all ages were arrested for 1,091 Part 1 crimes, of which only 38 were girls up to 15 and only 161 were 20 and under.

One reason for the huge incidence of juvenile delinquency, but by no means the decisive one, was an idiosyncrasy of the population trend here, topsy-turvy to every other in the country during the last 10 years. While the mean age of Americans was growing to such an extent that it appeared we were becoming a nation of old people, Washington's population increased 26 per cent—but its child population, as of birth records, increased more than 60 per cent. Nobody seems to know why.

If this has anything to do with the high influx of Negroes, the figures above quoted challenge it as a delinquency cause. Our observations led us to the conclusion that the principal influence is a system and habit of coddling found nowhere else. By Act of Congress, none but the Juvenile Court can take jurisdiction over offenders before they are 15; defendants under 18 must be transferred to it on the court's demand. This branch is dominated by fat matrons and skinny old maids who make a profession or a vocation of "child welfare." To them that means no punishment; everybody is innocent. In time the judges, New Deal appointees all, many from crackpot groups with socialistic and other distorted tendencies, have been conditioned to contempt of the law and slant toward paternalistic lectures and acquittals. The result is an enormous rate of recidivists, and the figures represent multiple arrests of such repeaters rather than of so many individuals.

In the rare instances when the punks are sentenced to confinement, they go to federal reformatories, where they get short terms and de luxe treatment.

Statistics are cold; many people skip them or disbelieve them. But cops are practical. And so appalling has moppet misbehavior become that an extra detail of 30 officers has been assigned on duty around the clock to watch and buzz the teensters, in an unprecedented campaign to ease Washington's biggest growing pain.

The vacuum in which federally appointed judges and officials responsible only to Congress can place a community is well illustrated by the juvenile delinquency procedure.

Judge Edith H. Cockrill, of the Juvenile Court, adjudicated in a star chamber, concealed from the public. Nothing came out of her court but rumors. One lawyer said her court is "a social worker's dream and a lawyer's nightmare." He said children and their parents are treated as "patients," none as offenders. The result is that about three-fourths of the kids processed through Washington Juvenile Court grow up to be adult criminals. Public pressure forced her to issue her first report last month, after more than two years on the bench.

Judge Cockrill is a typical Fair Deal beneficiary. She graduated from the University of Tennessee in 1939, then got her legal experience with the OPA. Figure out how that qualifies her to sit as a juvenile judge. Before her appointment, a couple of years ago, by President Truman, she had never tried a case in juvenile court. Her present calendar calls for about 60 cases a day, including bastardy, nonsupport and parental responsibility.

The previous incumbent on the bench was Faye L. Bentley, who voluntarily committed herself to St. Elizabeth's Hospital—for Mental Disorders—for treatment in 1948. This is a course we recommend to some other judges.

Convicted juvenile delinquents are sent to the National Training School for Boys, the National Training School for Girls, and the Industrial Home School.

The Department of Justice estimates three of every four graduates of these reformatories become adult criminals. And this though the Training School for Boys, known as "The Hill," goes in for all modern techniques and dodads, such as plastic surgery, psychotherapy and psychology. There are church facilities, athletics, television, radio and musical instruments. The boys are taught shoemaking, cooking, farming and other trades. The school specializes in group therapy, which has its advantages and its absurdities. Sometimes an entire group can be spoiled by one or two tough young kids who become ringleaders.

Except in the Negro sections, Washington has been spared the scourge of kid gangs. There are no major foreign-born settlements in town. Therefore the white kids seldom organize into mobs. Juvenile delinquency in other cities is often blamed on Italian, Irish, Jewish, Mexican and Puerto Rican under-age gangs.

But organization seems to be coming into fashion. While these lines were being typed, three local men were attacked and brutally beaten by a gang of 12 teensters in the 700 block, 6th Street, NW, apparently for the fun of it. The victims said the boys shouted insults at them from the sidewalk as they drove past. The three stopped and got out of the car. The gang then swarmed on them, beat them with bottles, belt-buckles, brass knuckles and improvised blackjacks.

Wherever young white criminals work together they are more often prone to choose school or college mates, or members of the same boys' clubs as buddies. For instance, police broke up the exclusive "Weekend Burglars" gang, whose activities had stirred up residents of an exclusive NW residential section when they discovered that the criminals were home on leave on weekend passes from a military academy in Maryland. The three boys, the oldest 17, all came from wealthy families. Their method of "cracking" a home was this:

They would ring a doorbell; if no one answered, they cut through the screen and smashed the glass in the door. Inside the house, they ransacked it for three articles, taking nothing else. Playfully they would toss furniture helter-skelter and break china. The money they spent. The whiskey they drank. The stolen guns they showed off with.

Kids of all ages and both sexes and races are smoking reefers in prodigious quantities. These are easily obtainable from peddlers who work outside the schools, and inside some schools, from students, themselves. The current price for the weeds to school-children is 50 cents each, sometimes three for a dollar.

The young dope-fiends are not confined to any neighborhood of the city or to any economic class. One high school in the area, attended by children whose parents are in the upper brackets, is reported to have 95 per cent addiction. A major kid crime element is marijuana. Youngsters go on from it to more potent narcotics, then commit petty crimes to obtain the funds to buy the drugs. Reefers and other dope sharply bring out latent lawlessness.

High school athletic events have become a scandal. Bootleggers purvey liquor openly in the stands. Hundreds of stinking-drunk youngsters are swept out of the stadiums after every game.

Professional gamblers attend these games and make book without any pretense, taking bets from the kids of from 25 cents up and giving tickets in return.

Neighborhood stores adjacent to schools also purvey bootleg liquor and take bets from the juveniles, not only for their own school games, but on the horses and numbers.

Juvenile delinquency is almost as bad in the suburbs. There kids have cars, and "hot rod" races are common.

Youngsters ape their elders when they see the callousness of parents to the processes of law. Laxity, favoritism, New Deal "liberalism," a general spirit of contempt for law enforcement are reflected in the growing generation. The solid virtues are "old hat." Youth is on a rampage.

Washington has no monopoly on young criminals, but it has more of them per capita than any other city in the nation.

Lame-brains like to point out that only colored people are confined to "slums" in Washington; that no whites live in ghettos in the capital. If so, how come that juvenile delinquency among the whites is as startling as among the blacks, more so, in fact? As reported elsewhere in this book, Washington's crime rate leads the nation. It is all the more startling to discover how many of these crimes are committed by children.

19. BOOZE AND BOTTLES

*W*_{ASHINGTONIANS} imbibe three times as much as you do, friend voter. Except for a few silly restrictions, no place in the country offers as many inducements to the potential alcoholic. The answer is, 14,151 drunks last year created a jail "housing crisis." The number more than doubled in the last five years. Liquor consumption of the District is three times the U. S. average. Every resident, including new-born infants, soaked up almost four gallons of hooch last year.

Even allowing for thirsty tourists, conventioners, and Virginia and Maryland commuters, Washington drinks more than any other U. S. city, including dissolute New York and debauched Chicago.

This is the place where price control was invented, yet the District has no peacetime minimum price law on bottled goods. You can buy standard brands for a dollar less than anywhere else. Many unnamed whiskeys and gins are cheap; it doesn't pay to cook your own. Whiskey costs less than $2.50 a fifth, and gin can be bought for $1.75. Yet the bootleg business is a major industry. Millions of gallons sold in the District, on which no tax was paid, swell the known figures.

The liquor control situation is an anomaly. Like the District of Columbia, itself, the liquor laws were born of compromise, this between Congressmen from the wet and bone-dry states.

You can drink hard liquor in restaurants and cocktail lounges, but only when sitting at a table. Beer and wines may be dispensed over the bar, but not to standees. You've got to find a stool. Some genius figured you can't get plastered sitting down, forgetting that many who drink and sit can't stand up again.

Hard liquor may not be sold on Sundays, though beer and wine can be. Bars can remain open until 2 A.M. every night except Saturday and Sunday, when they must shutter promptly at 12. You can't line drinks on your table; anything in your possession at the closing hour will be swept out of your hand. Most places issue the last call 15 minutes before the limit and in that final quarter-hour there are wild drinking scenes as customers try to get drunk all at once.

Liquor for off-premise consumption is sold in bottle stores, of which there are about 350. They close at nine on weekdays and at midnight on Saturdays and all day Sundays. A package store license costs $815 a year, but it will cost you $50,000 to buy one, as the ABC Board has frozen the rolls.

Those who can't get a bun on by closing time have no trouble locating an oasis after the curfew. At this writing there are 613 so-called bottle-clubs running in the District, in addition to hundreds of gin flats in Black Town, where almost any cab driver will steer you. Bootleggers work certain street corners, where you can buy bottle goods after hours.

The legal age minimum is 18 for beer and 21 for hard stuff, but this law, like almost all other rules and regulations, is breached more often than honored.

Citizens and Congressmen seek sporadically to rationalize local liquor laws, in hope of cutting down violations. But the dry bloc buries the bills in committees. Everyone was surprised when the House District Affairs Committee managed to bring up a bill permitting sale until two on Saturday nights. This turned out to be a piece of parliamentary jockeying in the fight against the President's FEPC Bill, of all things. That law, obnoxious to Southerners, would have come up for a vote unless one with legislative priority could be sent in ahead. And that bill, according to the calendar, was a proposed law to liberalize drinking habits in the District. So the Southerners brought it up, side-tracked the FEPC, and, a couple of weeks later, when it came time to vote on the booze act, roundly routed it.

The thirsty visitor finds it easy to find a bottle-club and become a full-fledged drinking member on the spot. The names, locations and owners of these after-hour spots vary from day to day. Occasionally, after clean-ups, all or most close for a couple of weeks or a couple of months. As these words were written the District was recovering from its most painful drought, brought on by revelations before the District Crime Investigating Committee, headed by Attorney Fischbach.

The front-page stories forced the cops and U. S. Attorney Fay to close some joints. Others lay low awhile. A murder in the Hideaway Club didn't help, either.

We made an intensive study of bottle-clubs. Of the score or

more we visited, we found only one apparently operating legitimately and according to law. That was the Lyre's Club, about which more later. Of the 600-plus such clubs in Washington, it is possible that a few adhere to the book, but we didn't hear of them.

On paper, bottle-clubs are supposed to be membership organizations, incorporated for social and benevolent purposes. Members bring their own liquor, which is held for them, their names on the labels. The clubs sell setups and food.

Charlie Ford, a Washington attorney to whom we will have occasion to tip our hats in much more detail later, is the lawyer for a number of clubs. He officiated at their births.

Here's how most of them really work. Regular patrons, i.e., "members," are supposed to pay annual dues of about $10, depending on the club, but most regulars pay nothing. Transients, i.e., guests, are charged a door-fee of one or two dollars, depending on the club.

Setups are sold, to those who bring their own liquor, at a nominal price of 35 cents and up. If you haven't your stuff parked or with you, most clubs will sell it to you under the counter or advise you it can be had from a guy seated in front of the entrance in a car.

These clubs are incorporated as non-profit private enterprises, not required to pay Federal amusement taxes even when they provide floor shows and dancing. Nor need they have ABC liquor licenses, because they are supposed not to be selling.

Many of them operate as follows: The prospective owner or owners and a couple of their friends or employes incorporate as a social or benevolent organization. The real owner then rents and furnishes the premises, which he in turn sublets to the so-called social club at a rent which will approximate all the "take" from membership and door charges. The "club" thereupon turns over the kitchen, the sale of setups and the hat-checking and cigaret stand to the real proprietor, as a concession, in return for a token payment, which in turn goes back to the proprietor with the rent.

In clubs that sell liquor illegally or provide gambling, records of such activities are not kept. The proceeds go directly into the owner's pocket. If raided or threatened by cleanup drives, the clubs disband. The owner organizes a new club under the same terms and repeats the process.

A new twist is being added since the Fischbach exposé. Some

club proprietors are making deals with units of legitimate bodies, such as veteran groups, labor unions, etc., whereby the clubs share some of the profits. One, the Amvets, closed after the Hideaway shooting, its charter lifted by the national organization.

Bottle-clubs find customers in a variety of ways. Some employes of licensed night clubs and restaurants hand out guest-membership cards to patrons who inquire where they can go after two. These steerers write their names on the cards and draw a kickback for every customer, usually a dollar a head.

Many cab drivers shill for the bottle-clubs, as well as for gin flats. Cab drivers' pay varies with the size of the party. They sometimes get as much as $5 a haul. They are the chief source of prospective patronage for the colored bottle-clubs. More than 500 after-hour spots in Washington are operated by Negroes or in the Negro district. All cater to blacks and whites. The twenty to thirty white bottle-clubs running are segregated as to Negro musicians and actors. In one club we saw three pretty blonde girls with two Negro men. They were all reefer-smokers, palpably.

Cabbies who hustle for the bottle-clubs not only do so in front of hotels and licensed cabarets and restaurants, but try to pirate customers away from opposition clubs. When they see a prospect waiting for the peephole to open, they tout him away "to a better place, where you won't have any trouble." The Hideaway, in Georgetown, depended almost entirely on such maneuvers, as it is far out and off the beaten track.

The pirates were acting so brazenly, police stepped in to curb the practice by giving tickets to drivers parked at strategic spots. The law requires cabs to cruise at all times, except in posted hack-stands, which are only outside major hotels.

Food, dancing, entertainment, and often dames are for sale at the clubs. Sometimes waitresses are available, but they work until 6 in the morning, by which time the average rounder has forgotten all about it. The price for a $10 girl picked up in a club is $20.

Some provide craps, stud poker and other games. The night we were there, a crap game ran on the top floor of the Atlas Club, on Pennsylvania Avenue, two blocks from the White House, and at the Stagecrafters Club, another hangout of General Harry Vaughan. The Atlas applied for a private club liquor license, which would permit legal sales, but the application was held up by the ABC Board until the club president, Sidney Brown, who was abroad, could return for a personal appearance. It happened that Mr. Brown, the sponsor of this after-hour spot, was abroad because he is an employe of the State Department. Some months previously, gambler Gary Quinn said he was the president of the Atlas. The license was denied, so it is still running as a bottle-club.

Among the after-hour clubs operating at this writing are the Top Side, 501 12th Street, NW; the Guess Who, 811 L Street, NW; the Acropolis, 719 9th Street, NW (patronized by Greeks); the Culinary Arts, 307 M Street, NE, and the Yamasee, 1214 U Street, NW. The last two are colored clubs.

The most notorious of the after-hour-spots speaks, the Gold Key, was closed by Committee revelations. It has since reorganized as the Downtown Club, with some of the same characters. Most of the others are patronized by unimportant transients or night workers, such as musicians, waiters and bartenders.

The Gold Key got the cream and they're back again. Among its regular patrons were local sports, including playboy Senators and officials. Waitresses there made as much as $150 a week in tips, whereas they are lucky to knock down $50 in other places. When lawyer Charlie Ford drew up the papers for the Gold Key, its original organizers were Albert Glickfield, alias Al Brown, Patsy Meserole, and Harry Conners, his brother-in-law. Meserole is a former New York gangster, one of the last surviving members of the late Legs Diamond mob. Glickfield is a gambler and associate of Frank Erickson. The accountant for this after-hour club was Henry W. Davis, a division head in the Accounting Division of the Reconstruction Finance Corporation, an agency of the U. S. Government.

Meserole left the Gold Key to open the Stagecrafters, 433 3rd Street, NW, and took a lot of the top political and theatrical business with him. His partner is Dominic Ferone, another ex-New York mobster. General Vaughan is a patron. It sells liquor openly and provides gambling, and waitresses will get women for them as wants 'em. Meserole testified under oath that many Congressmen and Senators were customers.

When Congressional investigations indicated the club was operated illegally, it was shuttered until the heat was off. But so heavy was the influence of its owners, through business ties with members of the New York Syndicate and the exalted position of its patrons, that as soon as the investigation shut down, the club reopened, not quietly, but brazenly.

We have before us an ad in a Washington daily which reads:

NOTICE . . .
Members and Their Guests
STAGECRAFTERS CLUB
NOW REOPENED
Same Place. . . .
Same Policy. . . .
Same Committees. . . .
Same Benefits. . . .
Membership Drive Now On
Help Get New Members!
EDWARD P. MESEROLE, Secretary

The Stagecrafters is the haunt of unsavory "introducers" who make contacts with wealthy chumps there, offering girls and gambling. Police recently arrested a lout, who, they charged, had become acquainted with William H. Engelmann, a photo-lithographer from Baltimore, out for a fling with friends in the Stagecrafters. The prisoner suggested a black-jack game and took him to a room in the Ambassador Hotel, which is owned by Gwen Cafritz's husband. Engelmann was soon a $1,500 loser, and asked his host to cash a check. He said he would, at the hotel cashier's booth, and left with Engelmann's check. Engelmann became suspicious when the man didn't return after an hour. He found the man had checked out. When the fellow was caught, police said, they found on him a deck of marked cards.

Another bottle-club that opened after the adjournment of the Congressional investigation is on the site of the Palm Grill, at 14th and Q, under a new name, the Sunrise.

The shuttered Turf-and-Grid was reborn as the aforementioned Amvets. The Turf's owner, Richard O'Connell, has been employed by the government since the beginning of the New Deal, in such agencies as the original NRA, the Department of the Interior (under "Honest Harold" Ickes) and more recently in the Red-infested Wages and Hours Division of the Department of Labor.

Another club that operates on and off is the United Nations

Social Club. When we visited it, its chief social activity was a crap game. Another is the Crystal Cavern.

When George P. Harding, a 39-year-old gunman and underworld fingerman, was shot to death by Joe Nesline, notorious Prohibition era bootlegger, in the Hideaway—an aftermath of last year's conquest of Washington by the Mafia—Washington's bottle-clubs took another shellacking.

Congressmen beat their breasts, newspapers shrilled, the DA promised action and the cops vowed to close all the joints. For a few days a couple of clubs went easy; at this writing most were again in action.

The Hideaway, scene of the crime, was reported "closed for good" by the precinct captain, but Joseph Horowitz, an owner, announced "business as usual" while the cops were telling everyone the premises were empty. At press time, the present and future status of the club was in doubt.

Legitimate clubs are a necessity until the District authorities amend the outmoded liquor laws. One which we liked is the Lyre's. Most members of this club are night-workers whose hours are such that they could never get a drink or relax if they had no place to go after 2 A.M. Among them are musicians of the big hotels and night clubs, waiters, waitresses, hatcheck gals, government swing-shift people and visiting entertainers. We spent considerable time at the Lyre's and noted everything was on the square. No patrons were permitted to enter who weren't members or their guests, and no drinks were served except out of members' bottles.

The Lyre's is chummy. There's a mainfloor bar and lounge and a basement dining-room and dance floor. Most of the musicians in town hang out there and put on jam sessions all night long. Its hosts are Vince and Mildred Carr, former Baltimore and Philadelphia night club operators. They have many friends in show business. The Carrs won't tolerate hookers and drunks, allow no soliciting, gambling or hoodlums. But unfortunately the Lyre's is unique.

Not all who want to drink late can afford to or can get into or know about bottle-clubs. Those who spend an evening in a licensed cabaret and find themselves still sober or out for fun at two, or at midnight on Saturday, are up against it. Licensed clubs and cocktail lounges can't sell for off-premises consumption. If you tip your waiter liberally he will dig up an empty

Coca-Cola bottle and let you fill it with the remaining liquor
at your table.

Some people who run dry at midnight Saturdays drive to
Maryland, where bars and package-stores close at 2 A.M.

Washington is loaded with bootleggers and blind tigers. We
have already referred to the gin-flats in Black Town, where
home-made gin—raw ethyl alcohol flavored with juniper and
sometimes diluted with apple cider—is sold. Prices are reasonable, as low as 50 cents a drink and $3 a bottle. The flats, usu-
ally five- or six-room affairs, have juke-boxes. Parlor floors are
cleared for dancing. Beds are handy. If cops come, it's a private
party. But cops don't come.

We pulled up in our cab to the NE corner of Popner and U
Streets, and waited five minutes. A colored man came over and
asked us what we wanted. He had gin, Scotch and corn. We
bought gin, trade-marked, $2.50 for a pint.

David Douglas Davenport, self-styled "Union Station bootlegger," has been selling booze in the railroad terminal for
years. He charges $5 for a pint of whiskey, which he keeps
stashed in an automatic coin locker. Davenport has a record for
court appearances, 115 in one year. He lost to the law once,
and did two years in the District jail. The day he got out of the
can he was in business in Union Station again and still was at
this writing, though arrested again and out on bail.

Many after-hour bootleggers sell legitimate stuff, which they
buy at Washington's low prices, and retail at 100 or 200 per
cent profit. Hundreds of other bootleggers, especially Negroes,
dispense moonshine. Most of this is acquired from mob sources
in Brooklyn and New Jersey, where the Mafia operates gigantic
stills capable of producing thousands of gallons a day. According to Carroll Mealy, capable and efficient head of the Alcoholic
Tax Unit, the rum-runners take this stuff to Washington in
1940 Fords, with Cadillac or racing motors in place of original
power. This model is preferred for its carrying capacity, ma-
neuverability and inconspicuous appearance. The souped-up
motors can hit 120 miles an hour against pursuit.

Much moonshine is made in Washington, though none of
the raided stills was found with a large capacity. The stuff is
cooked at 2nd and G Streets, NW. But legitimate Washington
sources supply liquor to be run into nearby dry and semi-dry
states and counties.

Not all who buy from bootleggers get drunk. Some get robbed.

"The tough part about it was that I never got the whiskey," Army Sgt. Filmore M. Broom, 41, moaned to police.

He said a Negro offered to sell him a bottle, but when the sergeant pulled out his wallet, containing $190, to pay, the Negro snatched it and ran—with the whiskey, too. This happened at 5th and Neal Streets, NW, and police are looking for a Negro with red suspenders and a white straw hat. No winter description available.

20. CAFE AU CORN

*F*OREIGNERS who have never seen the United States dream of beholding its wonders, of which the first two are New York and Washington. They envision not the monuments or the Government Printing Office, but a glittering world capital swirling with diplomats in colorful costumes, officers in dress uniforms, and pageantry punctuated with dazzling dames of the haute monde and the demi-monde. For this is the capital of capitals, and it must have everything, including what none of the others has—dough.

If there is any spectacular life in Washington, that is not for the eye of the uninitiated stranger. The days are vapid and the nights are stupid. Washington is dominated by elected and appointed functionaries who are schooled to believe they must never be caught having fun. Therefore, after dark it is more like Paducah than like Paris.

There are many hotel grills and lounges, which are night clubs after a fashion, and some cafes; but their chief patronage depends on visitors and government dependents. Both classes are drawn largely from farms and villages, with only a minor proportion from centers of laughter and light. Washington's night life is a dull, dismal and dreary reflection of our Main Streets, hard cider and juke-box roistering.

The few local sports and the free-fingered lobbyists seek their pleasure at private parties and behind closed doors of hotel suites, or fly northward to nearby New York with its El Morocco and the Stork Club.

The two principal night clubs in Washington are operated by Chinese, with American shows and dance bands. They are the Lotus and the Casino Royal.

Both are built for the mass-consumption trade, with popular prices and acres of dance floors. Hicks and tourists are dance-bugs. Dick Lam, host at the Lotus, is one of the town's best-known and best-liked showmen. He was one of the original founders of the China Doll, in New York, and has uptown manners and know-how.

The Blue Mirror, around the corner, specializes in hot jive. Kavakos, as mentioned, features nudes, as does the Players, opposite the Center Market.

Not only can and do some Washington cabarets get away with stuff that would land their owners in the clink in New York, but there seems to be no police control or regulation of acts.

For instance, Billie Holiday, the Negro singer who has served time on narcotics and prostitution falls, is barred from New York night clubs through the ukase of the Police License Bureau, which fingerprints all entertainers and thumbs those with records out of town. But while this was being written, Miss Holiday was starring in Washington's Brown Derby.

Washington caters to visiting theatrical celebrities. Holly-wood stars, to whom the capital spells spotlight, are flattered by attentions of politicians who, in return for free shows and broadcasts, flatter them. This racket was invented by President Roosevelt, and, ever since, theatrical headliners have been wel-come luncheon and dinner guests at the White House. In Washington they generally stay at one of the five leading hotels and may be found dining or drinking in the lounges and restaurants of the Mayflower, Carlton, Statler, Shoreham and Wardman Park. Autograph collecting is not a highly developed hobby in Washington; but some juvenile half-wits plant them-selves outside the hotels when such celebs are in town.

There is nothing the equivalent of Morocco, 21, Colony, Stork, or Toots Shor's. The Mayflower lounge, nicknamed "The Snake Pit," is that—the mad gathering-place at cocktail time for the local celebs: the Senators, lobbyists, army brass and blondest cuties.

Most Washington night-life is as flat as those who patronize it. The headwaiters are off the beam. The major-domo of the Wardman Park's Caribar, typical of most of the town's, is so provincial he doesn't know he could get rich trying to cater to the few spenders that stumble in. We watched him a whole evening and didn't see him snare a buck.

Patrons of Washington supper-clubs are lousy tippers. Most smalltown Americans adhere to a strict ten percent. When they think they can get away with it, they stiff even that. Captains, headwaiters, cigaret gals and retiring-room attendants they ignore. Southerners are worse.

We were twitting one Senator from a border state about the free haircuts the tax-payers provide for the members of the upper house in their private barber shop. This Senator replied, in all seriousness, "It's almost cheaper to go outside. When you get it for nothing, you gotta tip the barber."

The best palm-warmers are South American diplomats, who apparently have no regard for American money. Lobbyists, who like to flash big bills, especially when they are entertaining impressionable legislators, run for place.

Few Washington waiters deserve much. The service they give is as terrible as the tips they don't get.

Dance floors are crowded with jitterbugs. Rumbas never flowered in Washington. When a band plays one, flabbergasted hoofers try to jive to it.

Few clubs or rooms have rules against parties of unescorted women or stag men. If they did, they'd starve. It is not unusual to see half the tables in any room surrounded by all males or all females. The larger popular-priced clubs have signs on the tables reading, "Dancing permitted with your escort only." This is a dead letter, or there wouldn't be any dancers.

Prices are cheap compared with Gotham's. A few hotels impose cover charges when they book expensive name acts.

No room has more than one band, which plays both for the show and the dancing. During intermissions, the silence is broken by noisy drunks. Like all towns with early closing, people get loaded early. In Washington serious guzzling begins at cocktail time. Many of those who drink are oafs who don't know how to hold their hooch.

Most Washington saloon-goers are ill-mannered. On Saturday nights, when the last round is announced at 11:45, many arise as one and walk out, even in the middle of an act.

Washington has no cafe society. Its gathering places are utilitarian—for foods and drinks. No warm camaraderie, no light good fellowship, no wit, no animation. Corny commoners in stereotyped surroundings. Peoria on the Potomac.

21. CALL ME MADAM

THIS IS a brief brush-off of the social parvenus who scrambled up as Society scrammed out—through death and Democratic administration.

Faded and forgotten are the days and nights when Washington was ablaze with social brilliance and the gossip behind the fans reflected the sturdy foibles and feuds and infidelities of a class in superior strata of lineage, wealth and those graces which cannot be acquired with sudden fortune.

Society is always the shadow of one luminous, scintillant, predominant woman, such as Mrs. Potter Palmer was in Chicago and the dowager Vanderbilt remained until senility denatured her in New York. In Washington that woman, even though she seldom entertains or permits herself to be entertained, must be the wife of the President. She need not be a Dolly Madison. She can be a recluse, a Quaker like Mrs. Herbert Hoover; a New England villager, like Grace Coolidge; a grande dame like Mrs. Benjamin Harrison or an Ohio hick like Mrs. Warren Harding. But she is the undisputed ex officio queen bee of the social life of the capital. She sets its tempo, she elevates with a nod and she extirpates with a frown.

Few Presidents' wives would have won social preference had their husbands not squirmed through the labyrinthian catacombs with that miraculous luck which makes one man what they say any American boy can become. But once he takes that oath, his lady assumes a crown. Whether she chooses to wear it or not, she can and must exercise its power over her realm, Society.

And Society withstood the hostesses of gentlemen, soldiers, backwoodsmen, a sheriff, a tailor, a school-teacher, a railsplitter and a Buchanan. But it could not survive Eleanor Roosevelt.

Here came a woman of blood and millions, married to an equally high-bred, landed manor squire, perhaps the most charming and dynamic and handsome of all our Presidents. And the first tap of her flat heels across the White House threshold led off the funeral march of Society in the capital.

It is unnecessary to review her attitude and behavior; no First Lady was ever so unendingly publicized. That she became invested with certain homely and all-wooly virtues by the worship of millions is precisely why she choked the last breath out of social tradition with her Negro friends, her boondoggling, sweaty indigents, her professional Socialists, her dedicated slum-house guardians of gutter garbage, and her antics as the militant apostle of democracy and equality. The bedrock of Society is inequality, the existence and recognition of an aristocracy.

Whether it is good or not for fundamental Americanism, it was as lethal to the remnants of a baronial stratum in Washington as the Emancipation Proclamation was below the Mason and Dixon line.

No female in American history had ever been so despised in the drawing-rooms and so venerated in the kitchens and furnished rooms. But that hatred within the walls of the elegant was not enough to sustain even a social underground. A few dauntless matrons held out. They tried to continue executing the motions from memory, but they perished on the inglorious field of futility. They were the last. There were no wounded and no prisoners taken. A dynasty that had flourished for 150 years had been wiped out as were the Romanoffs.

And, surely, Bess Truman was not sent from above for the Restoration.

From the founding of the city until the recent demise of Evelyn Walsh McLean, who owned the Hope Diamond, Washington was celebrated for its intrigue, romance and scandal in high Society.

Eleanor "Cissie" Patterson and Mrs. McLean were the last of the city's great hostesses. Mrs. Patterson retired from the tea-table wars when she became active in newspaper work. With her death, and that of Mrs. McLean, the Washington Society pages were taken over by the climbers.

One needs no long memory to remember when social leaders from everywhere converged on this city. Dupont Circle was

Fifth Avenue refined and rarefied, the cream of established snobbery, wealth, officialdom and diplomacy.

Ambitious minglers from the Middle West, such as the Pullmans, the Leiters and others, bypassed New York's fatuous 400 and came directly to Washington.

Social history there begins with beauteous Elizabeth Patterson, of Baltimore, who wed Napoleon's younger brother. Its first tasty scandal was whispered in Jefferson's time, about the French Ambassador who was reputed to have married his jailer's daughter, who had saved him from the guillotine.

Early Washington Society was titillated by duels among high personages. The duel on the Hudson shore in which Alexander Hamilton was killed by Aaron Burr, in 1804, was talked about for years, until 1820, when a new gory sensation arose to take its place: the mortal wounding of Commodore Stephen Decatur in an arranged meeting of gentlemen across the District line in Maryland.

After a hundred years, Washington still talks about Peggy Eaton and President Jackson's Kitchen Cabinet. But, today's mundane morsels will make no interesting reading, leave no spice for the raconteur.

Society is on the wane everywhere. Taxes, Communist and New Deal propaganda, the high cost of living, make it virtually impossible to keep up huge menages. Now only rich labor leaders, black marketeers, gangsters and grafters can afford the expense.

There are a handful of rich dowagers like Mrs. Jay Borden Harriman and Mrs. Gifford Pinchot, but they are out of the running.

Cornelia Pinchot only entertains the "intellectuals," and they are legion in Washington. Where you find an intellectual in the District you will probably find a Red. Mrs. Pinchot does not know it, but the Commies have taken the elderly hostess over and are making hay with her name.

She lives in a Gay Nineties mansion on Scott Circle, where she often throws parties for the National Association for the Advancement of Colored People, attended by white and colored college professors, pansies and political economists. Mrs. Pinchot looks her age, though her hair is dyed the most amazing shade of carrot-red.

Mrs. Robert Low Bacon, the hostess of the Republican intellectuals, rarely hits the gossip columns. Even Evie Robert and her mother, Mrs. Helen Walker, have been dormant for years. Evie, the wife of "Chip" Robert, a brilliant political wire-puller, does not and never did give parties for social advantage. They were to advance the political prospects of her husband.

Today's Washington Society has no class levels. All you need is dough and the urge and the energy to spend it on freeloaders. If you can snag more important political people to your parties in any one calendar season, from October to May, than your neighbor, you are Number 1 social leader, regardless of whether you wore shoes before you were twenty.

Perle Mesta, a determined hostess who was lucky enough to have been gracious to Harry Truman when he was a secondary Senator from Missouri, is living proof of the potency of the Washington cocktail party. Her reward was the appointment as Minister to Luxembourg.

But Mrs. Mesta is by no means the only social climber in Washington, though she is and was the most publicized.

We would like to tell you about Mrs. Gussie (Gushie) Goodwin, formerly a Chicagoan. She is the wife of Federal Judge Clarence Norton Goodwin, who sentenced Harry Bridges in the Communist leader's first round before the courts. They were friends of the Woodrow Wilsons, which gave them some kind of claim to social standing. Meanwhile, Judge Goodwin started to go deaf, which handicapped him as a social figure. Gussie's star was setting.

Then came a turn to her fortunes. She met a charming Latin gentleman, Ramon Ramos, at a cocktail melee. He was a professor of Spanish. Gussie got an inspiration. She was going to cement Latin-American relations and her own social relations. She started a private class. Her little study group met once a week at her home. During the first year, there were eight women in it, each of whom chipped in a buck towards the professor's fee.

Gussie began calling the wives of the more important officials and Senators, and invited them to join her group. She was very careful to see that it was equally divided between Republicans and Democrats. One of the ladies who gladly became a member was the wife of Senator Harry Truman. After the Trumans succeeded to the White House, the Secret Service wouldn't allow Mrs. Truman to go to the lessons at Gussie's house, so all the meetings were moved to the White House,

though Gussie continued to be its leading spirit. Mrs. Goodwin was very offish. When Dean Acheson resigned as Under-
Secretary of State, his wife was not asked back.

Meanwhile, Professor Ramos showed he had hidden talents.
His hobby is cooking. The ladies were charmed. So an extra
feature was added. Each week the program was expanded to
include a luncheon, held at a different woman's house. The
Professor masterminded the menu, while the ladies did the
cooking and waited on the others. Mrs. Truman came to these
parties and pitched in with the work. The luncheons were run
on a Dutch treat basis, and each woman continued to pay her
dollar fee per lesson.

By this time there were sixty or seventy ladies in the group,
including good Queen Bess. Some took private Spanish lessons
on the side. Mrs. Truman was one of the few who was really
serious and wanted to learn the language. Most of the others
apparently came to the meetings because the Professor had
the personality to hold "menopause Minnies." Among the
students were a few who thought they should come along for
the ride without paying for lessons or the luncheon, because
of their social position. One was Mrs. Robert Patterson, wife
of the then Secretary of War. Mrs. Truman always paid.

When the Professor began to get too much publicity, Gussie
busted it up. After all, the whole purpose was to make Gussie
a figure, not the Professor. Gussie even went so far as to ask
newspaper society writers to use her name instead of his, saying
Mrs. Truman had complained about the Professor's publicity,
which was not accurate.

Anyway, no one learned much, but that wasn't the Prof's
fault.

In the absence of Madame Mesta, Gwendolyn Cafritz is
ballyhooed as Washington's leading hostess. She is a social
climber who invites only those in office or who she thinks are
due to be in. She sadly misjudged the 1948 elections. She ex-
communicated the Democrats. So she had a hell of a time
recouping her position. She still has her eye on the Republicans in 1952.

Compared to Madame Mesta, Mrs. Cafritz is a good-looking
woman, in early middle age. She may have been a raving
beauty when she was a slim, black-haired girl.

Her husband, Morris Cafritz, is a millionaire Washington
real estate owner. His office, in the Ambassador Hotel, which

he owns, is next door to the hotel's High Hat cocktail lounge, which is favored by the pick-up gals as a hunting preserve. Gwen drives her husband slightly nuts with her parties. He would prefer to play poker, at which he is adept. A lot of hogwash has been written about the Cafritzes since they zoomed into political and social prominence. Gwen was born in central Europe and may or may not have been the daughter of a college professor or a nobleman, as the stories go.

Cafritz's father ran a grocery store in Washington. The son's early days were spent in a bowling alley which he owned and operated. Then he turned to real estate in boomtime and found the Midas touch.

Gwen's enemies spread catty stories about her. One says she was a Broadway chorus-girl before she met her husband. If she was, she must've been a beaut. The other is that she was employed in Cafritz's bowling alley. The researcher finds it difficult to separate the truth from the chaff. There are no clippings about her early days in the Washington newspaper morgues. Cissie Patterson was her close friend. It is reported she destroyed the clippings in her own library and asked the publishers of Washington's other papers to do likewise.

Meanwhile, Mmes. Mesta and Cafritz had better look to their laurels, because a new assault is being made on Washington's social citadel, this time by a bullet-proof princess—Tawhida Halim, a cousin of King Farouk of Egypt, and immensely rich. She and Frank Rediker, a denizen of Gotham's cafe society set, were recently wed, repeat engagements for both.

The princess then acquired a mansion at 2339 Massachusetts Avenue, in which she and her bridegroom began to give lavish parties, designed to outdo any of the Cafritz woman's, with the elan that goes only to those born to the purple.

(*INSIDE STUFF:* The Redikers' social campaign is being managed by Leonard MacBain, elegant publicist and society arbiter of New York's plush El Morocco, where the snootiest people on earth gather. Leonard has steered royalty before. He could do marvels for Tawhida.)

Since the old aristocrats died or went into hiding, it is easier to get into Washington's society columns, if you care to horn in with inferior white trash.

Almost anyone, including justices of the United States Supreme Court, will go to any party to which they are invited. Many who aren't invited will also show up. The trick nowadays is to entertain lavishly and often, and sooner or later the papers will have to write about you, because there is nothing else to write about.

Ambitious hostesses buy the "Social List of Washington, D.C.," and invite names from it at random. The odds are 90 percent will show up, but the odds are as high that 95 percent of the 90 per cent aren't social. This list competes with the standard "Social Register." It contains most of the names in the latter, plus an amplification consisting of prominent politicians and diplomats. It is published by Carolyn Hagner Shaw. Mrs. Shaw told us a "board" selects the candidates for entry in the book. The board, however, is highly secret. One Washington newspaper insists it is as mythical as the balanced budget. Mrs. Shaw claims no one ever tells her why a name is added or dropped.

If you thought Maj. Gen. Harry Vaughan was part of the *crème de la crème* of the Washington social whirl, you'd better change your mind. He isn't any more. Not if you take the word of Mrs. Shaw. She omits the military aide to the President from her fancy green directory of the socially prominent. Mrs. Shaw doesn't know why General Vaughan isn't socially correct any more. She blamed it on the anonymous board.

About 200 who sought to make the list were turned down. Again no reasons given. Many bought copies at 12 bucks, hoping to see their names in. They didn't.

However, Guy George Gabrielson and William Marshall Boyle, respective chairmen of the Republican and Democratic National Committees, were among the new names added this year. The book also has the *dernier cri* on what to do about cards. They should not be left at Blair House, but given to the guard at the northwest gate of the White House.

"A courtesy call should be made on the President and his family once a year. This is a mark of respect that should not be neglected." (This was before two Puerto Rican enthusiasts tried it.)

Mrs. Shaw reminds her readers "During World War II, formal observance of the conventional days set aside for leaving cards on various officials was canceled. A return to formal recognition of these traditional days has yet to take place, and it is doubtful that it will ever again become obligatory to leave cards on certain days."

As to protocol, it notes: "It is well to remember personal

friendships do not count. The rank of one's guest must be the deciding factor."

If you are not sure of the comparative ranking of any guest, it is better not to invite him. Many of the biggest social wars were caused by such things. Still remembered is the feud between Alice Roosevelt Longworth, then wife of the Speaker of the House, and Dolly Gann, sister and hostess of Vice-President Curtis, over their respective precedence.

Officials and embassies receive advice on protocol matter from the State Department, but non-official hostesses are on their own. Mrs. Shaw supplies a service which gives assistance in seating.

An important fixture in Washington is the debutante party. These have almost disappeared in New York, where each year's crop of young hopefuls is introduced in a mass get-together. In Washington, the girl who doesn't get a dinner-dance on her own is a social slob. Washington's Elsa Maxwell for these parties is Mrs. Curt Hetzel, who succeeded Mrs. Merriam. Mr. Hetzel is a pianist in a restaurant—Ted Lewis'. Mary Stuart Price, a young woman, handles some debby parties as a sideline.

Club life is another sacred institution. Many important political decisions are reached at such places as the Burning Tree Club, the Chevy Chase Club, and the Sulgrave, famous for the McCarthy-Pearson battle of the century—more maybe than in the Senate and the House cloakrooms. The 1925 F Street Club, where ranking members of the Senate give parties, was once the exclusive home of Mrs. Laura Curtis Gross, who lent her house for parties. It is now a sanctuary for the whipped-cream of Washington society. Its dining-room seats about 60 and the club's membership is strictly limited.

Washington's newest aristocracy is evidenced by stone piles. The wife of the man who can build the biggest and plushiest office building is the reigning social leader.

Those currently with the highest batting average are Morris Cafritz, of course, Gus Ring, Garfield Cass and Preston Wire, all with gleaming new structures named after themselves. Much of the money of the real estate *nouveau riche* came from wise investments in Black Belt housing, or from refugee sources.

Until very recent years the august justices of the United States Supreme Court remained aloof from social functions, but during the days of the New Deal and Fair Deal, when the court was packed with soft-shirted politicians, the custom changed. Judges like Douglas are avid party-goers. The late Frank Murphy was a mixer with true CIO deportment, a hoofer and Saturday night sport. The result is that the opening of the fall season is now coincident with the convening of the Supreme Court. Then the jurists can meet the typists and clink cocktails with mobsters' mouthpieces.

The easiest way to get into what is called "society" is to be elected or appointed into it. Every ex-cow-puncher, dirt-farmer, smalltown lawyer and big-city ward-heeler who now has an "Honorable" in front of his name is as social as those who were born into it, bought their way in, or got in through a diplomatic passport.

All 96 Senators and 435 Representatives, nine cabinet officers, countless under-secretaries, assistant secretaries, judges, department heads and military brass are social, with a listing in the directory, though some never wore ties or socks until they got to Washington. These ex-officio lions became the life of the party in 1933.

Washington once thrived on dirt in high places. Grover Cleveland's bastard child didn't interfere with his electoral or social standing. Nor was Woodrow Wilson ruined when a certain lady was booted out of Washington by the Secret Service. President Harding's house on K Street is still remembered. There's nothing like it now. And his village sweetie and her baby have vanished. President Truman's poker games are penny-ante, not the lusty ones of yore.

The late Roosevelt administration is credited with more snappy spice than any other in history. Out-of-school tales were told about most of his children. The President and his wife were not spared by gossipers. But President Truman's personal life is treated as dull and austere.

His advisers are farmers or aging professors. They were pirates in the first Roosevelt decade. The sports, drinkers and rounders who held high cabinet and military rank then are either gone or too old. Now most official vice is grubby stuff, with call-girls supplied by a protected vice-ring, about which nothing is ever heard, and which no Congressman or Senator will admit he knows.

President Truman's pal, General Harry Vaughan, is comparatively quiet now, held to mama's apron-strings. There's gambling for him and the President in the White House.

There's no liquor shortage, either. The President likes his bourbon. He never smokes. He will not countenance whoring in his official family, though he doesn't put detectives on official tails.

Probably the only real sport in town is Senator Warren Magnuson. The others save their skylarking for New York. When they do it in Washington, they are as frightened as schoolboys at it, and often as unimaginative.

What a change from the Roosevelt days, when sex was the prerogative of all government officials, and usually paid for by the grateful tax-payers! Uncle Sam even had to help Harry Hopkins do it. A monkey-gland doctor grafted sex virility on Hopkins and two other aging administration stalwarts, one of whom recently resigned from a little-cabinet post.

The doctor billed the wealthiest of the three $3,000 for each treatment. He charged the other two $1,000. Hopkins had already stiffed the medico for three operations when he asked for the fourth, in view of his pending marriage to a young woman. The doctor's verdict was no money, no honeymoon. But Hopkins had a way out. He suggested the doctor needed a vacation anyway, so he offered to get him an appointment to make an inspection trip to army medical bases in the West Indies, with all expenses paid for self and wife, plus $35 a day fee until the $3,000 was paid. The doctor took the trip and Hopkins took the honeymoon.

High military brass is quiet today compared to the lusty generals and admirals of the '20s and '30s. Washington is still talking about how General Pershing, then chief of staff, ordered young General Douglas MacArthur to the Philippines after MacArthur married Mrs. Louise Cromwell Brooks, of the Philadelphia Stotesbury clan. Mrs. Brooks, after her divorce from her first husband, met "Black Jack" Pershing abroad. When she returned to America, she became his official hostess in Washington. She was 25 to his 60. Two months after their wedding, in 1922, the MacArthurs were shipped to the Philippines. Washington cats said Pershing sent his successful young rival into exile to get even. He had also exiled the captain of the Army polo team, who was attentive to the rich, beautiful Louise. She is now Mrs. Alf Heiberg, the proud owner of Washington's only private atom-bomb shelter, which she constructed under her Georgetown mansion.

The late General of the Armies, a widower, was quite a

man with the women. He kept a Roumanian babe and her mother at the Shoreham Hotel for 20 years.

"Thirty" was written to Washington Society when a local paper fired its social editor because she refused to print the names of Negro hostesses!

22. STRIPED PANTS

*E*LSEWHERE, men who wear them bury the dead; here, most of those who wear them are dead but not buried.

The decadence of the diplomats ran parallel with the fadeout of society, though not for the same causes. Continental and cosmopolitan life on Embassy Row was a war casualty.

The democratization and bolshevization of Europe turned their extra-territorial domains here into tawdry outhouses reflecting monarchies and empires riddled into busted republics and dictatorships, either scrabbling for the necessities of life or committed to the political policy of shabby proletarianism.

The kings are no longer king. The courts of Vienna, Berlin, Moscow, Madrid, Rome, and of the giddy little Balkan states are now the headquarters of Labor Parties and worse. The crowned heads of England, The Netherlands and the Scandinavian kingdoms are kept figureheads. Diplomatic display is a sin against poverty and the world rash for unilateral social and economic status.

There is not an embassy in Washington which does not cost far more than it did 20 years ago. That is because they have become workhouses where the press of international business is sordid and tremendous. Gone are the Thursday and Friday open-house hospitalities and grand balls in Technicolor, animated by gowns and costumes and uniforms of galaxies of all nations.

"These are difficult and different days," the deans of diplomacy sigh.

The old spirit has vanished not only from the governments, but from their representatives, who are living close to the vest, hoarding precious American dollars against revolution or overturn by popular vote of their countries. Ambassadors and

Ministers are salting away what they can skim off in Black Belt real estate, farms and U. S. securities. Some go much further. They are actual dealers in American goods which they can procure and can send home free of import duty to their countries. At the same time they blackmarket merchandise here, where they can buy liquor, cigarettes, cosmetics and other excised products free of internal revenue tax. For the best whiskey and champagne they pay $13 a case.

During Prohibition, a small Central American legation was actively in the rum-running business, importing huge quantities under diplomatic immunity, then reselling to Jack Cunningham, a local bootlegger. One day rival gangsters caught up with Cunningham in an alley in I Street, and there he was knocked off. The killing was hushed up. It would have involved too many untouchables.

These business opportunities and the degree of austerity which is still light as compared with most of the globe—all of it except Canada and South America—have made Washington the choice diplomatic plum, in place of London and its Court of St. James'.

The diplomats here are timid, precise and industrious. They are fearful of a false step which might mean recall, for here they are saving against eventual retirement. But their caution cannot withstand their greed and some smuggle dope in via their sealed and search-proof official pouches. They have discovered the glories of the American installment plan and buy not only land and houses, but cars and mechanical gadgets unobtainable at home. If they are transferred they rent out their properties here, which, in the only currency still reasonably dependable, makes them rich wherever they go, even into exile.

Another factor which helps reduce the gaiety and glamor of Washington diplomatic life is the competing diplomatic corps accredited to the United Nations, in New York. It is gradually getting the ace publicity breaks.

The question of sex looms big on the agenda of every ambassador. He prefers all his aides married, with wives in residence, so they will create no scandal. Many of the younger members of the various staffs, with modest jobs and salaries, are bachelors. These men are usually forbidden, under pain of being sent home, to fool around with women in Washington. Their chiefs, from time to time, order them to go to New York "to have a party."

If the press of business is too great to allow for long weekends, when the ambassador notes that the young men on his staff are getting hot britches he sends them to Baltimore, where they are unknown and nothing is barred.

Ambassadors, themselves, and senior diplomats with roving eyes, are taken care of by the Protocol Division of the State Department, which also handles the sex problems of visiting foreign brass. That's a job for specialists. There are so few girls in Washington glamorous enough to satisfy VIPs. Sometimes it is not politic to have them associate with local talent anyway, because of its tieups. So the State Department has compiled a list of amiable New York models, willing to come to Washington to spend a night with a foreign dignitary. They get $200 a night and expenses, from "contingent funds" coming out of the pockets of the American tax-payers. They are provided on an ancient reciprocity custom, in exchange for girls supplied to American junketeers who flit abroad.

This privilege is avidly utilized by American Senators, Congressmen and other officials, and is one reason why so many find it necessary so often to fly to Europe, Asia and South America at government expense. One prominent Republican solon, who never cheats in Washington, was shown such a good time by a French babe supplied by the Quai d'Orsay, he ended up in a Paris hospital for five days and has been a sick man ever since.

When the State Department procures women for foreign dignitaries, they are given security and VD tests. It is easy to see how delicate diplomatic relations might be ruptured by a microcosmic thunderclap.

Many embassies have their own "company- and party-girl" lists. They do not always want the State Department to know what they are doing. There's a girl named Mary Karrica, 1471 M Street, NW, who furnishes them to the diplomatic corps.

One of the major problems of such dialectics for the State Department's bright boys arises when a visiting notable plans to tour the country and doesn't plan to sleep alone. Protocol then makes contacts through local police departments, which are expected to know the best call-house madames in their own towns.

When the young Shah of Persia visited America a couple of years ago, the State Department had no trouble furnishing desirable girls for him in Hollywood and Chicago; but in New York, where he wanted a blonde that night, they had to get him a Powers model. Apparently his majesty liked it, because the next day he gave her an emerald worth $20,000. The guy from the State Department who told us about this sighed, "But the bitch still took our $200!"

Years ago, when Italo Balbo made his triumphal tour of the country, he turned his nose up at showgals and screen stars. The Italian air ace insisted on one from the Social Register. The Navy was in charge of entertaining him. Some of its younger attachés dug up a semi-society babe from Chicago, who was willing to take a fling with the Italian aviator. The Navy had no dough for the purpose, so the young officers chipped in $300 to buy her a watch, and told her it was from Balbo. Now a graying middle-aged woman, she still prizes the watch "given to her by the dashing Italian."

Most foreigners are discreet. Little rough stuff seeps out of the embassies. The Washington newspapers cover Embassy Row—there are two—16th Street and Massachusetts Avenue— but usually give their readers stories about cocktail parties, dances and weddings, instead of snappy copy.

Being confidential reporters we did not go through the front doors. What we know is mostly backstairs buzz, out of the kitchens and garages of the following embassies:

ARGENTINA—The Embassy, at 1815 Q Street, provided Washington with one of its liveliest tidbits. The real lowdown has not been divulged before. We got this out of confidential Congressional files, where the information was testified to under oath.

Nina Lund, niece of ex-Senator White, of Maine, was one of Washington's loveliest and most popular dishes. Her husband, Nathaniel Lautrelle, a local department store executive, suspected her frequent absences from home were not to go to the beauty parlor, so he and three men, whom he engaged, followed her to 3030 O Street, NW. Those with Lautrelle were Lt. Joseph Shimon, wire-tap expert of the Metropolitan Police who was recently under Congressional investigation; Joseph Mercurio, a dope addict and locksmith, and James Karas, former Pinkerton agent, who now operates the flower-shop in the Mayflower Hotel. Mercurio sprung the lock on Apartment

2 and the four entered. They found Nina and an Argentine Ambassador naked.

Shimon got five grand for his service. Lautrelle and Nina got a divorce. The Ambassador, sent here originally because Eva Peron fancied him, went back to Argentina for consultation.

But they have something else to occupy their minds these days. Many employes and upper attachés of the Argentine Embassy are feathering their futures by shipping electric refrigerators home, packed as personal household furniture.

This is simple, as it is not unusual for diplomats to buy enough personal furniture in the country of their station to furnish their homes. Hundreds of refrigerators can be packed into such cases, and each so smuggled brings a premium of $100 in American currency, worth ten times that in Argentine currency black markets.

BRAZIL—Hospitality in the Embassy, at 3000 Massachusetts Avenue, is in the best old-fashioned tradition. The Ambassador, Mauricio Nabuco, is a bachelor. His hostess is his sister, Carolina.

The Ambassador is one of Washington's best hosts. He constantly entertains at large formal affairs and at intimate gatherings to which statesmen, musicians and poets are invited. No scandal attaches to the Ambassador, but he likes to have pretty women around him. Maybe that's why he entertains so much. One 18-year old cutie told us, "Oh, the old guy is harmless."

CHINA—There's little gaiety as we write, in the Embassy at 3225 Woodley Road. But things were not always so. As witness:

Congressman Hale, of Maine (Rep.), is a short, white-haired, pompous gent, heavy with dignity. Not long ago he attended a formal affair at the Chinese Embassy.

Suddenly a woman came up behind him and "goosed" him. The legislator's dignity exploded with a scream. He turned around to confront his tormentor. The embarrassed lady apologized. "Oh—I'm sorry—I thought you were someone else!"

A good-looking, well-knit young man, employed by one of the government agencies, was showering in the bathroom of the YMCA, where he lived, some years ago.

Out of the corner of his eye he saw another man in the room, but thought nothing of it, as the bathroom is public.

When he came out of the shower the other was fixedly staring at him. Our friend grew embarrassed, and was not especially put at ease by the other's appearance. He was an elderly Oriental.

Our friend inquired what was doing. The Oriental, in a singsong voice, replied:

"You like go bed with rich Chinee lady?"

The chap was going to bop the guy, but first he tried to find out what it was all about. It developed that a high-placed woman in the Embassy liked American boys, sent her servant to recruit them in places like the Y, after having them looked over. What a switch on the oldie about "Is it true what they say about Chinese women?"

The son of a famous Protestant clergyman worked for the Maritime Commission, where he became friendly with the commercial attachés of many countries. He found some would take loot. This troubled him. He discussed it with an older man who had a desk in the same office.

This older fellow used to run errands for Lepke and Gurrah and their famed Murder, Inc. After Bill O'Dwyer destroyed the ring, he got a job with Uncle Sam.

He advised the young fellow to grab what he could while the grabbing was good. So the minister's son became the bagman for several embassies.

About this time the Chinese bought some gunboats and let out word they were in the market for repairs in American shipyards. The yards were in a post-war depression, needed business. Immediately, representatives called at the Chinese embassy. An official there, who spoke better English than most of us, mumbled in pidgin and routed all inquiries to "the young man in the Maritime Commission, in whom we have implicit faith."

The young fellow collected more than half a million in cash as the go-between, then beat it with the loot.

DENMARK—Ambassador Henrick de Kauffman and his family are so proper it hurts. The Embassy, at 2839 Woodland Drive, is like a morgue.

EGYPT—They are still laughing at this at 2301 Massachusetts Avenue. An Egyptian officer came to Washington recently on a buying mission. His embassy bespoke the American authorities to give him the A-1 treatment, the best. The Navy boys took him to Charleston to see the ships and set him up in style. The visitor wanted a blonde. But he was black, and

Charleston is down South. This posed a problem. They finally found a woman, but had to take her in through the back door.

The Egyptian was insulted. He returned home without buying.

FRANCE—No Parisian spice about the Henri Bonnets; however, there is no doubt the wife of a very exalted member of the staff is a Communist drop and transmission belt.

Mme. Bonnet has family connections interested in the sale of Lanson champagne. Important friends and guests pose with her, popping a bottle of the labeled bubble-water.

Latest to fall for the publicity gag were Averell Harriman and his wife, photographed with Mme. Bonnet while opening a bottle of the champagne. It got into all the papers.

GREAT BRITAIN—The embassy, at 3100 Massachusetts Avenue, under the Right Honorable Sir Oliver Shewell Franks, Knight Commander of the Bath, C.B.E., and Lady Franks is as dull and austere as England itself. But a former British Ambassador had as his lover his Russian valet.

ICELAND—Plenty of problems at the Icelandic legation. Lovely Margret Thors, debutante daughter of Minister Thor Thors, got too friendly with thrice-divorced Blaine Clark, Washington playboy, so Ma and Pa packed her off to Iceland, where Clark couldn't follow without a visa, which the old man wouldn't give. Margret promised to be a good girl and was permitted to return, but has to behave.

IRAQ—As we write, Abdullah Ibraham Bakar, Iraqui minister, has a headache. That's because Cham Chum Sesi was arrested for murder in his basement room of the Iraq Chancellory, 2205 Massachusetts Avenue. Muhmud Rodani, chief janitor, had been stabbed in the neck with a kitchen knife. Sesi told police he killed the janitor because he had made repeated improper advances to him. The diplomatic set talked about a lovers' quarrel there when a new homo came from Iraq.

NORWAY—The dean of the Washington Diplomatic Corps is Ambassador Wilhelm Munthe de Morgenstierne. The Norwegian Embassy, 3401 Massachusetts Avenue, generates no gossip.

SAUDI ARABIA—This country is orthodox Mohammedan, goes in big for polygamy. The Ambassador, Sheikh Asad Al-Faquih, had no desire to insult America by bringing extra wives with him, was afraid to affront his wives by choosing one and leaving the others at home. The result is there are no women in the Embassy at 2800 Woodland Drive, or in the homes of any of the attaches. When they want parties, they go to New York, or to the State Department, where Protocol provides.

SPAIN—America and Spain long exchanged no ambassadors. Don Eduardo Propper de Callejon, Spanish Minister, was nominally in charge of the Embassy. The wily Spaniards got around having no ambassador here by sending Don Jose de Lequerica, former Foreign Minister, as "Inspector General of all Spanish Embassies in the Western Hemisphere." However, the farthest he got from Washington since 1947 was Cuba.

Lequerica is a personality kid and a lobby genius. He entertains lavishly. His conniving paid off with the Spanish loan, and in time with full recognition. Ambassador Lequerica had cultivated the law firm of Sullivan, Cromwell and Dulles, until the 1948 election returns were in and Dulles was out—as potential Secretary of State. He switched to Max Truitt, son-in-law of Vice President Barkley. Smart guy.

Minister Propper de Callejon is married to an English Rothschild and is as proper as his name.

SWEDEN—Ambassador and Mrs. Erik Boehman are no exception to the rule that all Scandinavian embassies are tame and respectable. Theirs, at 3900 Nebraska Avenue, is.

TURKEY—The Turkish Ambassador, Feridun Cemal Erkin, insists on decorum in his Embassy at 1606 23rd Street. Turks there put on gloves and are fully clothed when they go to bed with their wives, an Orthodox Mohammedan custom.

UNION OF SOVIET SOCIALIST REPUBLICS—The Russians used to be the big spenders. Parties in the great white Embassy at 1125 16th Street were Washington's most brilliant affairs. Invitations were eagerly sought after. The Russian government paid all expenses of the Ambassador and his staff, even bridge losses. The Russkies were terrific gamblers and few locals could go along in games with them. Once when a Washington businessman was asked to play bridge at 25 cents a point he pleaded, "I'm only a capitalist, not a proletarian."

There was always plenty of food and liquor in the Red retreat. All members of the local press corps were remembered with presents, especially beluga caviar. But now the Russians don't go out except to official functions, and that goes for their satellites, too. And they travel only in pairs, one to spy on the other.

The Russians and their slave states bring their own females from abroad, because they're afraid to trust American women, Communist ones included, any more. In the good old days, the consecrated American left-wingers used to go to the Soviet Embassy, where they proved their party loyalty by getting in the hay with the men from Moscow. After many frightened American Reds got religion and betrayed the cause, Soviet diplomats were forbidden to Ostermoor with American women. This did not cause too much hardship, because most American Communist women are no dream-girls; even the Russians shrank from them.

Almost every member of the embassy set has a wife or a concubine posing as a wife with him. In Russian Naval Headquarters, a few handsome young orderlies are being used. There are said to be few homosexuals in Russia, where perversion is strictly punished, except for "Kremlin and world revolution."

As one humorist remarked, "There are no fags in Russia, because they like goats; but where can they find goats in Washington?"

As a further check on their own people, members of the Soviet Embassy staff are not permitted to live alone. Even couples must share apartments with others.

The Russians have been getting special kid-gloving in Washington since 1933, when the Embassy became the fashionable place to go. At Teheran, Stalin asked President Roosevelt for permission to set up a shortwave radio transmitter in the U. S. to enable his boys to contact Moscow directly. Roosevelt sent a memo to General Marshall, instructing him to cooperate. Marshall wrote back that the law absolutely forbade any foreign government to maintain a transmitter in this country. F. D. R. penciled across it, "Do it anyway."

Consequently, an entire wing of the Pentagon was turned over to the Commies, where they sent over a million words a week. The President ordered Military Intelligence not to try to break the Russian code, but some officers took their oath to defend the Constitution literally, and overrode the President without his knowledge. As these words are being written, thugs of the NKVD are sitting 24 hours a day with ear-phones and transmitters in Russian Naval and Military headquarters at Massachusetts Avenue and Kalorama Road.

* * *

When an embassy wife isn't worrying about a change in government at home, which may mean the recall of her husband, she's worrying about getting her daughter properly married. A lot of the debutantes of the embassy set are beginning to get American ideas after attending American schools. The foreign aristocrats don't like it.

Embassy wives have rarely been known to fool around. On the whole, embassy children behave themselves. When they don't, they get packed off to schools in their own countries.

With the exception of the Iron Curtain diplomatic slums, there is considerable camaraderie among attaches of the various embassies, though usually on equal strata. They go dancing in the hotels, visit at each other's homes, ride and play golf together. Some time ago, an attempt was made to start a United Nations Club at R and 19th Streets, by Meredith Howard, who is the twin sister of Mrs. Teddy Hays. Hays, a big Democrat and White House intimate, is assistant to Federal Security Administrator Oscar Ewing, the socialized-medicine man. The idea was to get younger members of the embassies together, but it blew up when Miss Howard left town with no public explanation.

When it comes to con games, the diplomats and foreign missions could show Yellow Kid Weil something.

Washington and New York are constantly being dazzled by members of foreign missions who come here talking about purchases in hundreds of millions (the dough to be put up by Uncle Sam).

Salesmen, sure-thing boys and big executives turn on every tap to entertain the foreigners and grab their business.

Girls are provided, expensive gifts are passed, and plenty of money changes hands. Then, suddenly, the mission packs up, leaves without buying, says it can't find what it wants.

Cooks and butlers in every Washington embassy get kickbacks from the merchants. Groceries, meats and other household goods are overpriced on a regular scale for the embassies, with a rebate going monthly to the aforementioned functionaries.

Lower-echelon foreigners have their wild parties in the Washington field offices of the United Nations. There is no central installation of the international body in the capital, but offices are spread out around the town.

One of the principal places for after-work revelry is in the U.N. offices in the Longfellow Building, on Connecticut Avenue, where booze and babes are available every day after five.

Employes of the embassies, foreign missions and the U.N. and such carry special cards which exempt them from the payment of all U.S. taxes such as DC sales, Federal amusement tax, etc. They are, of course, exempt from income tax, too.

It's a racket in Washington to borrow a friend's card when making any expensive purchase like a mink coat, where the sales and luxury tax swindle comes to 22 per cent by this means.

A racket begun in UNRRA and now going on in other foreign aid organizations is engaged in by top administration figures and important diplomats:

Most of the durable goods aid sent abroad goes with the proviso that it must be resold in the currency of the country to which it is consigned, and the money must be used to provide local home relief, such as food, clothes, etc.

So the way it works is this: The embassy wangles a shipment of, shall we say, locomotives. They arrive in the country of destination. They are then duly and dutifully resold in the currency of the country. But the law doesn't say for how much.

Some locomotives were sold in Greece for 10 drachmas each. The drachma runs about 1,000 to the dollar. The local poor get the ten drachmas. The local political bosses, gangsters and crooked diplomats split the resale profits with their opposite numbers in America.

That's big racketeering. A couple of Washington sisters have a petty, but profitable one. They operate a so-called Embassy social list and charge chumps to get on it, dangling invites to diplomatic balls as the bait, which they obtain from legation employes for a "cut."

Some fall for it. Our confidential advice is, don't pay. You can crash almost any Embassy party—but who wants to?

23. THE RIGHT TO PETITION

"Congress shall make no law abridging the right of the people peaceably to assemble and to petition the government for a redress of grievances"—First Amendment to the Constitution.

* * *

DON'T YOU believe it. Congress hamstrung lobbying by requiring practitioners to register. Then it appointed a committee to investigate them. Neither gesture got far. Lobbyists are among the most delightful people in Washington. They are the friends of everybody, including the Congressmen who are "probing" them.

Lobbying is like the Indian rope trick. Everyone talks about it, but no one has ever seen it done. It's one subject all Congressmen shy from, regardless of party. That's because there are lobbyists on both sides. You can hardly expect a Congressman to insult a supporter.

Many ex-Congressmen, who can't bear the thought of returning home after their defeat, remain in Washington as lobbyists. They enjoy an advantage, because, forever after, all ex-Senators and ex-Representatives have the privileges of the floor and the cloak-rooms. They can collar the ones they need while the legislators are in action. Thus, members, who are always aware of the possibility of being lame ducks themselves, keep these pleasant prospects of earning a generous living after retirement open and in good working order.

When you read about lobbying being a $100,000,000 business, don't believe that, either. Maybe they soak their clients that much, but most of it goes on padded expense accounts. Lobbyists are their own best press-agents. They are more responsible for the hue and cry against lobbying than are the reformers. By making it look more difficult, they can load their take.

Lobbying is as old as Magna Charta, which first granted people the right to petition their sovereign. Ever since, those who wanted something have hired someone to speak up for them. Washington is full of these hucksters. They are about the brightest spot on the glum scene. They spend, entertain, throw wild parties with pretty gals as souvenirs, tip lavishly and keep the hotel and liquor industries going. They are the only cream here in a welter of skimmed milk.

An Act of Congress, of doubtful legality, requires lobbyists to register and divulge the amount and source of their income. Some do, many more don't. Those who comply are the technical lobbyists—in other words, they are errand boys who merely transmit messages and appeals from their clients to the Congress. Many have no physical contact with Congressmen at all, reaching them through mimeographed propaganda mailed from a Washington office.

But most of those we consider lobbyists are the ones who feel they are not required to register. When we mention anyone in this chapter, we are not inferring that if he is not a registered lobbyist he is breaking the law. We group together for purposes of posing a picture, every Washington lobbyist, fixer, five-percenter, hot-shot lawyer, industrial press agent, and man from Missouri. They are a multitude, especially men from Missouri.

When a really big fix is made, it usually is not handled in Washington at all. The deal is consummated back home, as a quid pro quo for a large campaign donation, after which the county or state chairman sends word through channels to his men in Washington that the matter should be okayed.

Lobbying can be a delightful and well-paid occupation. The mouthpieces of the industrial petitioners are usually charming gentlemen who know how to entertain. Buying an uninstructed Congressman C.O.D. is obsolete. Giving him a high time will do it, and the lobbyist can pocket the money earmarked for bribing and tell his client he passed on the boodle.

Most solons are lonely uprooted rustics. Usually their wives are away, holy frights they are glad to leave back home. These men want to talk and drink with someone. You don't even have to get them girls, just invite them to a hotel and spend an evening with them. They'll be so thankful, they'll do anything you want.

The average big lobbyist doesn't bother with run-of-the-mill Senators and Representatives, who are in the bag without much trouble. He sets his sights on the key characters like committee chairmen and floor leaders, and even they can be snared at little cost, though naturally to corral a chairman means an even heftier bill to the employer. The procedure used in the case of VIPs is simple and cheap. Each lobbyist is on friendly terms with some local hostess, for whom he does favors or to whom he gives gifts. When he has an especially important deal on, he asks her to invite his prospect to a party. During most of the evening he keeps away from the man he wants to meet, until by a fortuitous accident he is placed next to him at the table. Even then the conversation is kept chatty and frothy. A couple of days later, the lobbyist phones his erstwhile table companion and invites him to a rubber of bridge or a game of golf, and from then on he's on his own.

Administrative heads and assistants are much more sought after than Senators. They are the ones who receive the deep freezes and their wives, the expensive gifts. In the final analysis, the best contact is a clerk, not a division head. The clerks do the work and make the decisions while their bosses drink cocktails.

Much of the big-time fixing is done by law firms. Many New York outfits maintain offices in Washington. These firms usually have partners belonging to both parties, so they are prepared for any political eventuality.

We would like to introduce you to some of the boys in Washington who can get things done:

First comes to mind an attorney, Charles Patrick Clark. Mr. Clark is a wonder-worker. When others can't score, Clark is called in. Even Max Truitt, the Vice President's son-in-law, had trouble getting Franco's loan, so Clark hit in the pinch and Congress voted it. It may be a coincidence, but Clark was a counsel for the Senatorial Committee Investigating War Frauds when Harry Truman was its chairman.

Part of Clark's success can be ascribed to the majestic manner in which he entertains. He used to project his parties in Georgetown, but now hosts it in a palatial four-story building near the Mayflower Hotel. It set him back a hundred grand to furnish its interior. The yard was landscaped at a cost of $25,000 more. Clark can muster more pretty girls than anyone else in Washington. You will always find enough of them at his parties. He has two stunners in his office, a blonde and a brunette, who frequently are escorted by his clients and his contacts.

Congressman Buchanan, Pennsylvania Democrat, chairman of the committee investigating lobbying, fell for Clark's charm. He and his wife visited Clark's play-place.

Clark is hot-tempered. He recently had a fist fight in the lobby of the Mayflower Hotel with Charlie Rogers, handsome former counsel of the committee that nailed John Maragon.

Dan Hanlon, a former law-partner of Democratic National Chairman Bill Boyle, has an office at 1727 Massachusetts Ave., where he handles internal revenue cases with much success. Hanlon is from Missouri. But as Boyle seems to be on the way out so is Hanlon.

The business is intensively departmentalized. Different lawyers have ins in different branches of the government. Persuasion on the Department of Justice is handled by Laughlin Currie, a former Truman appointee, through Tommy "The Cork" Corcoran, a Roosevelt favorite.

Treasury Department matters go through Joe Nunan, former Commissioner of Internal Revenue, who does not practice personally before the Treasury yet, because the law requires ex-employes to wait two years before they may represent clients in bureaus to which they were attached. But his associates are not so hobbled.

Former Senator Burton K. Wheeler is the man to see if you have any trouble with the Interstate Commerce Commission. Wheeler can have anything he wants in Washington. President Truman passed the word along. It was Wheeler who advised Truman not to resign from the Senate at the time of the Pendergast scandal. Harry has been eternally grateful ever since.

The law firm of Thurman Arnold, Abe Fortas and Paul A. Porter has practically everything for its field. All three are prominent ex-New Dealers. Porter's contact is with the Federal Communications Commission. Arnold, once a trust-buster, now defends trusts. Fortas, onetime stooge of Harold Ickes, is the boy to see for anything in the Department of the Interior. Among the clients of this firm is the Western Union Telegraph Company, for which they are the registered lobbyists. During their plugging for the telegraph monopoly it was brought out under oath that at least one block of 17 percent of its stock was owned by underworld figures. Since then, Western Union was indicted twice in New Jersey for engaging illegally in transmission of racing information, which the Grand Jury investigation indicated was the company's main source of profit.

The Arnold firm secured $200,000,000 for the Puerto Rican government. It also defended Owen Lattimore against Senator McCarthy's charges. The boys netted $600,000 last year. Drew Pearson's daughter is married to Arnold's son.

Arnold is the playboy of the firm, congenial and convivial.

When Dean Acheson's law firm swung the $90,000,000 Polish loan, its fee from behind the Iron Curtain was $1,000,000, plus an equal sum for expenses.

Leon Henderson, the social planner who admits he won World War II single-handed, deserves an important place in this chapter. As one of the brain-trust of the "progressive" Americans for Democratic Action, brother Henderson throws the weight of that organization's supposed voting strength around Washington for the benefit of his private clients. That is, when he is not too busy making a fool of himself with some young blonde on a New York dance floor.

The A.D.A. pipeline into the White House is David Garrison Lloyd, assistant general counsel to the President.

Robert Nathan, the CIO economist, who comes up with fantastic suggestions such as that the cost of labor has nothing to do with the final price of the commodity, helps support himself by "economizing" for capitalistic clients trying to borrow dough from the RFC. If they hire him, they usually get it.

Those who shed tears for Louis D. Johnson when he was fired as Secretary of Defense need have no worries about how Louis is going to make a living in the future. He is a partner in the firm of Stepto and Johnson, and he has high connections.

Louis, who put the stigma on five-percenters, is one of the biggest operators on government contracts in town. Incidentally, there's nothing illegal about five-percenting and the fee is now seven and a half percent—Truman inflation.

Though out of the administration, Johnson is so potent and powerful that failure to retain him is a death warrant on some deals. He specializes in alien property work.

Once again, as during World War II, the lobbyists and five-percenters' password is "Are You Protected?"

That goes for a lot of things. It means are you protected against the law, against competition? But, mainly, are you protected from your clients?

Too many fixers found themselves double-crossed. After they had delivered, they couldn't collect.

Now the smart ones won't unbutton a button until the cash

is put up in escrow. Fancy deals are worked out on paper to cover up the shady nature of the real transaction.

One contact man whom it was a pleasure to have lobby you was Howard Hughes' fat errand boy, Johnny Meyer. Johnny is a prodigal entertainer and check-picker-upper. During the Senatorial investigation into how come Hughes got some government contracts, it was testified that Johnny supplied gifts and gals lavishly. He introduced Brigadier General Elliott Roosevelt to his former wife, Faye Emerson, and picked up the tab for the wedding expenses.

Elliott screamed at the hearing, "You are persecuting me because my name happens to be Roosevelt." The Republicans who conducted it immediately got cold feet.

Their temerity in hounding Elliott and Johnny was not forgotten. Three years later, the radical lame duck Senator, Claude Pepper, conducted an investigation to try to prove that former committee chairman Brewster had tapped Johnny Meyer's wires.

If he did, he must have had a good time. We know. We were with Johnny in his Statler suite, and he was with us in ours. His "in" is former Washington Governor Mon Wallgren, who is an old drinking and poker-playing crony of the President. Wallgren has entree at all times to the White House and now holds a Government hand-out job so he can keep his lines and connections in order.

While on the subject of lame ducks, we mustn't forget Scott Lucas, former Senate Majority leader. He is now ready, willing and able to handle such Washington legal and contact matters as may be brought to the attention of himself and partner, Charles A. Thomas.

Many of the lawyers, lobbyists, fixers, five-percenters, etc., with wires into high places, do not actually practice in Washington, preferring to do their work through correspondents or connections.

One of these is Jake Arvey, the Illinois Democratic boss and associate of Mafia hoodlums, who operates through the Washington office of Louis Johnson. Arvey is the kingpin of the wire-pullers.

Often the extent of a fixer's ability is overrated. An intermediary needs only to be seen with a big politician to have the word get out that he's "in." Then, after spending thousands, a client sometimes gets the idea he's got to hire another lawyer to do the actual work. Sometimes the fixers themselves turn the actual leg work over to capable attorneys, sit back, and take the credit.

There are many of these bread-and-butter lawyers who accomplish what all the politicians and five-percenters can't, because they really know the law. For instance, one prominent politico told us that while few tax cases are "fixed" at the Washington level, many a fearful and repentant chiseler has been fleeced by smart operators who told him they were wonder-workers. For results, he recommended two relatively unknown but very successful practitioners, Bert B. Rand, Washington-wise attorney, and Nathan Wechsler, hard-hitting, astute C.P.A., because they had the staff and experience to meet the government on an equal basis.

Similarly, in the field of constitutional law and the intricacies of corporation procedure, and claim work, they look up Loring Black, a former Congressman from Brooklyn, who retired from the House in 1934.

One young fellow who can do more for you in Washington with less fanfare doesn't make it his business. He is Hal Korda, onetime newspaperman, who has many powerful friends on both sides. When the Dems found out he knew Republicans, and vice versa, they began to use him as a channel to square things they didn't want to talk about directly to each other, and he secured campaign contributions for both.

Many members of Congress lobby, legitimately, for their own communities, or the industries thereof, or for public organizations in which they have a deep interest.

For instance, Joseph Rider Farrington, the delegate from the Territory of Hawaii, who holds a seat in the House but no vote there, has been foremost in the fight to secure statehood for the Islands. Farrington has labored mightily in that cause, and could show the professionals a thing or two. If Hawaii ever achieves statehood, Farrington can take the bow.

Incidental to that great libertarian campaign, Farrington also plugs the produce and products of the Territory and is its chief booster for tourism. His office in the Old House Building resembles a cross between a steamship agency and a Chamber of Commerce.

On the other hand, Henry Latham, one of the three Republicans in the House from the City of New York—if you count Javits a Republican—is a strong and sincere booster for the

Navy. Were it not for his "lobbying" in committee, we would have no Marine Corps today.

Latham, a Navy officer in World War II, did not know he had been run for Congress or elected until his ship went into a South Pacific coaling station two months after the 1944 elections. He has been reelected ever since.

He spotted the joker which would have wiped out the Marine Corps in the administration Defense reorganization measure and tied the bill up until the Devil Dogs were assured of being more than a mere "police force."

Acey Caraway, finance director of the Democratic National Committee and longtime pillar of that body, is opening an office for "consultation" in the LaSalle Building. Acey, often referred to as the "junior Jim Farley," probably knows more Democratic rank-and-filers than anyone else in the party.

Among the law firms which have had the most success in lucrative immigration matters is the New York one in which Rep. Franklin D. Roosevelt, Jr., is a partner.

Thomas Shoemaker, a former Commissioner of Immigration, also shows remarkable results in such cases.

New York's left-wing New Deal Republican Congressman Jacob K. Javits is a partner in Javits and Javits, 1025 Connecticut Avenue. Several immigration matters have been settled successfully by them.

Wholly apart from such legal practices, the current price for bringing in a rich refugee who can't make the quota or other entry requirements is $75,000. This is split between three Senators and/or Representatives, to sponsor so-called "private" bills.

These bills are always passed, because the three interested members buttonhole other Congressmen, who themselves need support to pass their own private bills. That is called "Congressional courtesy."

An embarrassing incident happened recently when President Truman vetoed one such bill, after the 75 Gs had been passed and spent.

The Vice President's son-in-law, Max Truitt, lobbies for American flag steamship lines, and has had conspicuous success in obtaining government handouts. He is effective also for the Kansas City wheat pit, a favorite whipping boy of the administration he's married into.

Lobbying before the Maritime Administration is dream business. It had 17 billion dollars' worth of ships to sell after the war.

Much of this government property found its way into the hands of the right people, who floated their purchases, if not their ships, by borrowing from the government, then immediately reselling at double or triple to corporations they organized.

In addition, these purchasers charged off hundreds of thousands against their income taxes for expenses, on transactions which they frequently went into with no more than a few thousand dollars to start with.

Truitt is the most active in the ship field and is registered as a ship lobbyist with Congress.

The firm of the late Secretary of State Stettinius also dabbled in Maritime Administration work. His associate was handsome ex-Congressman Joe Casey, of Massachusetts.

One of the most up-and-coming of the lawyers with "inside" connections is Margaret Truman's "date," Marvin Braverman. It is doubtful whether he has much influence, but people are beginning to credit him with it, and he is no chump. He is taking advantage of the publicity.

Braverman is related to Harry Hershfield, the radio wit and cartoonist. And if his small talk is anything like Harry's, we don't blame Margaret for liking him. Because Harry is the funniest man alive.

Former Housing Administrator Wilson Wyatt, a roaring Fair Dealer, is lobbying for big interests to repeal war-time taxes as well as for the Dominican Republic dictatorship.

Clark Clifford, the President's former legal adviser and ghost-writer, is not starving in private practice, either.

Clifford says he "doesn't need law books." He uses the Mayflower Hotel menu instead.

Another law firm with great influence is Fulton, Walter and Halley, with offices over the Occidental Restaurant. Hugh Fulton was chief counsel for the Truman Committee. Rudolph Halley was on the staff. The firm has done handily representing Howard Hughes, owner of TWA. As special counsel for the Hudson and Manhattan Railroad, between New York City and suburban New Jersey, they secured a 50-percent fare increase from the ICC. In our book *Chicago Confidential*, we said that the underworld had large blocks of stock in the Hudson and Manhattan. Since then Halley, who was the counsel of the road, confirmed our statement, reluctantly, and we have affidavits to prove it.

A law degree is not always necessary to a successful contact man. Some of the most prosperous in Washington bill themselves as press agents. There is, for instance, a little man from Missouri, Victor Messall, who dresses like a race-track follower and has his walls plastered with pictures of the President. Messall was a beaver on the President's Senatorial campaigns. Later he was on his secretarial staff in the Senate. He has testified under oath that he has so many clients he can't remember them all. A witness charged before the Kefauver Committee he had given Messall $1500 to help him to get sugar-points illegally from the OPA during the war. The chairman of the committee was a Democrat. The counsel was the aforementioned lawyer for the Truman committee, Rudolph Halley. The subject was suddenly dropped.

Another who bills himself as a press agent and is blossoming into a power which some call sinister because of his connections, is a former newspaperman, Dave Charnay, who runs a publicity firm in New York and Washington, Allied Syndicate. Charnay is a long-time friend of Frank Costello, reputed king of the underworld, and has done public relations for Rep. F. D. Roosevelt, Jr., and Manhattan Borough President Robert F. Wagner, Jr., son of the author of the Labor Act.

During the administration of Mayor LaGuardia, when gangsters were ordered out of New York night clubs, Charnay, then still employed as a reporter for the New York *News,* was made "president" of the famous Copacabana at a salary of $500 a week. Charnay was known as Costello's press agent.

Among other clients, his publicity firm represents John L. Lewis' United Mine Workers, at a reputed annual fee of $175,000. Those who may seem mystified at his range of clients, may be surprised to learn that Lewis, though he doesn't know it, is a prisoner of the Mafia. It started many years ago, when the United Mine Workers imported Sicilian sluggers from the big cities. With this "in," the mob bosses began to cast greedy eyes on the colossal fortune owned by the mine union. The Mafia's policy is never to replace present management if it can take over a flourishing concern. The infiltration went on under Lewis' nose, yet the beetle-browed egomaniac does not know he no longer is the boss of the United Mine Workers. The boys let him think he is. Last year, the Mine Workers tried to take over New York's taxi industry, with an abortive strike in which Mafia associates took a part. Charnay's firm handled the strikers' publicity.

Charnay now has a pipeline directly to the White House, through the close personal friendship between John L. Lewis and Dr. John Steelman, assistant to the President. Some months ago, on his retirement as Secretary of the Navy, John L. Sullivan joined Charnay's firm as chairman of the board, but he resigned to practice law. Paul H. Griffith, assistant Secretary of Defense until he was replaced by Anna Rosenberg a few months ago, is now a vice-president of the company.

Charnay had a pleasant luncheon tête-à-tête with Kefauver counsel Halley, before the crime committee began its hearings, and offered to work for it without pay.

Another interesting lobbyist is Samuel Haines, whose contract with the hotel and cafe industry to try to get a reduction in the 20 percent amusement-tax was on a sliding scale, his fee to be determined by the degree of eventual tax reduction. The tax wasn't cut, but he got $46,000. Haines entertained Senators and Representatives in a playroom at his home, where he had slot-machines, reverse-rigged so the players always won.

A mysterious man about town is Dave Gordon, always seen with beautiful dames. Gordon is a close friend of Nate Lichtauer. Lichtauer is a shadowy enigma. Little is known about him. But this is to tell you he engineers the juiciest deals. ("Juice" is the capital slang for political pull.) Lichtauer is a collector for the Democratic National Committee. He makes the arrangements. When the contributions come through, he passes the word to Dave Niles, in the White House, who pulls the proper strings.

One of Lichtauer's closest associates is Milton Kronheim, another mystery man. He used to be in the bail-bond business in Washington and went surety for gamblers. He is now the city's biggest and richest wholesale liquor dealer. He is in on everything. He once peeled off 250 bills—$1,000 bills—to pay an OPA assessment, then put the balance of the still impressive roll back in his pocket.

He is close to General Vaughan and John Maragon, and thick with Jake Arvey, Chicago Democratic boss, friend and apologist for Al Capone's cousin, Charlie Fischetti, king of the Chicago underworld. Kronheim's son was recently made a Municipal Court judge in Washington. Truman nominated

Kronheim's lawyer, "Jiggs" Donohue to be District Commissioner. And Kronheim supplies the White House liquor.

One to watch as a power is a Boston lawyer, Paul T. Smith. He got that way because he and Dave Niles ran a forum in Boston called Ford's Lyceum, a sort of left-wing Chatauqua in which Frankfurter had a powerful say. When Police Chief Barrett was under Congressional pressure,. Niles and Smith interceded.

It was through the connections he made with dreamers and schemers like Harry Hopkins, who used to lecture for him, that Niles moved himself into the White House under Roosevelt and has remained under Truman, the only man Harry dared not fire. Niles, whose hand turns up in everything, may be the real ruler of the country.

Anyway, when attorney Smith gets a case with a Washington angle, he phones the White House. He usually gets what he wants.

Niles still operates Ford's, spends every week-end, from Thursday to Monday, in Boston. Niles' hatchet man is Donald Dawson, of Missouri, formerly with the RFC, now White House Liaison Officer in charge of personnel. He is the last word on all federal nominations and appointments, but his word is Niles'.

A couple of weeks before this went to press we saw Dawson lunching at the Statler with General Vaughan and Johnny Maragon.

If the impression was conveyed that after Maragon's conviction and denial on appeal that the pet five-percenter was out of action, you were so wrong. Up to this writing, Maragon has never served a day in jail, and he probably never will. News about Maragon is a scarce commodity in Washington, and bum steers are handed newspapermen. It was publicly reported that Maragon was ill and in the hospital of a Federal prison. The White House intimate had not spent one minute in jail. Maragon, the crooked fixer, is still in business and still has entree to the White House. The wise guys know that if he is ever punished, it will be perfunctory, because Maragon took the rap for a lot of way-ups and what he could tell would rock America. He is still being taken care of so he will never need to shine shoes again. If he isn't pardoned by the time this comes out, it's in the works.

From time to time, socialites and even foreign noblemen who need the jack lobby for it. A successful contact man is Baron Constantine von Stackelburg, who is with the World Bank. He and his beautiful wife host lavish at-homes for the benefit of such interests as the Florida citrus fruit industry.

Clients of lobbyists are divided into four groups. You may disregard the inspired baloney that they all represent the capitalists. Only a small fraction do.

The others who employ lobbyists are (1) Labor unions, farm federations and left-wing pressure groups; (2) nonprofit and nonpolitical organizations such as the Red Cross, American Legion, Elks, Knights of Columbus, etc., and (3) government bureaus.

The most powerful lobby in history was for the Anti-Saloon League.

By far the mightiest since then, at least until Senator Taft's overwhelming victory, were lobbies of the labor unions. By tradition and shaded reporting the representatives of the money barons are villains; but the labor boys are more vicious and intolerable. And they don't spend or entertain, which is even more heinous. The money charged against the unions for legislative purposes goes mostly to supply dames and hootch for visiting union chiefs.

The American Federation of Labor crowd hangs out at the Hamilton Hotel, where all the choice ringside tables in the supper club are reserved nightly for them. A stable of fillies is available to send up to the rooms of the dignitaries who dilute their champagne with the tears they spill for the sans-culottes.

The United Mine Workers frequent the Carlton.

The CIO also played at the Carlton until a Negro delegate was barred. Most of the boys quit in a huff, and moved across 16th St. to the equally tony Hay-Adams, where Negroes are also barred.

Many labor unions are represented by female lobbyists, and some of these will turn a trick in the hay if that helps the sacred cause. The labor broads still don't run as homely as some of the Congressmen's wives. For unions and other such pressure cookers do not usually offer money, call-girls or liquor. They threaten to withhold votes back at home.

As soon as a freshman Congressman checks in, the union harpies make a grab for him. One whom we know, a Republican elected to fill an unexpired seat in a Democratic district, received a visit from a couple of union goons the first day he moved into his office. They gave him orders how to vote on a pending measure. Congressman John Saylor, who is six feet four, grabbed them by the necks and walked them to the wall, where he showed them his certificate of election.

"I thought I read my name here, not yours," he said. Then he threw them out.

One of the most indefatigable female lobbyists is the daughter of former Senator Burt Wheeler. Though her father cleans up representing robber barons, her client is the left-wing United Electrical Workers Union. Congressmen report she's a pest who coaxes with a smile, and if that doesn't work, she threatens.

Old-timers in Congress will tell you about the dame lobbyist who represented some milk producers. She was a handsome woman, so voluptuously built that they referred to her as "Elsie the Cow." Her lobbying career ended in 1937, when she was caught in a hotel room with a Congressman.

For all practical purposes, lobbyists representing unions and minority groups do not often buttonhole Congressmen directly. Dave Niles handles all labor and left-wing angles, and arranges for the votes and rewards or punishments.

Anna Rosenberg, friend of Niles, former New Dealer, practiced industrial relations successfully until her appointment as Assistant Secretary of Defense.

Lobbyists for government bureaus often double as unpaid fixers for pressure groups, using government funds. Entertainments of Congressmen by State Department officials at cocktail parties are referred to as "smokers."

Sometimes pressure group lobbyists receive government favors and privileges denied the less favored. An intensive lobby was conducted against the Mundt-Ferguson anti-Communist bill by a former senatorial employe who was not registered as a lobbyist.

He is Palmer Webber, who was staff director in 1943 for Sen. Pepper (D) of Florida, and chief economic adviser in 1944 to Sen. Kilgore (D) of West Virginia. Webber bore down on his Senate contacts from a rent-free office in the Library of Congress. How he got it free nobody knows.

For two years Webber held a job as "legislative correspondent" on Capitol Hill for the Federation for World Government. Records in the office of the secretary of the Senate show Webber was not registered as a lobbyist for the federation and the organization is not registered to conduct a lobby. In addition to his arduous efforts to defeat the anti-Communist measure and his work for the federation, Webber was a demon, worked for votes for passage of the fair employment practices bill.

Webber was transferred by the World Government Federation from Washington to New York "to do research." The shift was for "political reasons."

He is an errand boy for the Lawyers Guild, which the House un-American Activities Committee cited as a "front" organization. It has also been active in another "cause" sponsored by Webber—the drive for an investigation of the F.B.I.

In 1947, Webber, a Ph.D., conducted a class in political philosophy at the King Smith school, where the democratic form of government was smeared to GI and other students.

A reporter attended Webber's class on May 27, 1947, when Senator Pepper was a guest. A woman student referred to J. Edgar Hoover as the American Gestapo head and declared the Catholic church was leading a crusade for war.

A woman in the audience, a secretary to a Republican Senator from the Midwest, jumped up and shouted, "Thank God for the F.B.I."

Webber was arrested in Charlottesville, Va., for distributing Communist Party literature. Police records show he paid a forfeit rather than fight the case.

He was at one time a research director for the CIO Political Action Committee in Washington and in 1948 was a paid director in charge of activities of the leftist Progressive party in 11 southern states.

Another who lobbies against anti-Communist bills, and is openly so registered, is former Democratic Congressman Jerry J. O'Connell, of Montana.

Utilizing his privileges of the floor, as an ex-Representative, O'Connell strides into the House and Senate while they are in session, and delivers advice, orders and inspiration to left-wing Congressmen, and threats to others.

When the Senate was debating the Communist control bill in an all night session last September, O'Connell took up a station at the Senate door with a reporter from the Daily Worker, and without any pretense of disguise, dictated the unsuccessful opposition's floor strategy.

But listen to the hue and cry when a manufacturer's lobbyist buys a Coca Cola for a Congressman.

Being a government lobbyist can produce desirable advantages, especially for a Marshall Plan press agent.

A survey reveals that the Economic Cooperation Administration information office has been giving several of its employes free visits to Europe and the Middle East. Robert Mullen, director of ECA information, toured Europe. He mapped a $7,500 'round-the-world trip, but postponed a visit to the Orient when the bullets began to fly.

Mullen sent an heiress to the J. P. Morgan banking fortune to London for a convention of clubwomen—to get new propaganda material on the Marshall plan to influence American clubwomen. He sent an inexperienced youth, hired as a "picture expert," to Paris and London, to see the sights and get new pictures for propaganda purposes here.

Though ECA has 73 American press employes in Paris alone, and 56 in 16 other Marshall Plan missions in Europe, plus 222 Europeans on these staffs, ECA sent a former woman reporter to Paris to get "human interest" stories for a clubwoman propaganda pamphlet.

The ECA press information office in Paris has a chief who gets about $20,000 a year in salary and expense money, has highly paid former reporters on his staff, but the ECA here sent a man from Washington to show a group of editors about Europe. Several others went to Europe on similar assignments.

Mullen has 48 on his Washington staff, drawing a total of $280,000 a year. Among these are the Morgan heiress, an ex-bullfighter, the daughter of a symphony conductor and a score of graduates from defunct war agencies. He separated a noted Negro Air Force pilot, who achieved some success as an author, from his Washington staff and dispatched him to Formosa at $15,000 a year to direct Marshall plan press information there.

The American press agents for ECA will draw $673,000 in salaries this year.

Congress gets around sporadically to investigating the lobbying "evil." The latest "crusade" was conducted by leftish Congressman Frank Buchanan, who muddled the issue so much, no one knows what happened, except that the National Association of Manufacturers emerged the villain. Congressmen don't hanker to expose lobbies, even if they're on the other side. When the investigation was first voted by the House,

Buchanan wanted to give the appropriation back, an unprecedented departure where committee chairmen always yell for
more. Buchanan tried to handcuff the lawyers engaged to conduct the investigation, though both were good Democrats and
good Fair Dealers. But they were also honest. Lou Little, of
Pittsburgh, a co-counsel, quit broken-hearted. Counsel Bene-
dict Fitzgerald, of Greenfield, Mass., a whiz of a prober, was not
even allowed to write the report. Buchanan refused to swear in
some witnesses; if they lied it would not constitute perjury.
When counsel called attention to that, he angrily shut them up.

The real brains of the investigation into lobbying was
Lucien Hilmer, committee staff director. He is regarded as a
left-wing lawyer. When George Shaw Wheeler was fired from
the government for consorting with Communists, Hilmer appeared as his lawyer and beat the case. Two years later, as an
economist with the U. S. Army in Czechoslovakia, Wheeler
vindicated the Civil Service Commission when he moved in on
Berlin Red headquarters. He announced he was a Communist
and always had been one. Hilmer shares a law office with John
F. Davis, who represented Alger Hiss before the House Un-
American Activities Committee. Hilmer had worked under
Max Lowenthal on the old Wheeler Committee.

And did we remember to tell you that the Kansas City
Chamber of Commerce has an office on 16th St., across the
road from the Russian Embassy? Both pressure groups have
displayed amazing influence in Washington

INSIDE STUFF: The law requiring lobbyists to register is
used as a racket by some. They advertise in trade papers: "Lobbyist, registered with the Congress of the United States," then
sell prospective chumps the idea they are "licensed" to lobby.
Anybody may file his name and set up his own "cause."

24. RACKETS BY REMOTE
CONTROL

*O*UR NEWSPAPER confreres, in the main, were willing to
be hospitable and helpful when we galloped in and made no
secret of our aims. We don't expect them to write our books.
But they often give us tips, which saves work.

The first question we asked was, "Who is the Washington Mafia boss?"

The invariable answer was that the local underworld was unaffiliated with the national setup, free and independent, self-contained.

All our experience made us reject that picture. We had traced and charted organized crime through the gang wars of Prohibition to this day. We had charged and it was being substantiated that no city of importance was left out of the clutches of the Mafia, with its brains in New York and its powerhouse in Chicago. It was inconceivable that a rich, large center on the Atlantic seaboard, almost a suburb of Manhattan, could be bypassed. So we found out for ourselves. This is the situation in Washington:

The National Syndicate, for reasons of prudence, has avoided first-hand operations in the District. You find few important Sicilian names in the police files. Vice, crime, gambling, narcotics and, to a smaller extent, contraband liquor, are farmed out by franchise to a cohesive local mob which deals with and pays tribute to national headquarters.

Despite tremendous influence, legal advice and guidance and the constitutional immunity against self-incrimination, the Mafia has an almost superstitious fear of Congressional committees. A city administration can be bought or scared or rigged. But nobody can capture 96 Senators and 435 Representatives. And any one of these is one of the immediate bosses of Washington; and any one of these can arise any day and demand a probe of anything. On the rare occasions when important racketeers were dragged to Washington on subpena, with all the assurances they got from many members beholden to them and the shocking obeisance paid them openly, they wet their pants in the witness chair.

Yet, these greedy gluttons can't find it in their miserly souls to declare it an open town, any more than they can force themselves to pay honest income taxes, though they awaken in their silk pajamas screaming, from nightmare dreams about Al Capone and Alcatraz.

District of Columbia is and was dominated by Emmitt Warring, Gary Quinn, Sam Beard, the Sussman brothers and Attilio Acalotti. The chief operation of these men is gambling, which will be traced in more detail later. They staked out locations in

Washington, worked together in harmony, well aware that the capital would not go for Chicago-style assassinations.

But the national Syndicate did not hesitate to work openly in the adjoining Maryland suburbs, where the late Jimmy La Fontaine, who died in bed at the age of 81 in 1949, was the local front man. Fontaine's rococo gambling casino, across the street from the District line, was as far as the Mafia cared to go openly. His chief lieutenants were Snags Lewis, Pete Gianaris and Mike Meyers. Snags has pleaded guilty to a mild rap on a bargain which will take the heat off others.

We have described the dope setup in the District, where local wholesalers send to New York for supplies, so that the Mafia does not have to deliver them in the capital. By a similar procedure, the gamblers and other racketeers procure their wire service from representatives of the big mob, across the border in Maryland. Snags Lewis was the local wire service man.

When it came to such things as numbers, whoring, illicit liquor and after-hour spots in the District, the local boys tried to hold on to as much as they could. They didn't want to divvy up with the Syndicate. The big mob didn't like that.

When the Mafia moves in, it gears its method to local situations. For instance, Dallas, one of the last hold-outs, is being taken over at this writing by strong-arm work and gunplay.

But when the beach-front bookmaking syndicate in Miami held out, it was cut off from its wire service, then local cops did the gangsters' work by raiding the recalcitrants, to make way for the Syndicate's own operators.

It was clear to Frank Costello in New York and Charlie Fischetti in Chicago, the operating heads of the underworld, that gat-work would not be tolerated in Washington. They knew the Metropolitan Police couldn't be counted on to co-operate, with J. Edgar Hoover on the grounds. Few understand why the F.B.I. has not acted against the Mafia. Its jurisdiction is circumscribed by Congress, and the black-handers have been smart enough to keep out of fields in which Hoover may act.

The outside mobsters adopted a third procedure to tighten their hold on the local underworld, one that had worked with great success in other towns. It came through with flying colors in Washington. Last year there was an epidemic of robberies of local underworld figures, and not by accident or coincidence.

One victim was Emmitt Warring. Three men forced their way into his home, at 3900 Macomb Street, and robbed it at gun-point. Insiders say the amount of cash lifted from Warring's safe was about $100,000. Warring told newspapermen it was only $20,000. He refused to cooperate with the police and would not admit or deny that the holdup had taken place. In the same week, the same thugs held up Johnny Williams, a numbers racket boss. Robert "Ryebread" Schulman and Theodore "Little Joe" Scheve also were held up. Williams' father-in-law is Dick Austin, a numbers king in Atlantic City and Washington.

Chief of Police Barrett said, "I am alarmed by the crimes. We can't have this sort of thing going on here. Pretty soon somebody's going to get shot." That was Scheve. But nobody got arrested. Then Washington racketeers saw a great light. They made peace with the Big Mob, which established its regency over the District, leaving the former operators in as partners with nominal control.

George P. Harding, victim of the recent slaying in the Hideaway Club, engineered the Warring robbery for the Mafia. Harding was born in Italy and had a long and bloody career as a gunman and killer, before being slain by his friend and associate, Joseph Nesline.

Nesline, who admitted the shooting, is a four-time loser. He told police it was either "Harding or me." His story was Harding had accused him of running out with his share of the gravy in a gangster-operated oil well deal in Texas, where Frank Costello and his boys are buying heavily into leases and royalties. The dead man had been sitting with George A. Clainos, white-slaver and member of the local Syndicate, who passed him a gun.

The actual cause of the killing, which we are telling you confidential, is that it was ordered from Mafia headquarters in Brooklyn, because Harding, who knew too much, was an intemperate drinker and was talking too much.

Harding had been warned "to be good or else" several months ago, through word transmitted by Tony Ricci, alias Tony Goebels, who is the message-center for the Unione Siciliano.

The formula of permitting local operators to retain management was followed last year when the mob moved into Tampa and Jacksonville, Florida, and was used also with much success in Newark, New Jersey, where the non-Italian mob of Abner "Longy" Zwillman was absorbed into the Mafia. The Cleveland branch, run chiefly by Jews and Irish, was given the same modus operandi and absorbed.

The chain of command and remittance from the District to top headquarters is through Prince Georges County, Maryland, where Gianaris handles the numbers intake from the District and Lewis superintends payments for horse wire service—which is utilized also as a clearing house to transmit receipts from all other illegal activities, entered on the books as payments for the services or as losses on bets.

La Fontaine's organization is kept together by Lewis and Meyers. Charlie Ford, Washington lawyer, who appears frequently in this book as counsel for gamblers, vice-hucksters and bottle-clubs, is the trustee of La Fontaine's fabulous estate. In this connection some complicated bookkeeping is required.

It develops La Fontaine was only a front man. Eighty percent of his holdings belonged to the Big Mob. His death brought intricate mixups, and what was his and what was the Mob's had not been identified in full detail. The situation is similar to that which followed the slaying of Edward J. O'Hare, Chicago mobster, who operated race tracks for the Capone syndicate. The stock of Sportsman's Park, Chicago, and the Miami Beach Kennel Club was in his name. He left it to his heirs and associates. It took years for the accounts to be straightened out, and when they were, some money was paid over in the form of a "loan" to Paul "The Waiter" Ricca, a close associate of the late Capone, who is one of the ruling heads of the secret Grand Council of the Mafia.

The La Fontaine payoff to the top was made through Nig Rosen of Philadelphia to Meyer Lansky of New York. Lansky is a tributary of Frank Costello and a gambling partner of Joe Adonis. Nig Rosen is a friend of Washington Police Chief Barrett.

La Fontaine was one of the most colorful men Washington ever saw. His legendary career as a gentleman gambler spanned half a century. This last of the gas-lit era gamblers was one of five children of a poultry dealer. He was apprenticed to his father's trade and might have carved for himself a similar career, except for a fatal flaw in his make-up: he could not bear to kill a chicken, nor could he stand the thought of others killing chickens he had raised. He hid his favorites in his father's attic.

A three-cent strike Jimmy made on the old St. Louis lottery

netted him $12. With this he set up shop across the Potomac in Virginia. He then went to work for the Heath brothers, old-time gambling combine. He soon had his own card table and he prospered. Subsequently he opened the Mohican Club, near Glen Echo, Maryland. Expanding, he purchased a large tract in Prince Georges County and established "Jimmy's Place." Around it he built a high green fence and within it men won and lost fortunes. Women never got past the door and no man who couldn't afford to lose was ever admitted again. It was staffed by more than a hundred carefully chosen attendants, all covered by social security. They made regular contributions to a retirement fund.

The house limit was $200 on craps, $500 a card on blackjack, and $10 on numbers, with no-limit games in private rooms for certain customers who could stand a tough tap. "Jimmy's" catered to as many as 2,000 gamblers a night.

Oddly, La Fontaine never got out of the poultry business. His passion was cock-fighting and he maintained a stable of 100 birds. Seeing them killed in action did not affront him. He also made horse book and traveled from track to track. La Fontaine bankrolled Tex Rickard, the fabulous fight promoter, in his early days. After Rickard's death he formed a silent partnership with Herman Taylor, Philadelphia fight promoter.

Jimmy served a jail term for income tax evasion and paid a fine of more than $200,000. The Big Mob had long cast covetous eyes on La Fontaine, who by now not only had his own profitable gambling enterprise on which he himself admitted paying off $100,000 a year for local protection, but he controlled also the entire underworld in the lush Maryland counties adjoining the District. About 20 years ago, emissaries from Philadelphia came down to muscle him out. One representative of Nig Rosen, a gunman named Milsie Henry, was mysteriously murdered, for which La Fontaine was loudly but not officially mentioned. The case is still unsolved. Shortly thereafter, La Fontaine was kidnaped by hoodlums from New York and Philadelphia. Before he was returned his family had to come up with $40,000 "expense money." And the Mafia was declared in on his enterprises.

Most naïve Washingtonians believe the appointment of attorney Charlie Ford as the trustee of his estate was a logical sequence, as Ford is a gamblers' lawyer. He testified before a house committee that he represented many gamblers, some of whom were such powers that they were unknown to the police or public as gamblers. He refused to divulge their identities. One is a liquor dealer and another, a local jeweler.

Ford has legal contacts with the topmost figures of the Mafia. When the wife of Charlie Fischetti, one of the most powerful men in the national underworld, the most powerful in Chicago, was subpoenaed before the Kefauver Committee, Ford flew to Chicago to represent her, though the Fischetti-Guzik gang has staffs of legal sharks who specialize in outwitting the authorities.

Quite often there is legal jockeying following the death of important gangsters like La Fontaine.

After Bugsy Siegel was slain in Beverly Hills, Morris Rosen showed up from New York at Siegel's ornate Flamingo and took over all of the murdered man's assets before his body was cold. They had never belonged to him at all. They were Syndicate property. So was 80 per cent of La Fontaine's.

25. WHO'S WHO IN MOBOCRACY

*F*OR TWO BOOKS and for the hundreds of newspaper stories we have done on American gangsters and their maze of intertwining organization we got enough to be publicly proclaimed America's top experts in the field.

We have been offered lectures and speaking engagements before bodies of bankers, merchants, criminologists, police conventions and on radio programs. But we have saved some new names and some newly-discovered secrets for this book, because a "confidential" without that factor would be regarded as a gold brick; and because our publisher knows us and trusts us and hasn't the rabbit in him that the owners of other media display, when they say:

"But you just can't publish that kind of stuff. You'll get us all killed!"

One magazine which paid for the rights to do a digest of *Chicago Confidential* weakened and, instead, did a piece speculating on our chances of surviving our tenure on the bestseller lists!

We have our own ways of getting this material, which so many think is so dangerous. It comes from many sources, all confidential. Some of it is right from the racketeers, themselves, for they have vendettas and jealousies and hatreds on which they don't dare to act in the open. The widow of a murdered hoodlum drove hundreds of miles and met us in a car in Central Park and gave us the tale of who rubbed him out and why. This was a woman who had told the cops and the prosecutors that she knew nothing, had no idea how her husband made a living, had never met any one who was even "shady."

Here and there a person who has been shaken down or shaken out, and thus knows a small angle which may be valuable as a tip-off on one or two people and authentic tactics gets to us and spills.

We don't believe all we hear. But facts mesh up and patterns form and truths evolve.

We have sketched for you the process whereby the pennies, dimes and dollars of the numbers-players, horse-bettors, hookers and junkies are harvested in Washington and funneled to the satraps who live in penthouses and mansions in New York, Chicago, Beverly Hills and Rome. They are big industry, our biggest. And while the principals hide in their drawing-rooms even if they pass through Washington, to or from Florida, they must maintain here high-powered lawyers, tax experts who study and report every decision of the Treasury, lobbyists, press agents and spies. Many of the vast legal businesses into which they channel their cash have branch stores and offices here. The Syndicate is an international conspiracy, as potent as that other international conspiracy, Communism, and as dirty and dangerous, with its great wealth and the same policy —to conquer everything and take over everything, with no scruples as to how.

This gigantic money trust has assets of billions, exceeding the combined wealth of Morgan, Rockefeller and all the Wall Street freebooters of old.

It owns, through legitimate sources of trade, incalculable commercial, residential, hotel and investment real estate, surpassing the holdings of insurance companies. Through its purchase of stocks and bonds it controls some and is attempting to control other transportation companies, as well as railroads, hotel chains, distilleries and breweries, department stores and chain stores, clothing and dress manufacturers, steel and iron works, franchised automobile distributors, trans-Atlantic steamship lines, a movie producer, a radio chain, a big-league ball team, phonograph recording companies, insurance corporations, banks, theatres, night clubs, laundries, oil wells; it has been buying into even newspapers. This is only a condensed catalog of its dishonest interests in once-honest enterprises.

A thief is always a thief. These modern pirates could not go straight. As soon as they dip their sticky hands into something legitimate, it goes crooked.

One of their favorite tactics is to buy in the open market enough stock of a company, to create a nuisance value. They organize a minority stockholders' committee and dig up proxies. They have no real intention of trying to get control, but some time before the stockholders' meeting, they approach the management and offer to sell at a premium, usually three or four times above the market listing. This is cold blackmail.

Another tactic, employed when they secure control of a transportation company, is to use their political connections to get a fare raise. That enhances the stock on the market, then they unload.

They buy into some companies to get enough stock to rig the price, a felony. In at least one instance with which we are familiar, the underworld put a representative in as an officer of a transportation company. He then sold company stock short on the securities exchanges. This is a violation of SEC law. When a complaint was made by other stockholders to the SEC, the man they talked to shrugged his shoulders and said, "Forget it. They have a fix."

Operators with such tremendous financial interests know their way around Washington. One of their chief sources of contact is through Democratic county, state and national committeemen, who are beholden for campaign contributions. Sometimes cash is handed over to sweeten the kitty. The committeemen and political bosses pass the orders along through their Congressmen in Washington, or, when the fix is important enough, directly to a specialist at such affairs right in the White House.

The Tammany and Flynn interests in New York and Jake Arvey's tight Chicago combine are powers. The Rhode Island organization of Senator Pastore and Attorney General McGrath, the crooked Connecticut machine that made Senator

Brien McMahon, and the Maryland organization, about which more later, get whatever they want. Senator Herbert O'Conor is the godfather of the Maryland outfit, and he is a member of the Kefauver Committee.

The Colorado machine handles the loot for the Mountain States. The errand-boy for the West Coast gamblers, dope runners and procurers is the California Democratic organization, of which at this writing, Jimmy Roosevelt is the National Committeeman, but the mobsters don't stick long with losers.

In *Chicago Confidential* we gave an outline of the organization and chain of command of the international underworld Syndicate.

The Mafia, an age-old institution, has existed in Sicily since before the beginning of written history. Sicily always has been, and to this day is, subject territory. It was owned by ancient Phoenicians, Greeks, Carthaginians, Romans, Imperial France, Italy and even Britain. The Sicilian peasants always worked for absentee owners.

In prehistoric times, the Mafia began as a patriotic terrorist society, somewhat like the Irish Republican Army. Venal leaders sold out, offered protection to some estates while they sacked others. They anticipated the protection racket by centuries.

The Mafia and the dread Black Hand are the same thing. The black hand was the sign over which the Mafia's threats were delivered. During several thousand years it came about that almost every native of Sicily had to have some tie or connection with the Mafia. Some were members, others were relatives of members, or partners, hired killers and spies. Others did business with it; still others were the terrorized unattached who dared not refuse its bidding.

Sicilians vie with Cantonese as the most migrating people in the world. Sicily, like Canton, is overpopulated and poverty-ridden. Another, more important factor, appears to be that at every change of government, Mafistas were forced into flight and exile in droves. They settled and colonized all over the earth. There are huge Sicilian colonies spread around Europe, in England, South America, North Africa, the Orient and the United States.

Every Sicilian colony had a hard core of black-handers, who set up an invisible government and preyed first on the other colonizers. The various groups were in correspondence with each other, cooperated in business deals, provided places for other fugitives and expatriates.

The first great influx arrived in this country exactly a hundred years ago, about the time Napoleon 3rd extended his influence to Sicily. Thereafter, every ten or twenty years found other large groups on their way here, especially after such periods of uncertainty as the unification of Italy, World War I, the Mussolini ascendancy, and after World War II. From time to time the Italian government tried to wipe out the Mafia, and after each attempt thousands more came to wink and leer at the Statue of Liberty.

Though the Italian government never could exterminate the Mafia, it did wipe out similar terroristic societies on the mainland, such as the Camorra, of Naples. The members of these other secret societies who could escape fled to Sicily, where they were welcomed and integrated as brothers by the Mafistas.

Their overseas affiliates were absorbed by local Mafia units. This process took place also among outlawed Greek secret societies, and the dread Black Hand of Serbia, which was akin in purpose to Sicily's Black Hand. Meanwhile, as Mafia bosses got fat and rich, they smuggled in new killers, many from Cuba and Puerto Rico.

The American Black Hand was content to operate exclusively in Italian circles for years. All Italians had to pay tribute, a tithe of their earnings, from the dollar-a-week of the corner bootblack to five thousand a night of Enrico Caruso. Failure to pay meant the Black Hand letter, and continued failure, death. Now the Mafia is smoother. It "owns" acts on a ten-per cent business deal. Frank Sinatra was discovered by Willie Moretti and is the pet of the Fischettis. He gave a gold cigarette case to Charlie Luciano, inscribed "To my friend."

Recent developments in New York again demonstrate how this works. A $4,000-a-year city fireman, an Italian who had changed his name, testified he was operating a $200,000 talent agency, which, in theatrical parlance, "stole" acts from other agencies. Two were "thefted" from agent Lou Perry: Alan Dale, another Italian who is the hottest crooning find of the year, and Toni Arden. The fireman, whose name is Gerry Purcell, booked these two and another, Terri Stevens, into the Copacabana, where all three "clicked" and started their climbs to fame.

In *Chicago Confidential*, we described how Big Jim Colosimo, then the local Mafia leader, set up the organization which under Al Capone and Johnny Torrio, was able to drive out of Chicago all the competing non-Italian and sectional mobs. Prohibition made them fabulously rich and potent.

The same thing happened in New York. While Colosimo was the head of the Chicago chapter, Lupo "the Wolf" Saietta headed the New York branch. After he went to prison, Joe "The Boss" Masseria took over, after a lot of mayhem.

They began to call the Mafia the Unione Siciliano then. At times it tried to pretend it was a respectable Italian-American benevolent society. Joe "The Boss" reigned at the top of the Unione for nine years, until he was murdered in 1931. His chief lieutenants were "Lucky" Luciano and Frank Costello. When Masseria was killed they moved in.

The Irish and Jewish mobs were being driven to the wall. The same thing happened in every important city. By the middle 1930s, the Unione Siciliano was dominant in every racket. Wherever there were non-Italians left, the only way they could do business was to accept the overlordship of the Mafia. If they were good boys they were allowed to come in and get rich. If they tried any monkey-business, they were assassinated, like Bugsy Siegel, or turned over to the law, like Lepke and Gurrah.

No one knows whether the top Italian hoodlums like Capone, Luciano and Costello took over the Mafia, or whether the Mafia took them over. That is an academic conjecture, as they are now one and the same thing, with the worldwide facilities of the Unione Siciliano the nucleus on which all organized vice, crime and corruption, not only in the United States but all over the world, has been built.

In *Chicago Confidential*, we stated in passing that since the exile of Luciano in Italy the American "president" or executive head of the Unione Siciliano is Frank Costello, and the vice-president is Capone's cousin, Charles Fischetti, in Chicago.

The worldwide Mafia is composed of a supreme head in Palermo, Sicily, a Grand Council consisting of high-ranking executives, subordinate officers, and a global membership.

Luciano, following his deportation in 1947, has been installed as the Supreme Head of the International Mafia. Members are divided into two distinct groups, inner circle and outer circle. The latter includes members of ordinary rank and standards. The former consists of those who command wealth, influence or proven underworld power. Membership in this group is kept at a minimum, since it derives a major portion of all proceeds from its general diverse illegal enterprises.

Members of the elite few are almost invariably, through ancestry or direct birth, from Palermo and its adjoining areas. A very few non-Italians have been taken into the ruling circle. According to the U.S. Bureau of Narcotics, American members of the Mafia are necessarily members of the over-all group, which therefore has continued to include former American gangsters who left the U.S. by deportation or voluntary flight. Prominently mentioned among these are John Schillochi (International List 298); Dominic Petrelli (International List 259); and Nicola Gentile (International List 133), all of whom were in Italy when last heard of, though informants tell us they have since been seen around New York again.

Other important members of the Mafia, such as Francisco Paolo Coppola and Sylvestro Carrolla, found their way to Mexico, where they took over the local Mafia. Other lesser figures represent the fearsome fraternity in Canada, Argentina, Brazil, France, and England.

The Bureau of Narcotics has compiled what is believed to be the only master list of the inner circle of the Mafia. It is based on documentary evidence in the form of address books, papers, interstate telephone calls, police records, screened informants, etc. During the recent Kefauver Committee hearings, Commissioner Anslinger supplied the document under oath to the committee. Extracts from this list are printed in the back of the book.

Even before the Mafia had organized the entire American underworld, it had strong communication lines into Washington. These were first built up during Prohibition, when the boys passed money back to the capital for their own protection. They also made liberal contributions to the campaign funds of dry Congressmen, without whose votes, for whatever cause, the racket was worthless. During the insane days of Prohibition, the underworld began the process of undermining the honesty and probity of federal officials, which has since been carried to an extreme.

Until the 18th Amendment, law-breakers feared Uncle Whiskers. There were few federal criminal laws. Most criminals didn't want to tangle with Washington. Only nuts got themselves mixed up with the postal inspectors or the Secret Service. After the wholesale bribery and corruption of the 1920s, all respect for national law enforcement had gone into the ashcan.

Now, due largely to the example of the F.B.I., the Bureau of Narcotics and the Treasury Intelligence, the public's faith in federal law-enforcement and investigative agencies has been revived, but the prosecuting and judicial ends have never come back. Most felons would rather be arrested by federal than state or city cops, because they know they can make a better deal with the prosecutors, and if everything fails, federal sentences are light and the prisons are soft.

Before the underworld was completely organized, Washington was a "neutral" city, where mob meetings and conventions were held. In such cities the delegates must not pack guns. Rough stuff is out by common consent. Other such open cities are Saratoga, Hot Springs, Las Vegas, Atlantic City and Miami. These were and are important resort centers, and are kept neutral because machine-gunning might scare tourists away. Washington was no-man's-land for obvious reasons; they knew tommy-guns wouldn't be tolerated in the Capitol's shadow.

Commissioner Anslinger recalls such a gangster convention in the Shoreham Hotel, two decades ago. The Commissioner dropped into the Blue Room for dinner and saw Luciano, "Machine Gun" Jack McGurn, Frank Nitti, "the Enforcer" of the Chicago mob, Izzie Bernstein of Detroit's Purple Gang, and three other hoods, each with a bejeweled blonde. They were registered at the Shoreham under assumed names and spent a week there holding meetings.

When Anslinger lamped the boys, he went to the lobby and had Lucky called out. Luciano was offended, beefed about the interruption of his party. He said, "You can't do anything to me. We got Constitutional rights. We're only sight-seeing."

Anslinger said, "That's all you'd better do," then glancing at the blondes, he added, "remember the Mann Act."

A few weeks later, Jack McGurn was knocked off. It developed that this meeting was called for his trial. He had been getting out of line. So he was summoned from Chicago to meet his peers from the other cities.

The organized underworld's influence in official Washington is incalculable. Its direct ties, even to the top, are so firm that in many instances even a political revolution will not dislodge them. They succeeded in doing that which the Communists failed to do; they infiltrated and took over the government. They are the true subversives, though that never comes out in Congress.

The Mafia's power is built around these factors:

1) The underworld's ownership of and contributions to local political machines. The mob has no politics or ideology. It pays liberally to both sides, so it will have a friend in court no matter who wins. Even the former American Labor Party Congressman, Vito Marcantonio, was on intimate terms with Mafia hoodlums, accepted campaign contributions from them, associated with and fronted for their racketeers in New York and in Washington, and welcomed them into his American Labor Party. He appointed the son of the infamous "Three Finger Brown" Luchese to West Point in 1946. Luchese was and is his contact in Tammany Hall.

2) The Mafia's huge cache of currency, hidden in private safe deposit vaults and in banks throughout the world. Its earnings from illicit sources are so great, and come in so fast, the boys cannot invest it fast enough. They must hide most of the money because they failed to pay income tax on the major portion of it. It is no exaggeration to say they have billions of dollars in U.S. bills. With this bankroll they can bribe at will, elect many officials, and swing public opinion to incredible degrees.

3) The Syndicate's interests in countless large legitimate businesses and industries give it a responsible, respectable voice in Washington through trade associations, lobbyists, law firms, banks, Congressmen who would do a favor for a local businessman but would not be seen dead with a gangster, and a considerable segment of the press, daily and periodical, and the radio.

4) The hoodlums' tie-up with some labor, which came about when unions needed sluggers, or when tough guys muscled in to grab union treasurers, or used them as part of their extortion rackets. Lobbyists representing the unions are feared and toadied to.

5) The Italian voting bloc now controls some of the largest cities in the country. It is the largest single unit in New York, where all three candidates for mayor in 1950 were Italians. Too many of their men in office have ties to the Mafia. They can count on the votes of their countrymen in nominations

and elections. The mass votes of Italians are bartered back and forth and usually can be delivered, by Black Hand threats in Italian neighborhoods, by appeal to blood relationship and national pride, or through the pages of powerful Italian language newspapers.

During his recent campaign, New York's Mayor Impellitteri charged that Gene Pope, publisher of Il Progresso Italiano-Americano, the biggest Italian daily in the country, was an intimate of Frank Costello. We have seen them dining together on intimate terms.

No book could comprehensively cover the mob's facets in Washington, but here are a few, at random:

The President's military aide and poker pal, Major General Harry Vaughan, has associated with Frank Costello. They were brought together through his stooge, the convict John Maragon, who was a pal of the late Bill Helis, Greek millionaire and partner in Costello's New York and Louisiana enterprises—as well as in a Scotch distillery.

Joe Adonis, New York mobster and lieutenant of Costello, had financial dealings with Harold F. Ambrose, former special assistant to the Postmaster General. Ambrose pleaded guilty to charges of operating a $600,000 fraudulent stamp-selling scheme. Adonis was questioned by the D.C. grand jury, but refused to talk, after which the United States had amnesia about his connection with the case. Ambrose is related to Democratic Senator O'Mahoney. His failure to go to trial protected his underworld associates.

Attorney General McGrath, who may be a U.S. Supreme Court Justice before this appears in print, was a Senator from Rhode Island and an important member of Rhode Island's Democratic machine. That outfit has tight ties with the underworld. Within days after McGrath was pushed upstairs to the Attorney Generalship, to make way for Bill Boyle as Democratic National Chairman, McGrath made a trip to New York City. There he or his double had dinner at the Copacabana night club with Joe Nunan, former Commissioner of Internal Revenue, and Julie Podell, manager of the cafe. It has been frequently charged in New York that Costello has an interest in the corporation. The late Mayor La Guardia ordered police to cancel the club's license if Podell, long an associate of Costello, was ever found on its premises again. Podell, while giddy, told one of your reporters that Costello had advanced $50,000 to open the club.

At the time of the dinner party there, the Copa was a possible defendant in a tax-action growing out of an investigation into the charges that it was owned by Costello. Since then, Podell was in Hot Springs with Costello and several other mobsters from all parts of the country, in an annual convention. McGrath has since stated there is no organized crime or vice in the country.

Former Attorney General Tom Clark, now a Justice of the United States Supreme Court, was closely associated with attorneys who represented underworld figures. There were no major underworld prosecutions during his term of office. A Congressional investigation elicited the startling information that Clark's boyhood pal, Maury Hughes, a Dallas attorney, was retained by five members of the old Capone mob, who had been convicted of extorting millions from the movie industry, to induce the federal authorities to nol-pros outstanding indictments against them and secure premature paroles.

Hughes, with other lawyers close to the administration, worked this feat of legal legerdemain. While these pages were being written, the same Maury Hughes secretly succeeded in keeping Alan Smiley, a notorious West Coast gangster who had been ordered deported, in the country. Smiley was Bugsy Siegel's buddy, and was seated next to him on a love-seat in Virginia Hill's Beverly Hills mansion when Siegel was ambushed and assassinated, in the only spot in the room visible to the torpedoes hidden outside, in bushes.

Until recently, Smiley had been passing himself off as an oil broker and real estate man in Houston, Texas, where he lived with his wife, a former movie starlet, in Glen McCarthy's swank Shamrock Hotel. Smiley took up with a Texas oilman, Lenoire Josey, who liked to gamble. Smiley said he liked that, too. He knew some good places.

He and Josey went to Sam Maceo's ornate casino, the Balinese Room, in Galveston. Then they went to the Mounds Club in Cleveland. After that they went to the Flamingo, in Las Vegas. A trip to Phil Kastel's (and Costello's) beautiful Beverly, outside New Orleans, followed. When Josey counted up he had lost $500,000. Smiley "admitted to being a big loser, too." If so, he got some back, because he owns a bit of stock in the Flamingo.

While these lines were being written, the California Crime Commission, headed by Admiral William H. Standley, Retired, castigated government aides for their ties with criminals. He said the relationship between the underworld elements and certain officials "must of necessity make it embarrassing for Federal officials to undertake prosecutions."

A specific example was Sam Termini, described as a godson of the late Charlie Binaggio, who would have had to earn $900,000 income last year to be able to afford the cash payments made on his mansion in San Mateo County. He paid income tax on no such sum.

It cited the case of Dorothy A. McCreedy as a specific example of tieups between criminals and government officials, stating:

"The McCreedy woman is a convicted madame, a major figure in the prostitution racket in California for years and operator of two large whore-houses in Honolulu."

She was reported to the Income Tax Bureau as a suspected evader, but "she is also a partner in a business called Safety Step Sales Co., and one of her partners is Ernest M. Schino, chief field deputy in the Office of the Collector of Internal Revenue."

They tell a spicy story about Dorothy, whom we know well—personally, not professionally. When F. D. Roosevelt made his first trip to Hawaii, the Secret Service failed to send ahead a black open touring-car of expensive make, familiar and standard for the President on open display. Honolulu was winnowed. Only one such car was found in the Territory. It was owned by Dorothy, who used to drive her gals through town, to show them off, for promotion.

Dorothy pridefully lent the car. Everyone in Honolulu recognized it on sight, but the President didn't know that. He flashed his historic grin, waved his hat, but couldn't understand why the cheers were accompanied by an obbligato of guffaws.

It was charged, and never refuted in the 1950 campaign, by both Governor Dewey and Mayor Impellitteri that Ed Flynn, New York political boss and intimate of the late President Roosevelt, is Frank Costello's contact in New York State. Flynn, who has, and retained after the debacle, the national patronage in the state, used it frequently to procure appointments in high places, including the federal district bench, the New

York State Supreme Court and some prosecutors, of men known to be friendly to associates of Costello. His defeated choice for governor of New York, former Congressman Walter J. Lynch, of the Bronx, had, while he was in Congress, introduced a "sleeper" which would have permitted the underworld kings, notorious for such frauds, to evade prison sentences for tax delinquency.

A report, in the possession of the Los Angeles Police Department, which we have seen, states that Flynn or someone who looked remarkably like him—with Frank Costello, Phil Kastel and others—was in Mexico City in December, 1948. Costello was in conferences that contemplated taking over the Mexican National Lottery. The group was partied by A. C. Blumenthal, expatriate New York showman.

Lynch, like his boss Ed Flynn, was a never-deviating New Deal-Fair Deal Democrat. He never voted against an administration measure. In the last Congress there was a mighty affinity between New Dealers and crooked dealers. For instance, former Senator Lucas, of Illinois, the majority leader, was beholden to the Nash-Kelly-Arvey machine. Appointments of shady figures to federal positions in Illinois cleared through him, the senior Senator, as all must.

Left-wing Democratic Senator Hubert Humphrey, of Minnesota, is a pal of ex-convict Charles Ward, millionaire calendar printer. Ward has many ties with the underworld all over the country, and was one of the financial backers of Anna Roosevelt's attempt to start a daily newspaper in Phoenix, Arizona. This was once he was outsmarted in a money deal. As is not unknown in the Roosevelt tradition, he got one cent on the dollar back. Bill O'Dwyer said he found a direct tie between Ward and Brooklyn's Murder, Inc.

Under such auspices, the underworld is establishing a firm grip on Minnesota. Its attempt to take over the Minneapolis and St. Paul traction systems is a part of the general picture across the land and was exposed by Lait last summer in his *Daily Mirror* column. It resulted in the indictment of one of the mobsters, Kid Cann, so called because of his many incarcerations.

The New Dealers have been kind to the underworld ever since their victorious election in 1932, after Costello and Jimmy Hines, with Ed Kelly, had successfully managed the convention fight in Chicago. While Frank Murphy was Attorney-General he saw to it that prosecuting attorneys laid off the boys. Internal Revenue agents prepared a tax case against Costello and Frank Erickson, but the U.S. Attorney was ordered to pigeonhole it.

Following Frank Erickson's conviction in New York on gambling charges, District Attorney's investigators seized his books and papers. Among them was a memo reading, "Phone Daddy Long Legs."

The sleuths jumped on this. They figured it was a code or nickname for one of the mob aces. That is one of the toughest problems encountered by racket-busters, i.e., breaking down the aliases used by the kings of the underworld on their books and in their records.

The gumshoes rushed over to the Island and interviewed Erickson in his cell.

"Who is Daddy Long Legs?" they asked. "And what did you want to call him for?"

Erickson laughed uproariously. "Why shouldn't I phone him?" he inquired. "After all, I'm related to him by marriage and he's the Vice President."

After the investigators had recovered from their shocks, this is what Erickson told them:

"An in-law of mine is an in-law of Barkley's. Barkley visited me in my Long Island home. My grand-kids are crazy about him. They nicknamed him 'Daddy Long Legs.'"

The story of the Binaggio killing in Kansas City, anticipated in *Chicago Confidential*, is recent, but the full background of the case has never been aired before.

President Truman is and was a loyal member of his county Democratic organization. And as such—a party man who never split his ticket—he was forced to go along, though unwillingly, when the Chicago hoodlums put Binaggio in as the leader.

When the President first went into politics, the Mafia was just one of the mobs. It had not organized the country. In the 1920s, most of the big city machines were owned by Irish bosses, who were tied up with the local Irish underworld gangs. Each city was independent of all other cities.

On the surface, the conviction of Tom Pendergast by U.S. Attorney Maurice Milligan was a smashing victory for law and order. But it was, at the same time, a greater victory for the Capone and Costello mob. There are high government cops— not friends of the administration, either—who have the wild idea that the only effect of Pendergast's conviction was to permit Charley Fischetti's ambassador to Kansas City, Tony Gizzo, to put in his own man, Binaggio, as county leader. Milligan's brother Tuck was counsel for Joe de Luca, a Mafia boss and convicted dope smuggler, during and after his brother's term as United States attorney. Milligan prosecuted few Sicilian hoodlums. T-men demanded 20 years for De Luca. Milligan's office asked for only 3 for his brother's client; he was sprung shortly thereafter and the stool pigeon who convicted him was murdered. We looked up the official record and that is so.

As new Democratic leader of the President's home county, Binaggio had great influence. Naturally, the President wanted to carry his own state in local and federal elections, so he had to work through his home organization. The presence in it of people like Binaggio and Gizzo may have turned his stomach, but that was politics.

We have explained that the Big Mob does not operate directly in Washington on the street and sewer levels, such enterprises being franchised out to locals. The Syndicate does do business in the District in connection with its legitimate affairs and some of its larger sub-rosa undertakings. In the latter category are black-marketing, the sale and resale of government surplus, padding of war contracts, etc. The boys had an office in the Thomas Circle Building during World War II, in which they dished out war contracts. One day a man was killed there, but so great was their influence that no record was made on the police blotter. The newspapers still know nothing about it.

A couple of hotels in Washington are owned by interests known to be backed by underworld coin. Many chain stores owned by mob money have branches there. Money of "Lepke" Buchalter, executed head of Murder, Inc., is in Jarwood's men's clothing store, across the street from the Department of Justice. The history of this chain makes a human interest story.

When Lepke surrendered, to be turned over to J. Edgar Hoover, he understood the boys put in a "fix" so he would be tried on federal charges and not turned over to Brooklyn's crusading District Attorney, Bill O'Dwyer, on the Murder, Inc., rap, which meant the chair in Sing Sing.

But Hoover would have nothing to do with such a deal, and gave him up to New York State. Lepke was convicted of first-degree murder. He knew he had been railroaded by the

Mafia, which had wanted to get rid of its Jewish partner. He threatened to blow the whistle, and was promised leniency if he would talk. His wife, an attractive brunette, went to see him in his cell and told him her life had been threatened, she would be croaked if he spilled. That was not so. Lepke loved her, so he went to the hot seat with his lips sealed to protect her.

Most of his illegal profits had been stashed away in secret safe deposit vaults. He told her where they were. While Lepke was in the death-chamber, his wife was often seen with Arthur Jawitz, a slick-looking young guy, who had attracted the attention of the Feds when they were looking for Lepke, whose bed he was keeping warm.

Shortly after Lepke's electrocution, his widow married the black-haired young man, and set him up in the men's clothing business. They changed their name to Jarwood. The underworld says Lepke left her $20,000,000 in U.S. currency. A former wife of Jawitz showed up, charged he had married Betty Buchalter bigamously. She said Betty was "keeping" Jawitz while her gangster husband was still alive.

After the Kefauver Committee quizzed Lou Wolfson, head of the Capital Transit Company, which owns the street-cars and buses in Washington, seeking gangster-ties, it went no further. There was no evidence. Wolfson, who lives in Jacksonville, Florida, says he is a legitimate businessman. We have no knowledge to the contrary. But it was developed under oath at a Senatorial hearing that Wolfson and one William B. Johnston had, between them, raised a fund of half-a-million dollars for the campaign of Florida's governor, Fuller Warren. Wolfson and Johnston each put $154,000 into this private, special campaign kitty, and were intimately associated during the campaign. Johnston is president of Sportsman's Park racetrack in Chicago, and several dog-tracks in Florida, which were owned by the late Al Capone. Johnston makes frequent payments to Capone associates as "loans." He admitted he had been associated with mob-owned enterprises.

Another witness, Leo J. Carroll, testified that it was general knowledge in 1948, that with the election of Governor Warren, one-third of whose campaign Wolfson financed, "the Mob would take over Florida." It did.

A few months after Wolfson secured control of the Washington transit system, he was permitted to raise the fare to 15 cents a ride, on the plea of extreme poverty. Right after that, the company doubled its quarterly dividends from 50 cents to $1 a share. Company stock scored a sensational advance, reaching $39. When Wolfson landed control he bought 109,000 shares at $20.

Wolfson's campaign to buy the local transit system was authorized by the ICC and the Securities Exchange after an adverse recommendation of the examiner and over opposition of minority stockholders. In less than ten months, the Wolfson group succeeded in dominating the board of directors and placing its own men in strategic executive spots, one of whom is Frank E. Weakly, president of the Wardman Park Hotel.

Now the SEC has granted Wolfson permission to sell some of his stock at the inflated price, which gives him the company and his money back. At this writing, he is negotiating to buy the Washington Redskins from George Marshall.

You can feel the presence of the mob in Washington. You can see evidence in many directions that it is there. John L. Laskey, immediate past president of the District Bar Association, resigned the chairmanship of its law enforcement committee because he had represented three witnesses called before the Senate Crime Investigating Committee in connection with Florida gambling. He was a former U.S. attorney.

When Frank Costello testified briefly last year before the Senate Interstate Commerce Committee investigating the transportation of slot-machines across state lines, the photo of a Senate attache calling a cab for him while Capitol policemen pushed nosy spectators away, was widely published. But what hasn't been printed is that a table was reserved for him in advance in the Senators' private dining-room in the Capitol, and while the great Costello dined with his staff of lawyers, a couple of U.S. Senators humbly waited for seats. The Senate dining-room is operated on a concession basis by the son-in-law of a Chicago vending-machine manufacturer.

It could be some of the Senators are on Costello's payroll. The law firms of at least 40 Senators and Congressmen regularly represent the wire service and local gamblers in their home towns.

Now let's gander the Kefauver Committee.

26. TERROR FROM TENNESSEE

THE HOUSE and the Senate have unlimited power and initiative in one function only—they can investigate anything.

No President can veto a resolution for an investigation or by law curb its activities or its scope. Theoretically, the purpose is to acquire facts on which to base future legislation. Some of the mightiest of our historical moves have sprung from such inquiries. Giants have risen in the course of them. Harry Truman would probably have remained an obscure little nonentity were it not that he became chairman of a comparatively inconsequential Senate body which got to asking questions.

One of the surest ways to grab public attention is for a legislator to propose a resolution for a special investigation. If it passes it is not submitted to a standing committee, but its author is by established custom chosen as its chairman.

This is the story of a special Senatorial investigating committee. In many ways it is typical of such things under the Fair Deal, where politics can strangle this last independent prerogative of Congress.

The central character of this tale is Estes Kefauver, who sprung a Senate motion to investigate crime. Your authors have a personal property right in this venture. For Senator Kefauver had read *Chicago Confidential,* and what he found there made his hair stand on end. This is no conjecture. His resolution was prompted by what we had discovered and published.

He was sincere, impulsive and ambitious—if you can call a yen to be Vice-President an ambition. He is our friend, and as such we wish him well and, as Americans who know a little more than most of their fellow-citizens about what is going on, we cheered the possibilities of an untrammeled turning of the turf that would show up officially any important portion of the staggering facts for which we risked our lives.

Kefauver began bravely. He realized that he had lightning bolts in both hands; that he not only could become one of the foremost men of his time, but that he could accomplish priceless service to his country. With the infinite power that was his, he could expose and perhaps destroy the Syndicate and the Mafia which rules it, and save us from the creeping, leaping conspiracy of criminals which already in many elements of our life has superseded constituted government.

But he wants to be Vice-President.

At this writing, he is 47; Barkley is 73. Political wisdom would dictate that the second man on the next national Democratic ticket should come from a border state. Kefauver is from Tennessee. He became a headliner when he licked boss Ed Crump. He is of Dutch-American stock and a Protestant.

He has four years more on his Senate term and could be re-elected. But for a national nomination one needs a majority of the delegates at a convention. Delegates are party men, designated by the party.

He had no more than taken his first bold steps when the party went to work on him. No Democrat can fight the Mafia and get anything from most Democrats except obstruction. They are so intimately and intricately interwoven with the underworld plunderworld through all political strata that they must protect it.

Kefauver was too naive to foresee this. He comes from one of the few states where there is no gangsterism except in picayune city and county affairs, and in those the Republicans share the chicken-feed rewards. Kefauver campaigned in a coonskin cap and unhorsed the Memphis machine, which had no great state-wide strength from within and no tie-ups to bring it help from without. But the explosion that followed when his bill passed rocked the whole national party.

Kefauver, in his innocence, had read our book of disclosures, but like thousands of others, he failed to grasp the significance of the political forces which have become integrated with the system, without which it could not have spread, and to which it has contributed and does contribute incalculable money, leadership and votes. It was inconceivable to him that mayors and governors he knew and many of the statesmanlike Senators with whom he mingled, could be beholden to, not to say slaves of, swarthy, sinister men, many of them ex-convicts, who traffic in bodies of women, making and supplying dope-fiends, dealing in extortion, smuggling, bootlegging, hijacking, bribing and murdering in the principal cities and states of the union; that these hyenas were a controlling influence in nominations and elections; that they owned vast commercial and industrial enterprises, labor unions, even some newspapers, and that their pirate hands gripped the steering wheels of enormous financial fleets.

He read it. But he couldn't believe it. And what he did believe of it he couldn't digest.

Now he finds himself in the middle of a giant whitewash. He is the chump whose good name is used to shield the key figures of the Mafia and obfuscate their tie-up with the big city Democratic machines. He does not admit it publicly but he is heartbroken.

Senate Republicans, seeking an issue, jumped in to support the proposed investigation. Kefauver's bill at once became a hot potato the Democrats couldn't drop.

Dave Niles, Bill Boyle, J. Howard McGrath, and Scott Lucas huddled. They found it was too late to sidetrack the proposed investigation; it had to go on, but with "sensible" safeguards. Suggestions that the probe be transferred to other committees were waved aside as impractical; it was necessary to have a front for this and Kefauver was perfect for the job. He is a man of personal honesty, with no embarrassing machine or underworld connections.

The committee was voted, but with the surprising proviso that the Vice President should name the minority party members. This was unprecedented. Minority leaders always choose their own committee members. The purpose of this tactic was to deal Michigan Senator Homer Ferguson, the Republican's top investigator, out. Membership was limited to five, three Democrats and two Republicans. Thereupon Vice President Barkley followed orders, named two GOPers, one harmless. Both were in the middle of violent primary campaigns, fighting for political survival. It was known they could not spend much time with the committee. Wiley, a good man, is a ranking minority member of the Foreign Relations Committee. He was kept close to that post by the Korean mess. Julius Cahn, Wiley's intelligent aide, was rendered impotent. And Tobey is more a New Dealer than most Democrats. He got campaign support from the administration, and in payment gratuitously but muddle-headedly blamed gambling in New York on Dewey.

The motor of a Senatorial investigating committee is its counsel and the staff. The members have other duties, must attend other committee meetings, must be on the floor for roll-calls. And they are not usually professional prosecutors. They are at the mercy of their staffs.

That's when the shenanigans began. Kefauver had no experience with such shenanigans. He didn't know whom to retain. Tom Murphy, Alger Hiss' nemesis and later Police Commissioner of New York, was recommended. But Murphy was persona non grata in Washington because he had guts enough not to throw the Hiss prosecution, after he had learned that would please the Attorney General's office.

Dave Niles told Kefauver to ask Ferdinand Pecora for advice. Pecora, then a Justice of the New York State Supreme Court, was getting by on the reputation of having exposed the money barons of Wall Street in the early 1930's. Pecora is a thoroughgoing New Dealer and Kefauver is one of the faithful. They failed to tell the man from Tennessee that Pecora is Bronx boss Ed Flynn's man. Flynn is head of the machine in which Frank Costello is a power. Pecora attended Costello's celebrated party at the Copacabana nightclub, with half the local bench, a number of jurists who owed their robes to Costello.

Pecora recommended his protégé, Rudolph Halley, of the law firm of Fulton, Walter and Halley, for counsel and Felix Frankfurter phoned to confirm it. Halley had been on the staff of the Truman Committee when Fulton was its chief counsel, so he looked good to Estes as an experienced prober. But Halley had been an attorney for the Hudson & Manhattan Railroad, in which it was alleged underworld characters owned stock. Kefauver told your reporters he had heard a rumor Halley might have represented them, and had asked him about it before hiring him. Kefauver looked us in the eyes and stated, "Halley said it wasn't so. Naturally, I took his word for it."

After the Kefauver Committee had been functioning some months, Halley admitted to your reporters before witnesses, that he knew there were large underworld holdings in that company, which had been his client. We have a sworn affidavit which reads as follows:

"Mr. Halley stated that the statement in the book *Chicago Confidential*, to the effect that the underworld syndicate has bundles of stock in the Hudson & Manhattan tubes, was substantially correct; that it was his own personal knowledge, as former counsel for the Hudson & Manhattan Railroad, that the underworld owned large blocks of stock in that company."

After a change in management, Halley was dismissed from the H & M, and went to work for the Kefauver Committee at $120 a week. The new management of the railroad said it had virtually eliminated suspicious stockholders and emasculated shady directors who could not be fired.

Among the investigators hired by the committee were ex-cops, disappointed lawyers and the usual Washington hanger-on-ers, recommended for jobs by influential friends.

Kefauver's principal source of information about the under-world was what he had read in *Chicago Confidential*. He knew no more. He asked Mortimer to take a leave of absence from his newspaper and act as paid adviser to the committee. Mortimer accepted, but said that he would take no compensation. Over the weekend, Kefauver withdrew his offer in a telegram in which he blamed other Senators. He said they feared other newspapermen would be offended. That was an alibi, quickly arranged when influential Democrats vetoed the idea. But he took advice from Nat Perlow, editor of the Police Gazette!

At the first open hearing of the committee, subpenaed gamblers were represented by Morris Shenker, St. Louis lawyer, formerly on the Missouri Democratic committee. As a result of his good work in obtaining campaign donations, Shenker was named by Bill Boyle to the Democratic finance committee. He hastily resigned after the deal was exposed in Lait's column.

Every effort was made to keep Kefauver concentrated on gambling. Syndicate heads know the nation is not shocked over bookmaking. Whenever witnesses or informers got hot on narcotics, the spine of the Syndicate system, or began to talk about the huge investments of the underworld in legitimate business, they were brushed off. There were rumors of fixes, payoffs and other such skulduggery, though Kefauver was ab-solutely in the clear. But whenever he was warned such things were happening, Kefauver, a softie at heart, who believes evil of no one, said it was impossible.

Though he promised your reporters his committee would hold open hearings in New York and Chicago before election, at which no punches would be pulled, he folded up like a frightened puppy. After one day in New York, at which no one of importance was questioned, the committee adjourned until after the election, with the statement that Joe Adonis, who had been allegedly sought for 90 days, was unavailable. Your reporters saw Adonis every night at the corner of 50th Street and Broadway while committee investigators were supposed to be searching for him. While the great man-hunt was supposed to be on, Adonis voluntarily surrendered himself to New Jersey authorities who wanted to prosecute him for gambling.

When asked why Costello hadn't been called before election, a committee spokesman stated "We have nothing to ask Mr. Costello."

Similar wariness was shown in Chicago. When former police captain Dan Gilbert, who was Jake Arvey's hand-picked candidate for sheriff of Cook County, was on the stand at a secret hearing, he was questioned about his wealth. Your authors had exposed him as the richest cop in the world, a millionaire. Gilbert's salary had never topped $9,000 a year, yet he admitted at the closed hearing he owned more than $350,000—which he said he had acquired through "speculation." The committee dropped it then. Senator Kefauver, in an interview, said, "Captain Gilbert was a forthright witness." When the *Chicago Sun Times,* a Democratic New Deal newspaper, got hold of the minutes of the secret hearing and splashed the text on Page 1 a few days before election, Kefauver threatened to hold someone in contempt for the leak. Yet the committee did not explain why this information of public interest had been bottled up before election, and why Gilbert's bank accounts and securities had not been scrutinized.

Later, Kefauver imperiously "directed" Eugene C. Pulliam, publisher of the *Indianapolis Star* and *News,* "to discontinue" publication of a series exposing gambling as revealed by previous committee investigations, under penalty of a contempt citation.

While Estes was threatening other newspapermen with jail, columnist Drew Pearson, his fervent supporter, was permitted to obtain access to secret committee records, including highly confidential income tax returns.

Wherever the committee held hearings, its staff tried to pick on the little guys, fingered as the goats. The procedure in Miami was to put six local Jewish bookmakers out of business. The Mafia was muscling in on them anyway. The dispossessed were scheduled to be closed up so the Chicago Sicilian mob would have clear sailing in Miami as soon as the hullabaloo about the crime investigation blew over next year.

Only half-hearted efforts were made to locate important fig-

ures. Where, at any time, any were questioned or threatened
with contempt, it was because the situation was so wide open
that no cover-up could be attempted without bringing the
newspapers down.

At this writing, Harry Russell, Chicago hoodlum, was the
only recalcitrant witness brought to trial. He's a small potato, a
Jew taking the rap for the Mafia. A judge ordered his acquittal.

The position of the Committee has been that witnesses could
refuse to incriminate themselves only on federal offenses, but
that if it was state prosecution they feared, they had no immunity—tenuous reasoning any way you look at it, though
many lawyers say it's legal.

But Kefauver has been letting his enthusiasm get the better
of him, and recently stated at an open hearing, "Don't think
we're going to let you get away with this. We are working
closely with local prosecutors and will turn our records over,
particularly where anyone defies this committee."

Though no comment appeared in the papers, the mob lawyers knew he had played into their hands. He might have made
the contempt stick before; now, however, since he himself has
stated he's acting as an agent for the states—though unofficial—
it's a million to one not one recalcitrant witness will be convicted.

The only state in which the committee got tough before election was Pennsylvania, where the municipal machines are Republican. In New York, boss Flynn and Tammany were un-
molested, and the onus was put on Dewey for having tolerated
gambling in Saratoga. There was no mention that when Lehman, F.D.R.'s "good right arm," was governor, gambling was
just as wide open there, and more so.

One of your reporters remembers seeing a limousine with
New York State license Number 1 parked under the portico of
Piping Rock, a notorious and expensive Saratoga gambling
joint run by Luciano. That was Governor Lehman's car. It is
possible his chauffeur was inside playing dominoes.

But the strategy of the Democratic brain-trust miscarried.
People in New York knew Costello was running the town and
trying to get control of the state, even when the Senate committee, with all its power and money, fiddled and twiddled.
Chicagoans knew the Fischettis and Capones, Boss Arvey, Dan
Gilbert and Senator Scott Lucas were political bedfellows,
which charge was aired daily in the papers during the 1950
campaign.

Wherever the committee gave the Democrats a clean bill, the people rebelled and kicked them out, most frequently on just that issue. But, where the committee had tried to show the underworld is tied up with Republicans, as in Pennsylvania, the GOP scored a great victory.

The two Democratic members of the committee, in addition to Kefauver, are Lester Hunt, of Wyoming, and Herbert O'Conor of Maryland. Where Hunt comes from, "crime" means cattle-rustling and claim-jumping. O'Conor, however, is the Democratic leader of the Maryland organization, which is in cahoots with one of the tightest and biggest Mafia concentrations in the country. Not only were no hearings held in Maryland before election, but Kefauver refused to send investigators into Prince Georges County, described heretofore as one of the most vicious crime spots of the country, even when citizens implored him to.

Instead of cracking down on murderers, procurers and dope-peddlers, the committee wasted time, money and effort on an investigation of comics. An effort was made to label the strips as the chief cause of America's crimes.

The Senate investigating committee has, through ignorance or by design, been playing directly into the hands of the Mafia. Most Syndicate key figures no longer have anything personally to do with gambling, except as bankers and protectors. Gambling is a seasonal business and investigations and clean-ups are discounted in advance, like rain in baseball economy and warm weather in Sun Valley. These catastrophes are averaged off over a long period. The computations contemplate temporary droughts at the street level. Except for a few who will go to the can for a few months and be paid for their time, nothing is disturbed. Bookmakers still take bets right outside the Senate committee room.

If no gambling casinos run in Miami this winter they will next winter. Meanwhile, those who want to gamble will fly to Havana, where the same mob operates the wheels and crap games. Anyway, you can still bet on the nags in Miami, clean-up or no. At this writing, at least two fully equipped casinos are operating in the area.

But while the committee was grabbing front pages with its gambling exposures, the big boys were immune in the affairs that really matter to them, like manipulation of the stock market, black marketing, smuggling, counterfeiting, dope and other forms of profitable deviltry, the proceeds of which they invest in real estate and securities, so that as of now, the crime cartel is more potent in the money marts of the world than all the highbinders so long hissed at, the "international bankers."

After Col. George White, Commr. Anslinger's ace investigator, on loan to the Committee, was withdrawn, Scott Lucas high-pressured Truman to penalize White. White had turned up evidence that beat Lucas in Illinois.

Purposely or not, Halley even helped the giggling gangsters get rid of the few rivals who remained. Few Sicilians got a going-over; but the heat was turned on the handful of Jewish and Irish cheaters who survived.

Personally, Kefauver is a delightful and appealing personage, tall, a former football-player with the charm of an F.D.R. and the fine, delicate features of a Woodrow Wilson. He may well be your next Vice President. After that—well, any American boy with no such start could be. His friends kid him and accuse him of saying "Good morning, Mr. President" every morning when he looks in the mirror as he shaves. Kefauver frowns at this. He says, "The Chief in the White House will get sore."

Kefauver's main weakness is that he is a Don Quixote for "causes" (except FEPC), has too much energy and tries to do too many things. He is on almost every regular and special committee it is possible for a Senator to make, so hasn't time to do justice to any. He is in modest circumstances, cannot be bought or bribed, though he could have had millions to throw the investigation—as it is being thrown anyway. Many believe some of that money went elsewhere, without his knowledge.

An employe of the committee, whose name will not be divulged by us, disgusted by what went on, unburdened himself. He said "a fix was made in Miami" to relieve a certain wanted hoodlum from testifying; and that another deal was put over in Chicago to protect some of the most important Mafistas. A fund was raised in Hollywood to choke off disclosures.

One investigator had as a chief recommendation, other than brief service with the F.B.I., that he had been a cop in a mid-Western city. With this background he was sent in to "bust" the mob in New York, a job that many District Attorneys couldn't do. He knew so little of New York that he had to ask how to get to Times Square.

This investigator, "unable" to find Joe Adonis during a 90-day search, was very diligent when it came to finding himself a

new, high-paying job. During the course of an investigation
into mob control of legitimate business, it was testified that one
Bill Giglio, now under indictment on a tax rap, had "muscled" into a sugar and candy company during the last war, and
that as a result of such activities he now owned a research and
development laboratory, the entire output of which was being
sold to a large and respected chemical corporation.

While going over Giglio's books the Kefauver man naturally
had occasion to call on the large corporation, and he ingrati-
ated himself with its officers, who were not called to testify in
Washington. The result was that, right smack in the middle of
the Kefauver investigations, this dick quit to head up the
plant-security set-up of the big corporation, which now has a
lot of war contracts.

But the payoff is that, a couple of years ago, before the
Kefauver Committee was thought of, the same fellow was in
charge of security at a Long Island plant making restricted
military products. There it was discovered that the future
Kefauver agent was protecting the bookmakers in the plant,
and he was booted out after the F.B.I. was tipped off. The
book at this plant was operated by Joe Adonis. Kefauver was so
informed, but did not fire his agent.

Federal and state enforcement agencies are squawking that
the mob is getting access to confidential files through leaks in
the committee.

But if the committee had wanted to probe, the goods were
in reach. Individuals all over the country sought to put facts in
its hands. Whenever possible, those who managed the investigations looked the other way.

Bill Drury, the honest Chicago ex-police captain, who was
slain by gunmen last September, might have been alive now
were it not for this committee. We were in constant communication with Drury, in fact Jack Lait received a letter from him
in New York the morning after he was assassinated. Almost his
last act was mailing it. When the committee first got under
way, your authors suggested to Kefauver that he hire Drury
and his partner, Captain Tom Connelly, as investigators. These
men knew more first-hand about the underworld than almost
anyone alive. Counsel Halley interposed. He told us the men
were not "reliable," because they had been fired from the Chicago police force. That was their chief recommendation to us.
They had been rooked out of the crookedest force in the coun-

try because they were fearless, honest and untouchable.

We told Kefauver the only way he could convince us his investigation was on the up-and-up was to hire these men. He promised us he would. That was in July, 1950.

Meanwhile, Drury and Connelly sought to contact Kefauver, failing which they tried to get in touch with Halley and the chief investigator of the committee. They hated the mob so hotly, they offered to work for nothing, though they were poor men. Had Drury been retained as an investigator, he'd still be living. No cop has ever been killed except in actual combat. The underworld never murders a policeman who is going about his business. But an ex-cop—yoho.

A lot of misinformation has been published about what preceded the actual assassination, last September 25. After his death, committee employes realized they would have to explain Drury's frequent phone calls. A story was dreamed up in Chicago to the effect that Drury was seeking "protection" and that Halley, after a couple of weeks' consideration, had agreed to arrange for it. That runs for the end book. Drury never asked anyone for protection. He was the bravest man we ever knew. He often traveled without a gun, but the mobsters feared his fists more than bullets. We spoke to him a few days before he died. He was not frightened. He was angry. He told us he had been trying to contact committee investigators for weeks to give them information. He said that ever since he had outlined to them what he was prepared to prove he got brushed off when he called again.

The Democratic *Chicago Sun-Times* charged categorically that Drury was rubbed out because someone on the Kefauver Committee "leaked" to the mobsters what Drury said he had the goods on. He told us his investigations implicated someone on the committee's staff.

A few days after the murder, Kefauver phoned us long distance to tell us to get all our records and correspondence concerning Drury together as he was going to subpena us at once, in an effort to solve the cowardly crime. That was October 1, 1950. As these words were being typed in February, 1951, the subpena remained unserved and the assassination unpunished.

On the other hand, Lait and Mortimer were under considerable pressure from important personages, Republicans as well as Democrats, "to lay off Halley," and place the blame for the miscarriage of the Kefauver committee on the chairman instead of on his staff. We refused to be bought, bribed, threatened or intimidated.

By resolution, the original life of the committee was until February 28, but it is probable that additional hearings will be authorized for March.

The plan, as this went to press, was to save all the fireworks for a final blow-out in New York, at which the glamor pusses of the underworld, such as Virginia Hill, dubbed by us "Mafia Rose," would be called for the publicity value. Virginia was served with much hullabaloo in September, but was saved six months to hypo the last act. Frank Costello was also slated to be called if he "cared to talk."

The big boys have brazenly stood on their "constitutional rights" on the advice of high-priced counsel who assured them their chances against conviction on contempt, which is a misdemeanor punishable by a year in a Federal "country club," were about a hundred to one.

It was decided by the Mafia Grand Council that if things got too hot, Costello would have to be the goat. He has been getting too much publicity for the conservative rulers of the Unione, who still live in cold-water tenements with fat old-country wives.

They resent the airs put on by the glamor-boy hoods, who, they feel, and with some justification, are putting the finger of the law on the syndicate.

One Mafia faction is for going further. In the event the spotlight hits Costello his number is up. He has so been told by Tony Ricci, alias Goebels, who manages many such things.

We have not seen it, nor have we any confidential information about the contents of the committee's final report, but we are willing to bet it will be along these lines:

1) There is crime.
2) No political party has the monopoly on it.
3) There seems to be a Mafia.
4) Gamblers should pay their income tax.
5) Kids should go to Sunday school.
6) Communities should appoint Crime Prevention Societies.
7) Because of the international situation, let's forget it and call the whole thing off.

The plight of honest Senator Kefauver is not unique. Wherever possible, the underworld uses such characters to do their dirty work. They fall for it, probably because dreamers and social planners are gullible, not practical like their more conservative brethren. That's why political bosses frequently back them and surprise semi-suspicious suckers who think they know things.

For instance, when the late Boss Kelly of Chicago, one of the most ruthless thieves who ever lived, thought he saw the handwriting on the wall, he nominated good men to run for Governor and Senator. At no time after Adlai Stevenson went to Springfield and Professor Paul Douglas got to Washington did these Utopians ever open their mouths or do anything, or even complain about the iniquities in Chicago, though we told plenty and a lot of other dirt wasn't confidential.

He hand-picked as his successor Martin Kennelly, a mild old bachelor who didn't know when it was Wednesday. This was a "businessmen's candidate." The mob and their Democratic sidekicks gave him the business.

Kefauver even has a soft spot for accused Commies. He was one of the seven Senators to vote against the McCarran Bill, which Marcantonio opposed in the House. Douglas, who didn't have guts enough to vote no, because that would have imperiled Lucas' chance in Illinois, did hop in to uphold the President's veto.

The only Senator running for reelection who opposed the McCarran Bill all the way was Lehman, a ticket-mate of mob-backed Pecora and Lynch, an old codger of eminent respectability and Wall Street millions, who is and always was "safe"—he's too wrapped up in Park Avenue dignity and too flattered by public honors to see or understand that with his silk-gloved hands he pulls hot chestnuts out of the oven for the dirtiest crooks, traitors and political plotters in the land.

27. LUCKY NUMBERS

THE FIRST thing a Congressional investigating committee gets, the sine qua non, is an appropriation. The next is a sheaf of time-tables. Then comes the joyful junketing-time to remote places—remote from the capital and remote from the subject.

The Kefauver committee made the grand tour—California

and Florida, Chicago and New York, about everything but Yellowstone Park. Its golden fleece was gambling. They could have cleaned up their quest for about $1.60 on a taxi meter.

All the evidence, all the interstate involvements and local conditions which are the particular province of Congress, they could find in Washington. We did. All gambling in the capital is interstate because it is inseparable from its lines into and out of Maryland and Virginia.

We outlined the setup of the nationwide underworld Syndicate. We brought it to the District line. At that point the on-the-spot gamblers take over.

They have been mentioned as Emmitt Warring, king of Georgetown; Attilio Acalotti, "mayor" of Thomas Circle; Sam Beard and his partner Gary Quinn, and the Sussman brothers. Of money gouged from suckers, 90 per cent clears through them, and "Black Jack" Kelleher, Frank Erickson's local observer.

A curious situation here is that "policy" or "numbers" gets a bigger play than bookmaking. The reverse is true almost everywhere else. The reason ascribed by the cognoscenti is that while everyone earns a fairly good living, few have enough surplus cash for important horse betting. But numbers tickets can be bought for from one cent up. That game is far more profitable for the operators, too. Bookmakers can't do much better than putting a ceiling on track odds. They must follow the mutuels, though they stop at a 20-to-1 payoff. Bookies who can't lay off enough often lose on a day.

The winning numbers pay only 600 to 1, whereas 999 numbers are drawn, and the draw can be fixed.

In most towns, the numbers play is predominantly by Negroes. In Washington it is general, with white government employes in the majority. The policy slips are usually sold by colored runners, often messengers and elevator boys in government buildings. The salesman witholds 25 per cent of the gross. Average booking is $50 a day.

The take from the numbers, in pennies, nickels, dimes and quarters, is deposited in the branch of the Hamilton Bank at 20th and Pennsylvania Avenue, in the Foggy Bottom section. The Congressional committee investigating local crime ascertained that this bank did not report the large deposits of small coins. The deposits are withdrawn each day and transferred to

Maryland, where local representatives of the Syndicate divide the receipts and send its cut to the Mafia in New York.

The sale of numbers is so widespread, the police can make only token arrests. Invariably, when the peddler, usually a Negro, is locked up, a representative of a bonding outfit appears at once and posts bail. Next day a member of the Charlie Ford law firm appears in court. Several defendants testified the lawyers paid their fines. The operation will be described in detail later.

Numbers sellers are picked up all over the town, and they are not coy. For instance, police got a squeal that two men were selling policy slips from an auto parked in the 1200 block of 7th Street, NW. Cops questioned them and numbers slips "just rolled out of a paper bag on the car floor." The prisoners were very "surprised," the more so when 200 numbers books were found in the car's trunk.

Vice squad dicks stopped in to get a shine at 209 K Street NW. They saw numbers lying on a chair next to two men. When they searched them they found many more in their possession.

Policy is a lottery. Under federal law, that is a felony. But the only way to cut in on the racket is to get tough. Twenty-five-dollar fines, paid by lawyers reimbursed by the bosses, are no deterrent. But Judge Thomas D. Quinn handcuffed the police even on that. He served notice on the U. S. Attorney's office that he "will not tolerate" prosecutors delaying court action on gambling cases until they can get grand jury indictments.

According to the Federal Rules of Criminal Procedure, the government is within its rights requesting these continuances, but Curtis P. Mitchell, an attorney for some arrested as gamblers, alleged the civil rights of numbers suspects were being disregarded.

Judge Edward M. Curran spiked the government's case when it attempted to clean up gambling in Thomas Circle. Though one defendant pleaded guilty to operation of a lottery, Judge Curran ruled police did not have enough "probable cause" to arrest the others, who were admittedly in possession of numbers slips.

Washington judges openly acknowledge the fact that the fines they impose are paid by the bosses.

Judge Henry A. Schweinhaut, of the United States District Court, frivolously presented a numbers operator named

"Lemon" a chance to prove there is honor in Washington's gaming fraternity.

He asked him to come forward and provide the $300 fine for an aged Negro who was convicted before him of taking numbers bets.

"Lemon put up bond for the defendant. Maybe Lemon will pay the fine," said the District Solomon. "I'll give him a chance to prove his loyalty to an old employe."

Defense Attorney Mitchell, who has figured in these pages before, quickly disillusioned His Honor. "As a practical matter, a numbers backer wouldn't be apt to pay a $300 fine for a man who only had a three-dollar-a-day numbers book," he explained.

But the judge winked and said, "If Lemon doesn't pay, it might get around that he will let one of his men stay in jail. It might reduce his prestige in the fraternity."

Did we hear someone talking about legalized and licensed gambling? This is it, with a bow from the U. S. District Court.

In recent years the top rulers of the netherworld have disassociated themselves as much as possible from street-level vice and crime, preferring to remain on the sidelines, where their take comes in clean.

The situation in Washington is a pattern and example for the rest of the country, because, for obvious reasons, the tygoons have preferred to have no direct dealings with lawbreaking in the nation's capital.

The method whereby the take from policy, Washington's chief form of gambling, goes upstairs is unique and ingenious, the product of brilliant legal scheming.

First of all, each local numbers bank is, for the records, completely independent. Its operator, who employs the runners who actually sell the lottery tickets, is supposed to be completely unaffiliated, and it would take a smarter guy than any government lawyer to prove him otherwise.

In the beginning, most of the local banks were really unaffiliated. Since then, on occasion, some have tried to remain that way. This is what happens when they do: The Big Mob sends in "customers" to bet a certain number; then, through its ability to control the daily winning number, that number comes up and the banker goes broke.

But if he wants to play ball, they sell him an "insurance policy" which guarantees him from undue loss—which is prevented by the control of the winning number. His daily premium is the payoff money.

The funniest one happened when a policy salesman asked police to lock him up because one of his clients had a $60 hit which the runner couldn't pay off—having lost the money playing the numbers. It came about when a cop admonished Lawrence Fields, obviously drunk, to quiet down. Fields begged to be arrested on the numbers charge. The cop asked Fields whether he realized the seriousness of what he was saying. Fields replied, "Nothing will happen. My boss pays protection."

The boss was identified in court as Sam Beard. Beard claims he is in the pickle business, but he once served 53 months in jail for gambling and 13 months for tax evasion. Fields got 90 days. His client is waiting outside the District jail.

But don't think bookmaking is a peanut industry either. Local authorities estimate the take of bookmakers within the District at $100,000,000 a year—not gross business, but net profits.

Horse money goes to Prince Georges, Maryland, as already described. Snags Lewis, the wire service representative, transmits the payoff and profits to New York and New Jersey.

Though Bernice Franklin, former sweetheart of Attilio Acalotti, testified in federal court that at least three members of the Metropolitan Police were paid off by gamblers in her presence, Washington authorities never show any enthusiasm toward investigating charges of corruption against cops.

When District Commissioner John Russell Young testified recently before a special grand jury probing Washington gambling, he was not asked about the possibility of bribes being paid by the gamblers. Assistant U. S. Attorney John W. Fihelly, conducting the inquiry, left it flat and started on "several weeks vacation."

You can freely make a bet on a horse in almost any place in Washington except a church—with elevator boys in government buildings, at corner cigar and drug stores, lunch stands and bellboys. If you still can't find a place, the ingenuity of the Washington bookmaker will solve your problem. For instance, the police said they broke the biggest gambling brokerage ever operated in Washington with the arrest of two men in a "doctor's office," on California Avenue, N.W. Police said one of the men they arrested was a physician. He told them he could make more money with betting slips than with prescriptions.

"There wasn't even a band-aid in the place." But there were the following items:

Betting slips; a looseleaf notebook which appeared to be a gambling broker's record, containing $75,000 in IOU's from all over the country; two promissory notes totaling $35,000; $134 in cash, an expensive radio, and a clock with a sweep second-hand. While police went through the place the phone rang. A voice on the other end "started to give me hell for a bum steer, saying the odds had dropped to 8 to 5," Sergt. James Roche said.

Police Lt. David McCutcheon told the District license board that a gambler paid the proprietors of Filo's restaurant, 1700-A 9th Street, NW, $200 a month for the concession to take bets there. At this writing Filo's is still in business.

During the seasons, Washington gamblers make book on baseball, football, basketball and hockey. Walter Lephfew and Skylar Wilson were arrested this year in what is described as a $2,000,000 football lottery.

We placed bets with bookies who hang out in the G & W Lunch Room, 17th and L.

Much of the local gambling is controlled by Greeks who operate in restaurants and private clubs.

We saw gambling going on openly on the second floor of a building on the northwest corner of 9th and H; also in the Greek restaurant on the second floor of 9th and G.

A dice and horse room was being operated over the Bazaar restaurant, at 17th and L. Say that Steve Akaris sent you. That's how we got in.

You can find roulette in a place at 5th and G., also over a restaurant in the 100 block of Vermont Avenue.

Don't think gambling doesn't account for plenty of violence in the District.

On recommendation of the District license board, the commissioners turned down a police request that they revoke a billiard hall license of William G. Heflin. Earlier in the year, Joseph H. "Big Joe" Scheve, a convicted gambler, was fatally shot there. Before that, James T. Skeens shot Edward Ryan in the leg there. Police charged the billiard hall was frequented by criminals. We saw bookmakers taking bets there.

A 25-year-old fireman with twenty pairs of crooked dice in his pocket was found stabbed to death in an alley as an aftermath of a crap game in which 15 persons participated. Every die was without 1, 3 and 5, making it impossible to toss a 7. The dice were of all sizes and colors, "suitable for almost any occasion."

One-armed bandits are banned by District and by the new Federal law. However, $100 federal stamps have been purchased for 50 such machines, operating at this writing in the city of Washington. Those in officers' service clubs have since been removed, but many operated brazenly in places open to the public.

Pinball machines, illegal in most big cities, especially in New York, and not permitted in the Virginia counties across the Potomac, are a popular indoor sport in Washington. They are found in restaurants, drugstores, bottle clubs and playlands. Many are used as gambling devices. The federal tax of $10 on each has been paid for 1263.

Federal records show 15,000 one-armed bandits and gambling devices registered for Maryland, of which 5,000 are in the District suburbs.

Most slot machines are manufactured in Chicago. Those destined for areas in D.C. or nearby, where they are against the law, were shipped to wholesalers in Danville, Va., then distributed sub rosa to Washington and Baltimore.

Payoffs are pretty lousy.

The new Federal slot machine law is a laugh. It was dreamed up in an effort to stave off Kefauver's investigation.

The only Senator who really fought it came from Nevada, where the one-armed bandits are legal, and into which, under the new Federal law, they can be imported freely. Nevada had nothing to lose and everything to gain.

The same Senator fought contempt citations against recalcitrant Kefauver witnesses, proving, to Estes' surprise, what we had told him about Democratic-underworld alliances.

The joker in any statute forbidding the interstate transportation of slot machines is they are manufactured from standard and interchangeable parts which can be assembled anywhere by any competent mechanic. Instead of shipping the finished device, the Costello interests will merely send the parts to local distributors who will put them together—and save freight costs.

The underworld's Washington representatives actually lobbied for the passage of the bill, figuring that its adoption would look like a solid accomplishment to the public, and take the "heat" off other monkey business.

Attorney General McGrath and the New Deal liberals who plugged for the measure had another reason. They hoped it would put the F.B.I. on the spot. Its enforcement being impossible, Hoover and his G-men would take the blame—either that or the F.B.I. would have to hire thousands of fly-cops and become a new, super Prohibition unit, exposed to wholesale graft and bribery, which would please the Reds and the crooks.

We don't think gambling will ever be eliminated. We don't think the public wants it to be. It is a human appetite, like sex and liquor, and no sumptuary legislation can wipe it out. But gambling corrupts law enforcement officers. While wagering is illegal and undercover, this is inevitable. When cops take bribes from bookmakers they feel they do no essential harm. But it's a start and soon they will sell out to anyone.

As to the cure, no two agree. Even your authors have divided opinions. One believes in legalizing gambling, the other points out Nevada, where it is legal, as the horrible example. There the same mobsters control it and law enforcement officers are bought up as usual.

28. IT'S A CRIME

*N*O THANKS is due United States Attorney George Morris Fay for the fact that figures and information regarding the local wave of crime are still available.

Shortly after he took office, in 1946, Fay rewrote the Constitution and closed off the court files from inspection by the press on felony cases. Not satisfied, last year he tightened up in Municipal Court, introducing a form of censorship for newsmen trying to check facts.

But we finagled some figures:

Per capita computations show Washington recorded one murder for every 25,555 persons in 1949. But Chicago, generally conceded the gunmen's playground, had one murder for every 26,902. Washington jumped to one for every 11,000 in 1950.

On the basis of population, Washington led 16 cities of 500,-

ooo or more in aggravated (felonious) assaults during the first
six months of 1950; and it was second only to Chicago in the
total number of such cases. Washington had 1,911, exceeded
only by Chicago's 2,184, and Chicago is five times as large as
Washington!

Though crime in Washington decreased slightly in 1950, as
compared to 1949, the District is high among the leaders, per
capita and in total number of offenses, in every major classification.

Crime has always been a popular pastime here. It increased
so alarmingly during the first years of the New Deal that a
group of public-spirited citizens formed the Washington
Criminal Justice Association in 1936 to help combat it.

The Attorney General in that year called Washington "the
crime capital of the world." The backers hoped for a virile,
hard-hitting body, similar to the Chicago Crime Commission,
which under Virgil Peterson, its executive director, has done so
much to spotlight the workings of the underworld there, or
like Danny Sullivan's Greater Miami Commission.

The original organizers of the Washington association included a number of do-gooders, such as Eugene Meyer, who
bars the identification of Negroes in his paper. The body soon
found itself struggling without sufficient funds. It is now supported by the United Community Services, which allots it only
enough to pay for a director, an assistant and a secretary. The
able director, Edward J. Flynn, is a competent, imaginative individual, handcuffed by lack of funds and public disinterest.
He can do little more than keep a record of crimes as they
occur, compile statistics and offer recommendations. They are
good, but no one wants them.

The situation has gotten worse rather than better since the
Attorney General castigated the city. In 1936 there were only
about 7,000 serious crimes. The number dropped to about
4,000 in 1944. But by last year it had skyrocketed to 13,000. It
is now slightly lower.

Washington is still the crime capital.

In other chapters we touch briefly on the so-called "organized" crimes—prostitution, gambling, and narcotics. This chapter deals mainly with offenses of violence and those against
property, which are usually regarded as unorganized.

But director Flynn agrees with your authors that, with the
exception of private crimes of passion, occasional robberies by

hungry men and juvenile delinquency, all crime is now organized to a degree. Flynn said:

"Highly organized criminal groups, carrying out skillfully planned operations, exist in Washington."

The police disagree with him, naturally. But the record is clear for any observer who follows the entire procedure through, from commission to arrest, bail-bonding and arraignment. The combine appears in the fencing of the loot. Burglars in Washington have a union to which they contribute a percentage of their take in return for bail when arrested, legal representation and fixes where possible. No professional burglars operate until they make arrangements in advance for disposition of their stolen goods, and, thereafter, the other services. Non-members of the union cannot secure bail at any price and are denied the services of the top criminal lawyers.

Why has the nation's capital more crime than other cities? Flynn says it is indicative of community lethargy. He thinks that is not unique in the District, but is equally true in every city. If that is so, there must be a special reason why Washington is more lawless.

Others blame it on the lack of home rule and local government. Yet every investigation and survey elsewhere shows that corrupt municipal city hall gangs are the protectors of vice and crime. The high rates in Washington cannot be blamed on the foreign-born, because only six percent of the population is non-native. As we showed earlier, Negroes commit most of the crime. But there are Negro criminals in other large cities, especially in New York and Chicago, where they do likewise. Why then are Washington's Negroes even more felonious?

There is no doubt that Washington is a cesspool of iniquity and a Utopia for criminals. The setup of the local government and the calibre of the men who enforce its laws and sit on its benches are partly responsible. Archaic and often ridiculous laws and regulations are a contributing factor.

For instance, guns are easy to buy in second-hand stores. There is no law requiring a license to keep a gun in a home. That forbidding the carrying of one in a car is a dead letter. It is a felony to carry a concealed weapon on the person without a license, but there are few arrests and fewer convictions for this, because the District courts and prosecutor feel it is no offense to carry an unloaded weapon, even if a clip of cartridges is in the same pocket. An expert could load the gun without removing it from his pocket.

The fantastic interpretation of laws by the U. S. Attorney and the federal courts has handcuffed the cops in their efforts to clean the town.

Not long ago a Negro was arrested for kicking and assaulting another man in a bus station. Though police found an unlicensed pistol on the prisoner's person, and bullets in another pocket, the U. S. Attorney refused to prosecute for either the assault or concealed weapon. When queried, a representative of his office said it was obvious the colored man was a nice guy, because he didn't load his gun and shoot his victim, who lay helpless on the floor. The prisoner had a record. When asked at a later date whether, in view of all the circumstances since developed, the D.A.'s office would prosecute, the spokesman said, "No. No judge will convict a colored man here for a minor offense like that."

The federal judges are lenient because they are federal judges. Of the 308 with life appointments throughout the United States, 224 are Democrats. During the first 17 years of the Roosevelt-Truman administrations, 289 judges were given such appointments, of whom 272 were Democrats. The same ratio shows up in the District of Columbia. The Democratic judges are the choices and flunkies of corrupt city machines or of unions, left-wingers and fellow-travelers' organizations. The city bosses' men are lenient to law-breakers because their masters order them to be so. The radicals' nominees seldom throw the book at a defendant, because Commies, pinkos and phony progressives hate cops, refer to them as cossacks.

A captain of the Metropolitan Police told us that even honest Washington coppers seldom make arrests any more, because they know what will happen when they get in court. The judge will harass, bullyrag and humiliate them. It is not unusual for a District jurist to castigate the policemen, call them liars and framers, then discharge the prisoners without hearing defense evidence. When the defendant is a Negro, the cops know they are going to get a going-over from the bench.

In 1937, after four years of Democratic administration, 90 percent of all major crimes went unpunished. Since then, largely through the efforts of Flynn's Washington Criminal Justice Association, and more recently of counsel Fischbach's revelations, about which more later, judges have been afraid to be too raw, and are giving stiffer sentences and holding prisoners in higher bail.

However, out of 811 of those indicted for major offenses in the last report period who did not enter pleas of guilty, only 281, about one third, were found guilty. Of those found guilty, the largest number received light sentences, far less than the maximum authorized by law. Even among those who pleaded guilty, more than 20 percent were permitted to assume lesser offenses.

An example of the penalties meted out for serious offenses is seen in those convicted of first- and second-degree murder: of 22, only three got sentences of 15 years to life; one drew 80 months to 20 years; all the 18 others got less than 20 years, with terms tapering down to one of three-to-nine on a first-degree murder, and one of one-to-four on a second-degree murder. None got the chair.

Disposition records on cleaning up major crimes are made to look good through an ingenious invention known as "Willie Pye" arrests. Whenever anyone is pinched in Washington and decides to take a plea, the cops induce him to admit every other unsolved crime of the same nature which is still open on the books. If the accused agrees to take the rap for these unsolved felonies, thus getting the police off the hook, they do not present further evidence to the grand jury, and the felon is not tried for the other offenses. Thus many complaints are charged off and police take official credit for solving crimes where no solution has eventuated.

The practice grew to such an extent about a decade ago that a public stench arose. After a conference between law enforcement officials and prosecutors, it was agreed to end it. But it goes right on and the evidence of it appears every year in tabulations of "cleared by other means." There were 667 so disposed of in 1949.

It is believed the term "Willie Pye arrest" first came into police parlance in Washington when a man so named lived there, about 50 years ago. His business was crime. Willie was indicted on two housebreakings and confessed to many more, which were then written off as closed.

An unnamed desk sergeant immortalized Willie by using his name for the practice of shutting numerous open cases by getting multiple pleas and choosing to proceed on only the last.

The blowup came when Leroy Mason, who was doing a

stretch in Occuquan Work House for three robberies, was still being charged for crimes going on on the outside. A nameless Washington newspaperman composed a deathless ditty, as offensive to grammar as the sentiment is to decency:

Willie Pye was a regular guy,
He took the rap for you and I.

Though the F.B.I. reported a six percent drop of crime in Washington this year, the local jail population reached a new high. The courts sent 21,062 to District jail in 1950, an all-time record. Meanwhile, the police had closed less than 60 percent of all cases involving serious felony, which by the way, was an improvement.

Arrests for the more serious crimes by race were as follows:

Offense	Total	White	Colored
Arson	34	13	21
Aggravated Assault	2956	342	2614
Embezzlement and Fraud	201	146	55
Forgery and Counterfeiting	100	72	28
Grand Larceny	1099	326	773
Housebreaking	2878	634	2244
Homicides	55	10	45
Incest	5	1	4
Rape and Carnal Knowledge	191	39	152
Receiving Stolen Property	59	31	28
Robbery	1033	230	803
TOTAL	8611	1844	6767

The high incidence of Negro and juvenile crime was dealt with in detail in previous chapters. One reason there are so many colored law-breakers in Washington is that many judges in nearby Southern communities order Negro defendants to get out of town, instead of holding them for trial, and these gravitate to Washington.

Tough guys of both races hang around on the streets and insult passers-by with impunity, snatch purses, stick up pedestrians and mug and yoke.

Most crimes in Washington are committed from Friday through Sunday. Almost everyone has a two-day weekend, and the drinking and celebrating begins Friday night.

The First, Second, Third and Thirteenth Police precincts account for 57 percent of all serious crimes. The First is "downtown," with tourists, transients and night life. The others are predominantly Negro.

Among the more profitable of the organized crimes are these:
Housebreaking, comparatively easy because of the large
number of private homes and two- and three-story detached
apartment buildings. The stolen goods are fenced in East Baltimore Street, Baltimore.

Auto thefts, growing more serious.

Bank robberies, not uncommon.

Pickpockets and cold-finger men find easy loot at the countless cocktail parties and other functions constantly given by
lobbyists, conventioneers and diplomats. It is a cinch to crash
these. Jewel-thieves have rich pastures. Social climbers and ambassadors' women are loaded with rocks and constantly display
them. A big gem haul is sent to Holland for recutting, via reverse channels used by the Mafia to smuggle dope. The reset
ice is smuggled back.

Because of the ease with which fixes are maneuvered, the lenient sentences, the failure of local courts to extra-penalize
repeaters, Washington is indeed a picnic-pasture for crooks
from all over the country. When other places get too hot to
hold them, they hop a rattler for the capital.

The pickings are easy. The pay-off is high. The risks are
minimal. The burg is a pushover.

Sex is a crime, too; a statutory felony. The incidence of such
offenses in the Nation's capital is so great as to be startling. The
nature of them nauseated even a couple of hardboiled reporters
like us.

The figures are public property, compiled by the F.B.I., the
local cops and the Davis committee. Howard Whitman, who has
been doing a series of articles based largely on newspaper
morgue material, printed the computations in *Collier's*, later
put them into a book on prurient misdemeanors.

Whitman slanted his findings to *Collier's* special-pleading
formula and found that "crime is a slum-connected characteristic."

That is a laugh. Washington is freer of depressed living areas
than any city in the country.

"And Negroes are ghettoized in these slums," adds Whitman
gratuitously.

Whitman quotes with approval the Committee for Racial
Democracy which urged that "training in minority group problems be instituted immediately as a part of the regular in-
service training of all policemen," the non-sequitur supposition

being that the colored folk out-rape, out-maim, out-steal and out-mugg whites eight to one because the coppers haven't been trained in minority group relations.

Nor are sex-criminals, white or colored, permanently taken off the streets after once being caught. Washington is a recidivists' paradise because of its ridiculous so-called "collateral rule" which takes the place of posting a bond.

A defendant could, and still can, despite a promise of the courts to tighten up, post a $25 collateral instead of a bond with a police captain. Thereupon if he does not appear in a court he is automatically found guilty and the collateral is forfeited as a fine. And that closes the case instead of the judge issuing a bench warrant as in other jurisdictions.

In the case of violent sex cases, the maximum collateral is $500 forfeit in the same way. A new judicial rule says all aggravated sex cases must be taken to court, but they are not.

Abortions are cheap and easy to obtain. Police are able to arrest only a few of the operators, and then only when complications arise. Even then, few are convicted. This racket is highly protected by an interstate ring allied with the Mafia. A ten million a year branch was uncovered in San Francisco, built around a prominent female Chinese physician, not publicly involved because of her high political and social connections. She is a close friend of Virginia Hill, gal friend of the late Bugsy Siegel.

Curiously, Washington is the nation-wide headquarters for the mail order sale of dirty pictures and post cards. Why this should be so is puzzling, though those who operate the business here face no tougher penalty than elsewhere because it is a Federal offense anyway.

29. THE LAW

WE MEAN the poor underpaid bulls, who enforce it—or, anyway, are supposed to.

Last year the Attorney General of the United States held a conference of mayors and other local law enforcement officers to try to figure out the causes of crime. When it was over, we button-holed a mayor of a Western city and asked him the following question:

"How come no one mentioned that hardly a crime or a vice violation is possible without the connivance of or the knowledge of local officials?"

The mayor replied, "That's an easy one to answer. We are all local officials."

We do not charge that the really terrible conditions in Washington are the fault of the Metropolitan Police. Most of the cops on that overworked force are honest. If given the opportunity they would love to do their duty. Most policemen all over the country are honest, too. They are slaves of a setup with the establishment of which they had nothing to do and which they are powerless to correct. Big payoffs are not made to men in the ranks. The orders go out from up above. Patrolmen follow orders. When they see others getting, they often ask what's the use of being honest themselves? Why make pinches when the prisoners are always sprung from up above?

For many years strenuous efforts have been made to sell the idea that the federal government and everything connected with it is straight and efficient. The Metropolitan Police force is an agency of the United States government. Only Gilbert and Sullivan could do justice to it, as a comic opera. But the laughs are costly.

The boss of the force carries the complicated title of Major and Superintendent. His name is Robert J. Barrett and he got the job because he was related to the former chief.

A fantastic story made the front pages last year, then was hushed and forgotten. Police Captain Anthony Richitt charged under oath, before a Congressional investigating committee, that he had been ordered by Police Inspector Jeffreys to turn in a false report on a gambling complaint. He also swore that the District crime investigating sub-committee was worrying the police chief, who, he said, was on intimate terms with gambler Emmitt Warring; and further, that Warring delivered messages from the chief to precinct captains.

Such charges elsewhere would have popped up a seething scandal, at least a grand jury to-do, with the probability of new brass in the police department. It took a long time, but even in Chicago the police commissioner, the county chairman and the millionaire chief investigator for the State's Attorney quit after publication of *Chicago Confidential*.

You think anything like that happened in Washington? In this home of laissez faire the grand jury wasn't interested even to the extent of whitewashing the mud.

The incident was treated as a private feud. It was officially settled on the records when Richitt apologized to his boss, in a public apology, six words long:

"I regret the incident ever occurred."

No explanation, no retraction, no withdrawal of the charges. Barrett's reply was nearly as short:

"Richitt has complied with the orders of the department as far as I am concerned."

Thus was departmental satisfaction restored. But there was no satisfaction for the public. No determination was ever made as to whether the chief had ordered his subordinate to falsify arrest records. It was decided by all concerned that this was of no interest to the tax-payers, the grand jury included.

Barrett had forgotten he had told the press he had what he called "evidence tending to show perjury" on the subject of Captain Richitt. Chairman Davis of the House District Sub-Committee, before which the stink started, got into the act and announced he, too, had closed the book on the affair.

The terms of the deal apparently were such that neither Barrett nor Richitt are ever again to question the other's activities. Some months before, evidence was brought forth that Richitt had bought seven autos in addition to the one he was driving during 27 post-war months, when civilians could get cars only in the black mraket. No explanation was volunteered by anyone, though Richitt had sold most of the cars as soon as he bought them.

Your authors know this is a common practice in police departments all over the country.

A sergeant of the Bridgeport, Connecticut, force was fired for similar activities. Many cops used their emergency priorities to order cars which they then transferred to dealers, without ever taking possession. The cops rarely handled the money. The dealer went with them to accept delivery and paid the purchase price, the cops chiseling from $500 to $1,000 on each transaction.

When we arrived in Washington to dig for this book, we asked: "Who makes the fixes?"

In other cities, contacts are closed with precinct, ward and district leaders of the political party in office. If you want to retail women, make book, land pickpocketing privileges or get a summons or a violation squared, you go to see this local boss.

If money is to be passed it goes through him. Many favors are granted in return for party loyalty, votes or campaign contributions. He takes care of those, too. The leader passes the word along to city hall, where it is relayed to the local police station. In some towns, Chicago for example, the channels are short-circuited in advance, so the leader can go direct to his police captain.

But what happens in Washington, where there are no voters, so there are no district leaders? How do you fix the cops? Who is the collector?

Some naive Washingtonians said there is no such thing. There is no collecting. There is no graft.

That is cockeyed. The payoff is through the local police captain, who acts as the collector for anyone in the District Government who is to be fixed. The captain retains his own percentage of the boodle, plus anything he can steal, then passes the balance up above, through the regularly established channels.

Such a system plays hell with the poor cops on the street. The guy who pays the captain for protection knows he doesn't have to take care of underlings. The most the uniformed patrolman is good for is a meal, a cigar and an occasional five-spot. Vice squad men and detectives can sometimes do a little modest shaking, but not enough to get rich on.

A police captain told us this story: Two Chicago detectives came to Washington to pick up a wanted prisoner. It is the custom among all police departments to entertain cops visiting on business. Washington has no fund for such purposes. Its men are so poorly paid, they can't treat. But the two assigned to keep the visitors happy had worked the bright-light belt, so they knew where they could cuff a few small night clubs. During the evening, one Chicago detective asked the Washington cop, "What is your job worth?"

The reply was, "I get $3,300 a year?"

"No, I don't mean your salary; what's it worth?"

The Washingtonian looked puzzled. The policemen from the Windy City said, "You can talk freely. We're friends. No wise cop in Chicago would take the job unless he could pick up at least $10,000 a year on the side."

Washington policemen who can average $20 a week extra consider themselves lucky. Not so many higher officers.

Internal Revenue agents, who never allow themselves to be quoted, told us some officers have safe deposit-vaults choked with big bills. But many others are honest, like chumps. They have to go along with the crooks to hold their jobs. They can't squawk without implicating too many important higher-ups.

Salaries of Washington policemen range from a take-home pay of only $200 a month for the lowest-grade patrolman to about $10,000 a year gross for the chief. Military ranks are used. Private, sixth grade, the highest non-officer rank, pays $3,750 a year. A corporal gets $4,025, a sergeant $4,228, a lieutenant $4,600, and a captain $5,300. That's the salary on which Captain Richitt bought eight cars in 27 months.

If the fix you're after is of a nature which the local precinct captain can't handle, you go through a certain District Commission employe who is the bagman for one of the three District Commissioners. The Commission is the immediate boss of the police department. Any commissioner can issue orders to the chief.

There are occasions, however, when a really strong in is needed. Washington is federal territory and is ruled nominally by the national administration. In such an instance, the guy who wants to call the cops off has to try other doors. The odds are, even if he is in business in Washington, he has his roots elsewhere. Many Washingtonians maintain voting addresses in the states from which they originally came. Others have friends, partners and relatives in various states.

The procedure is to make the connection through a Democratic county committeeman back home or through a member of Congress in the home state. Congress is the ruler of the District, and almost every Congressman is as busy as a Chicago alderman fixing everything from parking tags to felony warrants.

It is similar when a cop needs influence to square a rap or get an appointment or a promotion. Elsewhere we know that being a paid-up member of the local political club never hurt the career of a policeman. Here there are no political clubs, and most cops are not even Washingtonians. Their jobs are not confined to locals, but are open to all American citizens, regardless of residence. You can take a civil service test back home in Oskaloosa, then arrive in Washington a full-fledged policeman.

Most Washingtonians don't even want to get on the force at the penny-ante salary. But $3,000 a year looks good to a cotton-picker in Mississippi, where the annual per capita income is $600. When he gets to Washington he finds the $600 back home goes further than $3,000 here.

So, what does a cop do when he needs help? He follows the procedure outlined above. If he comes from out of town he corresponds with his local ward-heeler or goes directly to his Congressman on Capitol Hill.

We asked one cop, "What do you do if you're a native of Washington and have no vote?"

He replied, "You're just out of luck."

That is, unless you're a Negro.

The Washington force had some fine colored cops and detectives, native-born men who decided to make a career of police work in the days before Washington was flooded with the displaced from the plantations in the Deep South. In those days Negroes got no special privileges in Washington. Now almost all of the 300 colored policemen are political appointees. The white applicant undergoes a rigid and rigorous investigation; Negroes are forced on the force even over the disapproval of the department's intelligence squad.

Many colored policemen have rackets on the side, are gamblers, operate whore-houses or do a little pimping.

The frequency with which the following happens is too great to set it aside as a mere isolated example: White cops tell you colored ones often stop pretty white women drivers, bawl them out and threaten them with arrests until they cry, then offer to square it for some petting.

Testimony under oath, reported in a previous chapter, in which a former sweetheart of gambler Attilio Acalotti charged she had seen hush-money slipped to three cops, was not pursued by police brass, the District Attorney or the grand jury. Several defendants were convicted for trying to influence her to change her testimony, though Acalotti, "Snags" Lewis and Frank Billeci were granted new trials on the gambling charges.

Our indictment is not against Washington's police. As we said, most of them are honest, conscientious, decent citizens, thwarted by something above their reach.

The culprit is the system. That is responsible for the childish, irresponsible atmosphere of everything in this dizziest of American cities.

Don't think, despite the annual yaps for more assistance, the Washington police force is radically undermanned. Compared to numbers in other cities, it is not. The Metropolitan Police have the second highest manpower per capita of any large outfit in the country. It is not up to authorized strength, but that goes for most cities. That doesn't tell the story, because, as we indicated, there are at least five other police forces operating in the city, with several hundred more cops on tap. Generally speaking, the jurisdiction of each force is limited to the particular area for which it was created. All Washington policemen have the right to make arrests for crimes committed in their presence in any part of the District. For purposes of convenience, deals are made between various forces, so sometimes one patrols a district which really belongs to another. For instance, if a small square or park is situated miles away from the next nearest park, the city police often relieve the National Park Police of the necessity of sending squad-cars far off their regular beats.

There is a reverse, too. The Metropolitan force has about 1,800 men for its 14 precincts and one harbor station, but men are continually called for and assigned to guard visiting diplomats and dignitaries, and for special duty at the White House, government establishments, and even as ushers at tea-parties. With days off, sick leaves and men on special assignments, the force is lucky when it can put 300 cops on the streets on any shift.

The police are used for many duties delegated to others in well-regulated cities. For instance, policemen must act as collection agents for wives with delinquent husbands. Any Congressman can call and ask for police protection, which means he may want a cop in front of his house as a parking attendant for his private parties.

Any time the President or an important official drives through Washington, special cops are strung along the route to clear traffic. Wives of Congressmen and expectant mothers with a drag rate a police escort to a hospital. Even the circus can call for a special detail of 22 men.

It is almost impossible to keep any foot patrolmen on the streets. The force is all-motorized, that being the only way it can get around the sprawling District. Meanwhile, there are no harness-bulls on beats to keep toughs and thugs in line. So serious is the shortage of personnel that the black marias attached to each of the 14 precincts roll the streets 24 hours a day instead of being in their garages. The patrol-wagons are equipped with two-way radios and respond to calls the same as do squad cars. This is a help for spot work, one up on most towns.

One chief trouble with the police department is that so few of its men are natives. They have no local civic pride. Another factor is the constant turnover in personnel, because of the lousy salaries and lean pickings down below. There is no adequate pension system. In New York they can retire on a minimum of half pay after 20 years, regardless of age, which means a man who goes on the force at 21 can get off at 41 with a life pension. But in Washington you cannot apply for retirement before age 55, with 25 years' service. And even then there is no guarantee you will be allowed to quit, as retirement is not automatic, but at the pleasure of the board. Usually only one-third of those who apply are permitted to quit.

On the other hand, Washington cops work an eight-hour day on an authorized five-day week, and are not restrained from holding jobs on the outside which don't conflict with their assigned duties. Many own or work in stores. Several are chauffeurs. Embassies hire them for body-guards. Some drive cabs. A few owned fleets of them, but this was forbidden when it was found they were using their police pull to get their drivers off for traffic violations.

One policeman, Private John U. Carroll, managed a chile parlor in the 700 block, 11th Street, SE. There was nothing wrong with that, according to regulations, but the police trial board nabbed him when he failed to report that he had been in a fist fight with some customers in his place. According to testimony, Danny Petro, a former professional pug, walked into the "parlor" and slugged Carroll's pal. That brought on a four-man melee in which the cop was injured. The trial board fined him $75. After being restored to duty he retired, claiming a veteran's disability.

Though the department lowered standards because of the difficulty of recruiting men, its record for solving crimes is still good. But convictions and sentences are far under the American averages. The present laws and regulations so hamper the police that even if all were honest and intelligent, which they aren't, serious inroads into the crime situation would be impossible.

One of the most serious roadblocks is the fact that after they make an arrest and hold a prisoner for the magistrate, they cannot make their complaints to the court direct, or tell the judge what it is all about. Washington rules require policemen to go to the U.S. Attorney and plead with him to book a case. The prosecutor thus sits as practically a committing magistrate, as the defendant and his lawyers are heard at the same time, and they can bargain with him for a nolle pros or a lesser charge.

If the U.S. Attorney decides not to handle a case, the police are sunk. They cannot ask the municipal judge to hold or commit. In many other jurisdictions, New York for instance, the arresting officer acts for the state at the preliminary hearing, before a magistrate, and not only tells his story to the judge, but can question the prisoner.

The U.S. Attorney is usually reluctant to prosecute. Even if he decides to, the cops are due for a browbeating from the judge. This story is no isolated incident—it is typical of what constantly goes on in the local, politically appointed courts:

Many policemen told us the courts work against them. When they make arrests they have to go to trial on their own time and are usually kept sitting there all day at the pleasure of the defendant and his lawyer. The defendant may wander around, but the policeman is required to remain in the court until the case is called. He is not even permitted to go to the washroom. If he does, the eagle-eyed shysters call the case immediately, with court consent, and the defendant is discharged—for lack of prosecution!

Several policemen who went to the toilet were threatened with contempt citations.

From the time a policeman makes an arrest, until the final disposition of the case, the entire atmosphere of the District enforcement machinery is mined against him. The District Attorney's office is skeptical of anything he says, and is inclined to side with the accused. The courts, frequently presided over by gangster-appointed judges or left-wingers whose constituents are rebels against the accepted code, bend backward. They make defendants of the cops instead of the prisoners. So most policemen shrug and forget about it. For instance, in the Black Belt, not one of every three known crimes is reported. The experienced cops take it easy, go to the ball games and dances.

The most absurd straitjacket in which the Washington police are confined is the law which forbids them to serve warrants. They may be served only by deputy U.S. marshals.

This completely screws up the orderly procedure, because District judges, who are hot hell to protect the civil rights of murderers, pimps, dope-peddlers and gamblers, refuse to hold a prisoner in most cases unless he is arrested on a warrant. And they never uphold a John Doe warrant.

For instance, on one occasion, two cops assigned to the vice squad at night, working undercover on prostitution, got into a house and nabbed several bottles of whiskey there. They called for a police car. When it arrived, further search turned up narcotics. Twenty-six were arrested without a warrant. The police knew the courts would not hold them for even disorderly conduct, because arresting officers could not specify which offense each and every one had committed. So the prisoners were not photographed or fingerprinted. All were allowed to post $5 collateral, which was, of course, forfeited.

A cop can arrest a man whom he sees in the process of housebreaking on burglary, but if he then fans him and finds a gun he cannot charge him with a concealed-weapon violation, because he had no warrant for the search. When police have information that a crime is being committed on a premise, they must first get in touch with the U.S. Commissioner or a judge, then locate a deputy marshal to come and serve the warrant.

But don't you assume you can get away with anything in Washington. The cops are death on jay-walkers. If you cross against the light you'll be jugged. That in Washington is more serious and more culpable than murder!

30. HOW TO STAY OUT OF JAIL

THESE ARE the steps:
First you break the law.
Then you get pinched.
Then you hire Charlie Ford.
Who is he? Charles E. Ford is the "Fifth Street Cicero."
Ford, a behemoth of 220 pounds, is 52. He has been practic-

ing law in Washington for 28 years. His father, a New Jersey
Democrat, was the public printer of the United States in 1913.
Since then a lot has been printed about his son in the public
records.

As noted, Ford was the late Jimmy La Fontaine's lawyer
and is a trustee of his estate. He appeared in Chicago to convince the Kefauver committee it couldn't force Anna Fischetti
to testify against her husband, Charles, the notorious Capone
gangster. And he convinced it.

But not all Ford's work is so aristocratic. He and his associates take them as they come. Hardly a day passes without
defendants in criminal court being aided and comforted by
Ford or someone from his office.

He is the darling of the gambling and prostitution fraternity.
His clients seldom go to jail. The police don't feel so bad when
they lose to Ford as they do when other lawyers oppose them.
For Ford is a great friend of the cops. Whenever a policeman
gets in trouble, Ford takes his case, usually without fee.

Charlie is one of those big, brash, bluff guys everyone loves,
especially the newspapermen. He feeds them plenty of copy—
and liquor—and never hesitates to give them a lift when they
need background material on gangsters and criminals, without
violating his fiduciary ethics. He is a social guy who likes to
entertain and who loves to eat. One of his clients was the late
Tom O'Donnell, and under the terms of his will Charlie operates the two celebrated O'Donnell restaurants and patronizes
them freely.

Whenever his waist gets out of bounds, he goes to Hot
Springs, Arkansas, for the reducing baths and a few days of
friendship and cheer with Owney "The Killer" Madden, retired gang chieftain, now Hot Springs' most eminent elder
statesman.

None of Charlie's clients has ever gone to the electric chair.
One was sentenced to death for murder, but saved Charlie's
record by considerately hanging himself in jail. So he is one
up on Sam Leibowitz, whose lone mistake waited for the minis-
trations of the public executioner. But Ford is that kind of a
guy. Everyone loves him. No one would embarrass him.

We have sworn testimony before us which shows the operations of Ford's jail-thwarting apparatus. It usually works this
way: The prisoner, who may be a numbers peddler, a bookmaker's runner, or a street-walker, is booked at the police sta-

tion. He or she puts in a phone call to a certain designated unofficial party. Thereupon one of a half-dozen bail-bond brokers gets a call, and within minutes a runner for the bonds-man appears at the police station and puts up surety for the prisoner.

Among bailers-out utilized by the organization are James H. Conroy, Isaac P. Jones, William P. Ryan, and Leonard, Louis, Max and Meyer Weinstein.

The legal fee for a $500 bail bond in the District is $75. The foregoing bondsmen charge the combine only $37.50, half-price, for springing a protected person. The rules regard-ing their surety are sketchy. They may register a $25,000 piece of property, then lay a hundred or a thousand $25,000 bonds against it.

On release, the defendant may visit the law offices of Ford, on 5th Street, where he is interviewed by Ford or his asso-ciate, Clifford Allder since the resignation of James K. Hughes. But sometimes the defendant does not speak to his counsel until the case is actually called in court, when his lawyer—Ford or an associate—whom he has never seen before, stands up for him at arraignment. If the defendant has no previous convictions, Ford's office often pleads him guilty; whereupon the judge imposes a fine of usually not more than $25. We have proof that the fines for many of these defendants are paid on the spot from the lawyer's pocket.

The system is keenly organized. Not one in a hundred peo-ple arrested pays his own bail-bond fee or knows who contacted the bondsman or paid him. Records of the bondsmen are kept so cryptically that in the rare instances when they are queried under oath they can say all they remember is they got a call from someone who only gave his first name, to put up bail, and they have no record to show who paid them. The rules are being changed. They must obtain a full name—but not for public record. And they won't ask for birth certificates, either.

The Ford office has been able to pass the buck between its members. They cannot remember who retained them, who paid the retainer, or who put up the money to pay the fines, if "they actually did it," which they "doubt."

Ford successfully defied a Congressional committee which tried to make him divulge the names of his clients, though he

admitted Emmitt Warring was one. The others, he said, were
known to the public only as respectable businessmen. They
were "more powerful" than Warring or even the late Jimmy
La Fontaine, who were only peanut-peddlers compared to
them, he said.

When pressed, Ford remembered a man by the name of
Bettis whom he represented; and Earl MacDonald and Attilio
Acalotti. He said he thought he had represented another defendant, named "Washington—I think it was George Washington, and that's all I can remember now."

Ford's business is not confined to the gambling and hustling
fraternity. You see his name bob up in court on almost every
kind of criminal case. One of his recent ones was the arrest
of two men on charges of violating the alcohol tax laws.

"Did you have a warrant?" Ford thundered at the ATU
agent. When he conceded he had not, Ford asked, "How did
you know this is alcohol? Don't you know it is illegal to
arrest people without a warrant?" "I smelled the alcohol,"
declared Agent Sweeney. "I've been in this business for 17
years and I've developed a keen sense of smell—especially for
alcohol."

Ford's clients were accused of unloading a truck with 127
gallons of moonshine whiskey.

Ford's office has practically a monopoly on the setting up
of and organizing after-hour bottle-clubs. He is generally given
credit by the local legal fraternity for being the genius who
figured out the way to sidestep the 2 o'clock closing ordinance.
His associate is defending the confessed killer in the recent
Hideaway shooting; Ford himself secured the Hideaway's after-
hours charter.

Ford's operations are not confined to the District, but lap
over into nearby Maryland, where, as trustee for the multi-
million-dollar estate of gambler La Fontaine, he finds plenty
of activity. Many of the gamblers and other shady citizens
whom he represents operate across state lines. The bounda-
ries often come to the aid of his clients. For many offenses,
especially most of those before the District Municipal Court,
there is no method whereby authorities can extradite defendants from Maryland or Virginia, and vice versa. It is very
much as if a law-breaker could take refuge in Brooklyn when
wanted in Manhattan, both boroughs of New York City. There

is no more physical difference between Prince Georges, Maryland, and the District than that.

This all-service Ford is chairman of the Criminal Law Committee of the District Bar Association.

Another lawyer who frequently appears in court for arrested hustlers is Ed Buckley.

Fifth Street, between Indiana and D, is called "The Fifth Street Lawyers' Association," because so many bondsmen, shysters and good lawyers have offices there.

We asked a friend to name the real sure shot mouthpiece who could spring you if you were arrested for murder and knew you were guilty.

He said William Leahy was the best trial lawyer in town and one of the most respected. James Laughlin, who himself was once arrested but not prosecuted after a reversal, is another successful practitioner.

Others who do considerable criminal defense work are Denny Hughes, Saul Lichtenberg and Myron Ehrlich.

Another interesting criminal lawyer is Robert I. Miller, who shot and killed a St. Elizabeth's Hospital psychiatrist whom he suspected of playing with Mrs. Miller. The shooting took place at about noon one day, in the heart of the shopping section at 11th and G Streets. He was represented by H. Mason Welch, who sob-storied the jury into an acquittal on the "unwritten law."

Miller is not the smartest lawyer in town, but he does a tremendous business defending Negroes and other superstitious criminals who engage him sometimes just to sit at the trial table for good luck, because he beat his own case. Miller, an ostentatious person, often wipes his glasses with a $100 bill while addressing a jury. He claimed close friendship to Roosevelt and Garner and decorates his office with photos of them. He ran a Republicans-for-Roosevelt club.

Some lawyers win their cases through merit, others through a fix. Still others, who weren't envied by their colleagues, had to do it the hard way when a certain former bachelor-lady judge, who shall be nameless, rendered her verdicts in favor of clients of the mouthpieces whose persuasion grew between covers not on law books. She was an awful tomato, and many attorneys preferred to lose their cases.

Judge Hitz, the humorist of the local bench, got off a dilly when he discovered the plaintiff in a matrimonial action was still living with her husband, the whole divorce proceedings being a sham to swindle creditors. Said the judge, in dismissing the action, "You can't litigate by day and fornicate by night."

31. THE BOSSES

THE LAST orthodox political boss of Washington was Alexander Robey Shepherd. When he finished with the city treasury, Congress voted to end home rule and took back the government.

From the time of its incorporation as a city, in 1802, Washington was run by elected mayors and aldermen. In 1871, in President Grant's administration, it was turned into a territory, similar to Alaska or Hawaii, with delegates in Congress and a large measure of home rule. Shepherd was a pal of General Grant, who had numerous smelly friends.

Shepherd's stewardship was modern in every respect. He went in for a New Deal on a big scale. The town was torn up while Shepherd paved streets, installed sewers—sometimes two sets to one avenue—went in for slum clearance, built squares, parks, circles, gas-mains and sidewalks. Shepherd began life as a plumber, and showed partiality for anything with pipes.

Shepherd had built up a small Tammany to keep his boys in power. Votes were bartered, crimes were fixed, laws were perverted. When the end came, Shepherd skipped and hid out until the statute of limitations ran out. When he returned they greeted him with a brass band, like New York did Jimmy Walker, and built him a statue.

The Congress was more interested in the welfare of the District of Columbia 75 years ago than it is now. Unable to stomach the stench, it decided to exercise its Constitutional right to govern the District, and substituted the present commission-form of government in place of home rule and local suffrage.

Under the present setup, the executive is a three-man commission, appointed by the President for a three-year term. One must be from the Corps of Engineers of the Army. On the law

books, these commissioners have no more power than a New
York City Borough President. They can do practically nothing
without approval from Congress. But by virtue of the apathy
that prevails in Washington, these men have become little
czars. Congress, by statute, has empowered the commissioners
to make building and plumbing regulations and to create and
enforce all reasonable police and other city rules. But they
do not levy taxes or make appropriations. That is done by
Congress. And that's the District's chief squawk.

Every buck collected in Washington goes into the general
funds of the U.S. Treasury; not earmarked for the District.
All payments come out of the same general fund. The result
is that, while Congress pays up to ten percent of the cost of
local government, the citizens bear the other 90 percent. But
52 percent of all the property is tax-exempt. The government
owns more than 40 percent, the rest belongs to embassies, tax-
free organizations like the Red Cross, etc. So the residents
complain that the rich U.S. government is riding along on a
free pass, leaving local property to bear the cost of supporting
the huge Federal establishment.

The present commissioners are John Russell Young, president of the Board; Guy Mason, and Brigadier General Gordon
R. Young, the engineer commissioner. Mason's term expired
in February, 1951, but he was permitted to serve until Donohue's confirmation.

Under them, the commissioners have a large staff of special
assistants, private secretaries, administrative assistants and
others who have access to their offices. We are just telling you
this in case you are thinking of making a fix, for one of these
persons is the guy to see.

One of the three commissioners is noted for his ability to
bollix everything up after a big, bad night—which is almost
every night. Even his enemies consider inebriation a valid ex-
cuse for his befuddled condition. A Congressman investigating the Commission said, "After all, the poor guy always has
a hangover. You can't blame him for what he does when he
feels awful."

Under the commissioners are such usual municipal executive
officers as assessors, auditors, tax collectors, license commissioners and bureaus of public welfare, recreation, traffic, police,
fire, health, corrections; and—oh, yes—the corporation counsel.

The observer who takes a gander at the judicial branch of

the District government sometimes wonders if he followed Lewis Carroll's Alice down into the rabbit hole.

The judicial powers are exercised by the District courts, which sit not only for federal cases, but for felonious breaches of the local law, too, and by municipal courts, judges of which are appointed for six years. They have jurisdiction over minor suits and unimportant law and ordinance violations.

Members of the federal judiciary for the District of Columbia need not be local residents. They may be appointed from anywhere in the country. Usually these plums go to deserving Democrats from elsewhere. At this writing there are 15 District judges and 13 municipal court judges, in addition to justices of the United States Court of Appeals for the District of Columbia, the Municipal Court of Appeals, and the Juvenile Court.

The District courts serve a two-fold function. They act both as federal courts and as superior state courts, handling civil and criminal matters. No judges of either court are elected by the local citizens or by their representatives. They have no interest in the community. They do not partake of a legacy of local common law and custom.

If any courts should be impartial, those of the District might be. But they are not. Some of the judges are venal, inefficient party hacks or militant propagandists for left-wing philosophies.

The U.S. Attorney for the District of Columbia has the most overworked office in the land. He not only functions as a local district attorney and as United States attorney, but triples in brass with a job corresponding to a state attorney general. But his budget and the number of assistants allotted him are on a per capita population basis, as though he had to prosecute only federal cases in any city the size of Washington.

In the prosecution of some minor cases in municipal court alone has he any assistance. The city Corporation Counsel's office handles those. To demonstrate again what can happen when a bureaucracy turns dictator—the criminal division of his office has no law library. It does not have a secretary.

If he or his assistants want to check a law or a decision they have to buy their own books. He is given no fund to keep records, so no records are kept. It is almost impossible for him to find out the disposition of cases. He has only five low-paid assistants assigned to municipal criminal courts, and these are so overworked, sometimes they have to prosecute cases on an average of one every three minutes. Under District law, defendants are permitted jury trials in all cases where the penalty is in excess of ninety days or a $300 fine. It is no wonder the Corporation Counsel is usually willing to take a plea of disorderly conduct, instead. The maximum penalty for that is $25, no jail.

Persons accused of serious crimes under federal law must be booked immediately before a United States Commissioner, as all crimes in the District, even those like assault, robbery, drunken driving, gambling, homicide, and rape, which elsewhere belong exclusively to the state, are federal matters here.

We gave you a rough idea of the volume of such criminal activities in the District. If those defendants had been arrested for the same offenses in states, they would be booked before a magistrate, a police court or a justice of the peace. There are none such in Washington other than the judges. The chief committing magistrate is the United States Commissioner, and he has no assistants. He not only performs the federal duties that U.S. Commissioners in other towns assume, but he also acts as a committing magistrate on all local felony charges in the District.

A U.S. Commissioner is not a judge. He is chosen by the local Federal bench. He serves without salary on a fee basis, but is limited by statute to a maximum of $9,400 a year, out of which he is required to pay office rent and stenographic expenses. The law permits a U.S. Commissioner to practice law on the side, and many in other jurisdictions do, but, because the D.C. office is the busiest in the country, he has no time to handle outside cases. The Commissioner is on duty 24 hours a day. There is no night court. He is it. Police awaken him at any hour of the night when they make important arrests or require warrants, and he is busy at hearings, setting bail, and presiding at arraignments all day.

When you get into the U.S. Attorney's office you really see how things are loused up here. The rich Federal government apparently has dough to toss away everywhere else, but not in its own home. Of course, there are no faithful voters to be placated here. District Attorney Fay has only 34 men on his staff; his office is required to do more work than the entire Second Judicial Circuit, which includes the entire states of Vermont, Connecticut and the four districts of New York. His budget is so limited, most of his assistants receive only about $4,000 a year, and so the turnover is terrific; young men just out of law school go to work for him for a couple of years, then go out to make a living.

His office is so understaffed, there are not enough employes around to handle all complaints. It is possible to walk in and rifle the files at will. Many shyster lawyers often do that, killing the cases against their clients.

With such a small, unseasoned staff, it is no wonder the complaint desk in the U.S. Attorney's office has been compared to "a bargain grocery counter." It looks very much like one. It's a long wooden shelf behind which a deputy district attorney stands and does business with plaintiffs, defendants, cops and lawyers across it. We noted that police may not enter their own complaints. They must bring them to the complaint bureau of the U.S. Attorney, before the hearing in court. It is then up to the U.S. Attorney's office alone to determine whether the complaint will be made.

What happens is that, every day, thousands of people mill around in this complaint room. An onlooker can't tell who are cops, lawyers or prisoners. When the arresting officer speaks to the deputy D.A., he does so in this cut-rate counter atmosphere, before the defendant and his lawyer. There is no privacy. The cop has to spill his case to the opposition. The defense lawyer then sets up an argument for dropping the case or reducing the charge. The officials are so harassed, they try to dispense with as much work as possible, which accounts for a hefty proportion of pinches that never get past this bureau.

Sometimes a youngster just out of law school is the "grocery clerk." He makes such grave rulings as deciding not to prosecute a homicide charge. These law clerks arrogate to themselves the rights and prerogatives of the courts. When the D.A. decides to go before the grand jury, he usually asks for an indictment for only one offense, even if the accused has been charged with twenty. Elsewhere the custom is to indict on each count and try on one or two, leaving the others hanging over the defendant. That does not happen in Washington. After a prisoner is discharged and commits a crime in some other jurisdiction there is no record for probation officers there of other outstanding charges against him. That's another reason why the professionals like to practice their trades in Washington.

There's another booby-trap for the law. The prosecuting and corrective branches of the government don't take the cops into their confidence when a prisoner is paroled. Elsewhere the police are notified when a parolee is back on the streets, so they can keep an eye on him. In Washington this is considered an invasion of the convict's Constitutional rights.

If the defendant cannot make a deal before the complaint bureau, his lawyer is entitled on demand to get possession of the file on his case. The place is so understaffed, with not enough stenographers, that the only notes in these files are brief pencilled memoranda jotted down by the Deputy District Attorney. There is never a complete record. It is simple for defense lawyers to sneak some of the notes out of a file; they'll never be missed, because no carbon copies are made. The overworked deputies can seldom remember what they wrote.

When the trial is scheduled, the deputy prosecutor seldom has an opportunity to read the files, even if there were complete data. Felony cases are often ground out in District Court at the rate of one an hour, including time out for picking juries. When a U.S. Attorney finishes with one case, the clerk hands him a folder on the next. That is the first time he ever saw it. Add to this the fact that the prosecutors do not work with the police in preparing a case, and you can see what "confusion twice confounded" means.

One of the most unusual features in the setup of the District government is the office of the Coroner. Until recently, this functionary, who need not be a physician, had no laboratory. What he has now is incomplete. He has no medical examiner and only a few low-paid researchers.

But he has a swell job, with a ten-year tenure and a courtroom better than the U.S. Commissioner's. The present Coroner has virtually set himself up as a judge, with no authority in law, and is said by his critics to work with a gavel instead of a scalpel. He is one of the town's most powerful functionaries.

Among the many strange quirks of local law is one which requires the Coroner at times to serve as a constable and to make levies. When the Coroner acts as a coroner, he holds court like a judge. And he thinks he is one, too. He has frequently discharged from custody persons accused of homicide, who had been held without bail by a U.S. Commissioner. He often sets bail and discharges defendants on bail, though there are no statutes authorizing such procedure, and he has so admitted under oath.

There have been instances when the Coroner has ruled a death was justifiable homicide and released the prisoner. Though this is no bar to subsequent indictment, prisoners often flee the jurisdiction before the prosecuting attorney knows what has happened. The law does not permit the Coroner to discharge any person.

Coroner's juries are impaneled by that official to meet his own preconceived ideas and prejudices. There is no requirement that a coroner's juror must even be able to read or write. The salary is $7 a day, and the Coroner has his favorites. Some men served as many as 31 times last year.

The Coroner frequently discharges the accused prisoners on grounds of justifiable homicide, despite evidence that they had committed other crimes at the same time, such as carrying concealed weapons or selling narcotics. The Coroner then shrugs his shoulders and says those things are none of his business.

There have been known instances of jury fixing. Through the proper channels, a charge of a death caused by reckless driving has been reduced to an innocuous misdemeanor or dismissed completely. One of the Coroner's deputies was a notorious abortionist who performed the autopsies on his own victims.

Too bad Boss Shepherd isn't around today. He could appreciate what the backroom boys have done to the District government.

32. MONARCHS OF THE METROPOLIS

*S*INCE wood-cuts added to the native press the element of pictorial illustration, cartoonists have caricatured the American alderman. His heavy foot is on the bottom rung of the legislative ladder. The "gray wolves" of Chicago were known around the globe for venality, degradation and cold-blooded chicanery. The Tammany members of the board, the San Francisco, Kansas City, Philadelphia, New Orleans, Boston, Albany and St. Louis "city fathers" were in their most nefarious days gangsters, brothel-keepers and police court shysters, overlaid with a refined sprinkling of saloon-keepers.

That mixture does not reflect the complexion of our Congress. But when, twice a month, they sit as the Board of Aldermen of the city of Washington, they are about as dignified and statesmanlike as the city council of Peoria.

The Constitution says, "The Congress shall have power to exercise exclusive legislation over such District."

The actual detail of city government is delegated on the committee system and for all practical purposes the rulers of everything within the Columbia confines are 13 Senators and 25 Representatives on the District committees. In an extremity they can be overruled by their chambers and the President could veto any of their acts, but no one remembers when such a thing happened.

There is a certain local prestige about being a D.C. committeeman. He probably could with impunity drive through a red light or spit on the sidewalk, or even jaywalk, which no unprivileged person this side of an ambassador may dare without at least a stiff bawling out. But the members of Congress assigned to weighty national and world problems shun the task of managing the municipality.

Of the 38 who are completely responsible for every law, appropriation and tax measure in this city of almost a million, only two in the 81st Congress came from communities as large as or larger. They were Congressmen Arthur G. Klein, of New York City, and John F. Kennedy, of Boston. Only three others in the last Congress came from cities with a population in excess of 100,000—Senator Estes Kefauver, of Chattanooga, Tenn., 130,000; Senator Harry Darby, of Kansas City, Kans., 130,000; and Congressman John J. Allan, of Oakland, Calif., 380,000. Darby is not in the 82nd Congress.

In other words, 33 of the 38 Senators and Representatives who ruled this metropolis in the 81st Congress were from farms, villages, and rural towns, that include Fairmont, W. Va.; Lander, Wyo.; Bristol, R.I.; Middleboro, Del.; Madison, S.D.; Skowhegan, Maine; Burley, Ida.; Florence, S.C.; Okolona, Miss.; College Station, Tex.; Scottsboro, Ala.; Stone Mountain, Ga.; Cedar City, Utah; Hammond, La.; Kennett, Mo.; Carrollton, Ill.; Frostburg, Md.; Glencoe, Minn.; Decorah, Ia.; Rosemont, Pa.; and Farrell, Pa. Even those who were sincere did not and could not understand the problems of a giant city.

In the current Congress there are a few more city slickers on the committee: Senators Butler, of Baltimore; Bennet of Salt Lake, and Pastore of Providence.

From time to time, about once every ten years, Congress gets appalled at its own reflection and decides to investigate its own municipal creation. After such probes a few anemic recommendations are submitted to the Congress, a few minor corrective bills are passed. Then the speakeasies and gambling houses reopen, the dope peddlers and murderers come out again, and once more life goes on, as Washington life goes.

The last time Congress got in a mood of righteous self-examination was in 1950, when a sub-committee of five was appointed by the House District of Columbia Committee to investigate crime and law-enforcement in the capital. The sub-committee chairman was James C. Davis, of Georgia, a sober and sincere lawyer with a distinguished record as a crusading superior court judge and member of Congress. The Congress originally voted the handsome sum of $10,000 to this committee, with which it was expected to dig up the dirt on a billion-dollar-a-year vice establishment.

Davis determined not to get a political hack as counsel. If he had not chosen a dynamic attorney, this committee would have been as innocuous as most others. As it was, it uncovered plenty that should have rocked the nation and shocked the Congress. It was no fault of Davis or Hyman I. Fischbach, committee counsel, that it did not. But Congress, as expected, ignored the report and skipped the record. Davis and Fischbach came up with suggestions—some far-reaching—for a reorganization of the District police, court system and method of prosecution. But to guarantee that nothing would be done about it the Democratic leadership put road-blocks in the Committee's path. Nevertheless it is now before the Congress. It will go the same route others have, or establish a precedent.

Fischbach, with many years' experience conducting such investigations for other Congressional committees, turned out what a committee counsel should be—in happy contrast to the sad picture of the Kefauver group which was operating at the same time. No one could see him getting far with his beggarly budget. It hardly allowed for an office staff, let alone investigators. But Fischbach hired John Woog, a 27-year-old war veteran and member of the New York bar, as chief investigator and practically the whole staff. Working 18 to 20 hours a day they uncovered enough rottenness, funny business and stupidity to fill more than 1200 closely printed pages of terrifying testimony.

When Fischbach started stepping on some sacred toes the ceiling fell in. Rumors were whispered around the House Office Building that Fischbach would be canned. Plenty of Congressmen were a-tremble; Fischbach was getting too hot. One who tried to throw a barrier in his way was Representative Wayne L. Hays, a Democrat from Ohio, whose Congressional district includes tributary territory dominated by the Akron and Youngstown mob which is ruled by Frank and Tony Milano, cited before the Kefauver Committee as organizers of the infamous Mayfield Road gang, Ohio branch of the Mafia. Hays tried to hold up money for the committee unless Fischbach were fired. He was joined by Mrs. Mary Norton, who retired at the end of the 81st Congress, and who represented Hudson County, New Jersey, and was sent to Washington by the notorious Boss Hague. She did not stand for reelection after Hague was run out of Jersey politics.

Another who opposed Fischbach was Edna Flannery Kelly, of Brooklyn, who was chosen by the Democratic leadership to spearhead the campaign. Mrs. Kelly, who serves by grace of Irwin Steingut, minority leader of the New York State Assembly, has been an errand girl for the Brooklyn bosses ever since her election to Congress.

Mrs. Kelly's reluctance to expose crime in the District may be understandable to New Yorkers who know that among her constituents are some of the most evil gangsters who ever slit a throat or lived off the proceeds of a prostitute.

These three button-holed other Democratic Congressmen and said they were opposed to Fischbach because, as a New Yorker, he should have been cleared through the New York County Democratic Committee. That Committee's other name is Tammany Hall. To Davis the mere mention of Tammany Hall is like defaming the Stars and Bars. Lack of Tammany endorsement was the highest recommendation. On such little things is history made.

It still remains for the Congress to follow the Davis recommendations. Meanwhile, all the law-breakers who hid while he was probing slid back into business as soon as the "probe" was over.

Few solons really want home rule, not even Northern New

Deal Congressmen who scream for it because the Negro press does.

Most of the members shirk the committee meetings, because while membership gives them great prestige locally, it means nothing nationally or to their constituents. The District Committee is a "minor" one, and membership on it does not count against the legislator's allowed minimum of committee appointments.

Few remain on it for long, and assignment to it is, in a manner, in the way of punishment. First-timers, especially in the Senate, are hazed that way.

A typical majority member of the House District Committee is Representative Arthur G. Klein, of New York City's 19th district. We give him to you not because he is the most active or prominent, but because he is closest to our home. His district begins a block away.

Klein, an exasperating and annoying pleader for left-wing causes, has been on the public payroll for 16 of his 46 years, the first six spent on the legal staff of the S.E.C. He has been in Congress since 1941.

Klein's district, which runs between the Bowery and the East River, below 40th St., contains not only the worst slums in New York, but some of the newest and finest housing developments, as well as large hunks of the city's financial district. He promoted the former for his constituents at the expense of the latter.

Also in it is Manhattan's downtown Mafia stronghold—parts of Little Italy—whose voters sent him to Congress and demand favors in return.

Operating in his district is New York's most evil and notorious fairy-haunt, the disgusting 181 Club, at that address on Second Ave., where every cabaret law and ordinance on the books is fractured nightly. This profitable venture is overseen by Alan Bono, a cousin of Joe Adonis, and a contributor to Klein's campaign funds.

Former Congresswoman Norton served 10 of her 26 years in Washington on the District Committee. She had strong backing for the appointment as District Commissioner but was nosed out.

Even when not a member of the committee, Mrs. Norton always had a soft spot in her heart for it, and frequently interested herself in District affairs, being given a respectful hearing because of "the woman's angle."

But Mrs. Norton was and is and always has been a creature of Boss Hague, one of the most corrupt and thievingest municipal overlords in the world. At this moment the Hudson County grand jury is working overtime grinding out indictments against ex-officials appointed by him.

Many Hague specialties were exported to Washington during her tenure as mayor ex officio, among them a high tax-rate, municipal corruption and official protection for gamblers.

Mrs. Norton's home town, Jersey City, was, until last year, the national clearing house for the laying off of horse bets from all over the country.

While she was in Congress, Hague was the absentee chief magistrate of Washington.

33. WIRE-TAPPERS, SNOOPS AND SPIES

AFTER you've exchanged conversation with a number of Washingtonians, you wonder what made them decidedly different from others. Then it dawns on you. They are whisperers.

They all seem consciously afraid that they may be overheard. That marks them even in casual conversations, and when they utter secrets they are theatrically overcautious. These are acquired habits, not without foundation. All mankind has a common weakness for spreading gossip. Most people can retail only minutiae. But in Washington, matters that may rock the world are entrusted, or pass through the hands of, those who otherwise would have little to tell beyond back-fence piddle. Furthermore, for one to say his wires are tapped is a mark of self importance.

The capital is overrun by snoops and spies, not only using every cloak-and-dagger device for foreign transmission, but assigned and trained to catch and report inter-bureau information, rumors included.

An observation at a dinner table by a member of Congress

or an executive may cause an uproar in Moscow, London or Calcutta. Or it may bring a midnight huddle in a cabinet department or the President's sound-proofed den.

You meet almost no one of any importance who converses at ease. The thinnest statement or flattest opinion can be amplified and multiplied. If it escapes an official listening post, it may reach a columnist, which is worse.

There has been considerable furor on the subject of Washington wire-tapping.

That is a topic which every seasoned editor has learned to recognize as having extraordinary human interest appeal. The phone is such a common, yet tricky instrument, that kitchen-maids who have affairs with delivery boys shiver with horrible fears that their big secrets are being tapped. And this is not confined to small people. In Washington such suspicions are justified.

Many mentally connect wire-tapping with the F.B.I. The two have been joined in recurrent publicity. Deliberate left-wing propaganda has exaggerated and exploited the notion. The F.B.I. uses this method, as does any other efficient police force. But emphasis thereon is disproportionate. The practice is widespread with only a modicum of use in criminal investigation. The F.B.I. itself makes a daily check against cut-ins on its own wires, including J. Edgar Hoover's own private lines. He and his bureau are Enemy No. 1 to the Reds and all their sycophants and sympathizers, the only man in the country who called the shots on the Communist situation since the beginning. And as the eyes and ears of the Department of Justice, the G-men handle dynamite affecting interests from car thieves to disloyal U.S. employes to chairmen of the boards of trusts.

Tapping F.B.I. wires is not a profitable career. The bureau knows all the tricks. New electronic developments now make it possible to intrude on some communications without physical contact with the wire. No instruments can detect such espionage. This is a hazard beyond mechanical defense.

We said everyone in Washington lives in constant fear and dread of being overheard, even if the subject matter is of importance to no one. It becomes habit. Congressmen and officials are cagey when they talk on the phone, though after a few minutes of cryptic conversation they forget and loosen up. When you visit the average office holder in his sanctum he steers you away from the walls, then speaks in an undertone.

In your hotel room his eyes wander around the walls, searching for "bugs" which can pick up and record every sound.

Wiretapping is a merry indoor sport in Washington, engaged in by dozens of agencies—public and private.

When the White House wants to know what's going on it employs Secret Service experts. They ferret out information about the President's political enemies, inside and outside the government. It is filed away for future reference to be used for retaliation or guidance. Some Democratic Senators and Congressmen use Congressional committee wiretappers. Investigators get the dope on political enemies in Washington and back home. Administration leaders tried desperately to "get" Senator McCarthy and no method was beneath them. Minority party members, deprived of the services of official wiretappers, hire private detective agencies. Kefauver complained his committee's wires were being tapped.

Many cabinet officers and other high officials usually have their own intelligence services for spying on associates, the opposition, Hoover, and even on the President himself.

Foremost among these administrative intelligence sections are those of the Department of State, Treasury, Defense, and the Post Office, with its sureshot inspectors.

Oscar Chapman, Secretary of the Interior, has a fine intelligence, headed by Mike Reilly, former chief of the White House Secret Service.

The political cross currents are such that at any time five or six sets of wire-tappers, each unaware of what the other is doing, may be listening in on a subject's wires; while the subject may have his own dicks listening in on the principals whose agents are cutting in on his conversation.

Like lobbying, wiretapping is an insidious system used by everyone, acknowledged by no one, so Congress shrinks from delving deeply into it.

Communists recently forced the issue into the open, as they did with lobbying, both of which they use extravagantly. The Senate came up with a weak-kneed investigation of wiretapping. Senator Claude "Red" Pepper, of Florida, already a lame duck, was appointed to head the committee. Pepper tried to slant the hearings to make it appear the only wiretappers in Washington were Republican leaders. He named Senator Owen Brewster of Maine as the goat. About all the investigation brought out was that the Metropolitan Police Force is a chief offender.

Police Lieutenant Joseph W. Shimon, the cops' expert, admitted he did some outside work on these lines for private clients and for Congressional committees. Senator Brewster said he paid Shimon's expenses to investigate a man who, Brewster thought, was "shadowing" him. It turned out also that Shimon was paid to tap Howard Hughes' wires when that eccentric nabob was probed in connection with his wartime airplane contracts.

After the Senate committee spent a lot of time and money investigating wiretapping, its counsel, Gerhard Van Arkel, who also wants to be District Commissioner, made a brilliant discovery. He said the group already had proved its chief point, namely, "There is a good deal of wiretapping going on in Washington and it is difficult to act against the practice under present law."

Foreign government operatives compile volumes on the words of our officials, as well as from embassies and snoopers of other foreign countries. Wiretappers do not expect to garner much direct information, but they winnow a thousand talks for one bit that will compromise the object of the tap and make him vulnerable to power pressure.

Lobbyists and labor unions get the goods on people they need. And government wiretappers often listen in on them.

Add to all this private intrigue, suspicious husbands and wives, and you have an industry.

Because Washington is federal property, its telephone setup is governed by the Federal Communications Commission. FCC rules forbid unauthorized listening in on phone calls. U.S. law makes it a crime to divulge such information. Evidence secured by wiretapping may not be used in federal courts. Supreme Court Justice Holmes decreed it "a dirty business." The strict rules hamper legitimate law enforcement officers, but do not hinder those snooping secrets for blackmail or political pressure.

In many other states, New York especially, any evidence, obtained legally or illegally, is admissible in court, though the detective who breaks the law to land it may be prosecuted, but never is. He's decorated, instead.

New York law is liberal in extending the right to local peace officers to tap wires by judicial sanction, ex parte, for specific inquiries, never refused. Federal agents working on cases in New York and other such states usually tie up with local cops and prosecute in local courts, because the Feds are restrained in their own. In the District there is no local law, so the authorities are handcuffed.

Wiretapping is rarely used to procure actual evidence. Judges and juries don't like it. But eavesdropping alerts officers and then they go after collateral evidence and don't reveal where the tipoff originated.

Instead of developing more stringent legislation which is what the Communists, who break every law, want, the radical-sponsored Pepper investigation failed so miserably that many Congressmen agreed the government should have more power to protect itself by means of wiretapping. The Department of Justice is sponsoring a bill to permit, under some circumstances, the use of evidence in court so obtained; to be accepted after a Federal Judge issues an order on application of government intelligence agencies, and to sanction such agencies to engage in wiretapping directly, not for court evidence, subject to approval by the Attorney General.

Many sober observers feel that to forbid the F.B.I. any reasonable means for counteracting treason and espionage is childish prudery, and that its bitter opponents are not in good faith.

You hear a lot from pinks and phony progressives that the nation's capital is a police state where no man is free to utter his thoughts. But most of the spying is done not for legitimate government sources, but is privately sponsored by politicians, office-holders or subversive and inimical interests. Washington is no OGPU camp. Most of the work done in the headquarters of federal investigative agencies is administrative. They decentralize their field work. The Washington offices of the Federal Bureau of Narcotics, the Alcoholic Tax Unit and several others are branches of the Baltimore division and report to the superintendent there.

The Washington field office of the F.B.I. is as remote and as independent from the director as, for instance, the ones in New York, Chicago and Los Angeles, and like them is run by an agent-in-charge, through regular channels like out-of-town offices, via Clyde A. Tolson, the skillful associate director, and brainy assistant directors Mickey Ladd, Hugh Clegg, Lou Nichols, Dick Glavin, Rolf Harbo, Al Rosen and Stan Tracy before Hoover handles any matter.

The agent-in-charge of the Washington field office has as much authority and autonomy and is as locally independent as Ed Scheidt and his assistant, Bill Whelan, in New York; George McSwain in Chicago, and Dick Hood in L.A., all solid and seasoned chiefs of ability, integrity and patriotism.

The same lefties who are moaning about Washington being a police state recently tried to slip a fast one over, to make it so, and at the expense of embarrassing and possibly destroying the F.B.I.

When the House Committee Investigating Crime and Law Enforcement in the District was drawing up its report, certain sources tried to sneak a sleeper into it, recommending that the F.B.I. be given final responsibility for policing the city of Washington.

We have determined that the suggestion was made to subcommittee Chairman Davis by District Attorney Fay who said he concurred in it with Peyton Ford, an Assistant Attorney General, with a long record of sympathy for "progressive" causes. Informed observers wonder if Ford, who helped whitewash Amerasia, was acting for higher-ups out to "get" J. Edgar Hoover.

The plan was to slip this through into legislation. That would mean the end of the F.B.I. as we know it. It would then become a city police force. Its organization would be disrupted, as was the Treasury during Prohibition. It would have to take on thousands of new agents, waste time with drunks, whores, policy-slip peddlers and punks, and meanwhile it would have to take the odium for the conditions portrayed in this book, which go deeper than mere failure of police.

In recent years it has become the fashion in the movie industry to produce whodunit pictures about detective agencies of the Federal government. The Hollywood geniuses think they have covered all but they missed plenty.

(Note: In all cases their duties are regulated and catalogued by statute. None, including the F.B.I., is a genuine and general secret police force—such as Scotland Yard.

Generally speaking, their powers and duties are in one of four categories.

The Federal Bureau of Investigation "investigates."

The Postal Inspectors "inspect."

The Treasury Agents "enforce."

The Secret Service "protects"—the President and the currency.)

The Narcotics Bureau is covered elsewhere in some detail; but this is as good a place as any to assure you that Federal cops are human beings, not machines assembled to turn out convictions. A principal function of the Narcotics Bureau is to combat the dope evil, not to imprison its victims. This was demonstrated when a famed Hollywood movie star went on the junk. The Bureau, in checking prescriptions, found she was in the hands of a quack who was ruining her life. Commissioner Anslinger made a trip to Hollywood to plead with the head of her studio to give her a year off, so she could go to a sanitarium for a cure. She had two pictures in the works and the studio factotum demurred. He mentioned her contract, said the company had millions invested in the films. He "couldn't possibly see my way clear."

Anslinger warned him she would collapse and the company would lose an asset worth even more. The young woman was being kept alive during the day on benzedrine. Afternoons the doctor tapered her off on secanol. After work she was dosed with morphine. The inevitable eventuated. She blew up completely, tried suicide, was hospitalized and suspended. Then the government stepped in and gave her the cure. Now she is dehabituated and rehabilitated.

The Intelligence Unit uncovered the huge tax fraud that sent Henry Lustig, former owner of New York's Longchamps Restaurant chain, to the pen. Many stories are told on how the prosecution began, including the apocryphal one that Henry Morgenthau, then Secretary of the Treasury, was forced to stand in line and wait for a table in a Miami cafe when Lustig was ushered in ahead of him; Morgenthau asked who the man was, exploded and ordered the Feds to get him.

But the real story is this: The New York hideaway office of the unit is at 253 Broadway. There's a Longchamps Restaurant in the basement. Federal agents don't earn enough to afford its fancy prices. They usually lunch in a counter-joint around the corner. But one day it rained. Some agents were tied up on a big case, didn't have time to wait, so they ducked down in the elevator.

Many Wall Street financiers lunch there regularly, have tables reserved and waiting. The only empty one had a "reserved" sign, but the Intelligence boys grabbed it over the protest of the hostess. When the millionaires arrived they had to wait. They fumed. Lustig was there. He shouted, "Why did you let those bums take that table?"

Service to the "bums" was cut off. They wondered whether the imperious Lustig's returns were clean, whether he wasn't the sort of individualist who would probably steal. They checked. He had sequestered $5,000,000 in unreported hat-check money.

When the Intelligence Unit, nicknamed "The U-Boats," sent Atlantic City boss Nocky Johnson to the can, they got him by counting the towels sent to the laundry by the local cat-houses. This established the intake of the madames, and their kick-backs upstairs.

The Intelligence Unit has been working on the hidden holdings of the Mafia for years. When evidence in hand is collated, 30 of the most important hoodlums will trade in their tailor-mades for prison denim. There's terrific pressure from higher-ups to stop the forthcoming prosecution. Only orders from the President or Attorney General will do it.

Sometimes Intelligence runs into amusing situations like the case of the rich Chinese and the blonde model. He was a wealthy importer, named Hsieh, in America on a diplomatic passport as the representative of the Bank of China. Nationalist Hsieh fell for Marion Saunders, a sensational slick chick with platinum hair, from Indiana. It became a terrific romance. Cafe socialites kidded that he bought her a new mink coat every day.

The Treasury heard about the dough he was lavishing on her. They looked him up, discovered that as a nonresident alien he was exempt from American income taxes. But Mr. Hsieh had forgotten gift taxes. Under the law the donor, not the recipient, is liable for payment—25 percent. The Feds tracked down gifts aggregating $1,000,000—the untraced value was far higher. Mr. Hsieh was soaked $540,000—tax plus fines. He was allowed to pay in three installments. He pulled out a roll of bills and peeled off 180 G-notes for the down payment.

Some months later, Hsieh and Marion were married. Gin-mill habitues said he married her to get his dough back. That couldn't be so, because one day, last year, the *Queen Mary* came in with $2,000,000 in gold consigned to him. It was landed under guard of six armed Chinese, toted off in steel-lined limousines.

Which reminds us of the story never told before, too good to keep.

One of the benches in Lafayette Square, gathering place of the faggots, across from the White House, is wired up. You ought to hear some of the gay conversations. We did. Then we squirted penicillin in our ears.

PART THREE

THE ESCAPE
(*Confidential!*)

34. THE TUESDAY-TO-THURSDAY SET

THE MOST itching urge in Washington is to get away from it. Few have the conventional home ties there which bind the average American to the hearth, or the radiator. Weekends are dismally dull and shop shuts up from Friday night until Monday morning, with few exceptions. Civil servants rate thirty-day vacations. The winters are sleazy and frosty. The summers are insufferable in that swampy, flat region which enjoys no ocean breezes.

Where to go? Anywhere. Those who can afford it scram to New York or Atlantic City. The next layer hightails it for Baltimore or Philadelphia. Some fly to far points. Eastern Congressmen and officials rarely bring their wives and families to Washington, an arrangement of mutual consent after the rookies have tried domestic life there for a few months of high anticipation and depressing disillusionment. Most Congressmen from east of the Ohio River don't wait for Friday. They are known as the "Tuesday-to-Thursday" set, because that's the point of departure and return. Frank Roosevelt, Jr. is its most consistent member.

The great hegira starts Thursday, when the Congressional Limited leaves, at 4 P.M. For the rest of the day and throughout the night every outgoing train and plane is packed and the stragglers fill them up on Fridays, too. For these trips and returns, hundreds of regular reservations stand during sessions.

Weekenders who have no fences to mend or wives to mollify or private practices to superintend hie to resorts in Virginia and the Carolinas. But the pet dreamland of escape for the hiatus is Atlantic City. During spring and summer the Pennsylvania Railroad runs a through Pullman car daily to and from there, via the Delaware River bridge. This is hooked onto or off the New York-Washington train at North Philadelphia, where there is a rush for the club car. The drawing-rooms house either poker games or shut-in shebas who long to smell the sea. Teetotal-voting, Bible-Belt solons stagger up and down the boardwalk with potted patooties on the arms that beat the righteous breasts in the hallowed chambers.

The politicians favor the Claridge in Atlantic City, but the Brighton, across the street, is rapidly becoming the gay spot, much patronized by those who go up for laughs. Those who want seclusion usually stay at the Ritz-Carlton, at the end of the boardwalk and off the beaten track. The Ritz was once owned by Enoch "Nocky" Johnson, former Atlantic City political boss, recently discharged from federal prison. Nocky is on parole now and not supposed to drink or go to public places or engage in politics, but he does and is still a power in the town and is called on by visiting Washington G.O.P. dignitaries.

Nocky was one of the few leaders with underworld tie-ups prosecuted during the Roosevelt administration. Of course, Johnson was a Republican, not a Democrat, and the orders went out from Boss Hague in Jersey City to get him.

Many Washingtonians seeking fun go to Philadelphia, of all places! Philly is a natural for married men who want to do a little cheating, because who would ever think of looking for them there? "Sleepy" old Philadelphia is not so sleepy. It is one of the hottest towns in the country, loaded with after-hour spots which offer fast floor shows and run later than anything in New York.

Philadelphia is Mafia-controlled, run by the same branch of the mob which owns South Jersey and its domestic wine industry, and Atlantic City. Many Philadelphia spots break the law brazenly and openly, protected by the Mafia.

But Philadelphia has one of the finest restaurants in the world, operated by one of America's best-known hosts. This is Jack Lynch's Zodiac Room in the Warburton Hotel. Lynch has more friends in show business and high politics than any other man alive. Many top actors break their trips from Washington or Baltimore to New York to stop overnight for an evening with Lynch.

Philadelphia is two hours from Washington on fast trains. Many show-starved Washingtonians, who don't have the time to get to Broadway to visit the legitimate theatre, find they can ride to Philadelphia, catch a show—there are usually four or five big-time productions playing—have a drink, and get back to Washington in time for bed. Washington wolves go to Philly to howl. Mention New York or Atlantic City and a bimbo knows that's a weekend and all that goes with it. But invite her to Philadelphia for an evening, then a few drinks after the show —and the last train has left. A lady can't sleep standing up.

Of course, New York remains the chief target for weekenders. Those on small budgets stay at one of the popular-priced West Side hotels, visit the usual tourist traps, occasionally see a Broadway show, and have a hell of a time without spending too much. Government clerks come away to New York for a weekend, a man and a woman, going Dutch. Groups of government girls save up for a trip to the big city. They go sightseeing and gawking, send home colored postal cards and eat box-lunches in Grant's Tomb.

Most good New York cafes will not serve unescorted women. So the best the typists and filers can do is wander around, oohing at the bright lights and dreaming up lies to tell when they get back.

The guys in the bigger jobs have a hell of a time when in New York. Embassy people come up regularly and are provided with introductions to top models by the State Department. Key Congressmen and high officials are brought up on junkets by lobbyists, entertained in the swank joints, and if they don't have their wives with them they can have the best. If wives are along, they are invited by the lobbyists to go shopping at places like Saks-Fifth Avenue, Bonwit Teller, Bergdorf Goodman and Hattie Carnegie, and charge anything they want on the lobbyist's accounts.

The favorite hangout of the New Deal set in New York is the Stork Club. The attorneys for the Stork Club are Goldwater and Flynn. The Flynn is Ed Flynn, New Deal Democratic boss, campaign manager of the late President Roosevelt. The Stork became a hangout for the left-wing and do-gooder crowd during the 1930's, when the late Supreme Court Justice Frank Murphy used to cut up on the dance-floor with cuties.

Harry Hopkins, the ex-Mills Hotel flopper, who addressed envelopes at a cent each, favored its rich menu—on the cuff.

Many of the important bleeding hearts, labor union leaders and spokesmen for the have-nots spent and still spend their time in New York in the Stork Club, where the have-nots they bleed for are rigorously barred by silken ropes.

Here such union bosses as the musicians' Petrillo, a pal of Truman's, and the truckmen's Tobin, a Roosevelt favorite, are served by a nonunion restaurant staff. Sherman Billingsley, the Stork's owner, had to cough up more than $100,000 for back salaries and unfair labor practices. But while he was fighting organized labor the chief union bosses, all the Roosevelt sons and half the cabinet frequented his place. They still do, though the restaurant unions still consider the Stork unfair. But Sherman's friends see the place is never picketed any more.

The diplomatic set, visiting nobility and royal guests of the State Department, and the older Washington dignitaries visit John Perona's El Morocco, the swankiest in New York. One may meet ambassadors, princes, a dispossessed king and some South American presidents in Morocco at one time. On these occasions there is more law scattered around the room than there are customers in most other clubs. A visiting potentate like a sultan or maharajah, in addition to rating a couple of Secret Service men, gets four New York detectives.

When the boys come up from Washington with nothing good on their minds they head for a retreat in a private house in the West Sixties, right off Central Park West. This place is run by a couple of sisters who used to operate a well-known night club. One of them is close to Joe Nunan, former Commissioner of Internal Revenue and intimate friend of Boss Ed Flynn. This place gets away with anything and has for years. It freely sells liquor at any hour without a license and without regard to closing ordinances.

The manager knows a lot of amiable dishes who hang around there. If there should happen to be none when a visiting padrone comes in, they soon get there. This spot is practically unknown to New Yorkers, few of whom, including newspapermen, ever heard of it. It is patronized almost solely by august Democrats from Washington.

Visiting New Dealers pour also into Toots Shor's restaurant, where they are almost as welcome as baseball players and prize fighters. The late Bob Hannegan, postmaster and Democratic

Committee Chairman, was a regular. Sometimes he brought an unknown Senator from his home state with him, Harry Truman, who liked the conviviality of the place and bent an elbow with the boys. When the Senator was Vice President, he stopped in and played the piano in the private room. Toots, a genial giant, fat and wide and tall, had lunch at the White House with the late President Roosevelt and made him laugh. Sometimes at dinner there's more Washington brass at Toots' than there is in Washington. Toots also runs all non-union. But he can call a cabineteer a crumb-bum, and is then set down as a character and a wit.

35. BALTIMORE, CONFIDENTIAL

(*Authors' note:* This is a chapter, not the going-over that a Lait-Mortimer excavating job on our sixth biggest city, our second port in tonnage, truly rates. It is a by-product of this work, because aristocratic, historic Baltimore is the slumming-ground for thousands of escaping Washingtonians, only 36 miles away over fast rails and modern autobahns.)

STIR up your memory and try to think when and where you have read an "exposé" or any other study of Baltimore. You can recall pieces, kindly or vicious, about San Francisco, Los Angeles, Denver, Chicago, New Orleans, Philadelphia, New York, and discussions of the peculiarities of Boston. But Baltimore, a main-line metropolis, with atmosphere and tradition and volume and character, is by-passed.

We were almost complete strangers there on field-work, though our tortuous delvings into the continental Mafia-managed Syndicate long ago fixed for us its place in the national network.

Baltimore is perhaps the perfect example of a Mafia-controlled city in action. For practical purposes it is a contraction of Chicago and an expansion of Galveston, extreme gangster-throttled cities with the same core of Sicilian manipulators who push the buttons and pull the levers.

Italians constitute one of the largest foreign elements in Baltimore and can always be depended on to vote in a bloc. Little Italy is centered around Albemarle and Fawn Sts., where much of the deviltry is hatched over "dago red" wine. Add to this the huge colored vote, which also is pretty solidly Democratic, and you have the makings of a perfect boss-run burg.

Our investigations into other American municipalities have shown where the Mafia dominates there is a disintegration of public morality and private conscience.

To this major seaport huge numbers of Italian and Sicilian immigrants have always been drawn. They formed the base for its underworld colony, made it a star on the Mafia map. It is a concentration point for illegally-entered Sicilians, stowed away on the freight steamers that ply between the Mediterranean and Chesapeake Bay, by a smuggling-ring. As these aliens become Americanized, grow rich and powerful in the rackets, they import new waves of Sicilians for the underworld's menial tasks.

Baltimore is a favorite hide-out for Mafistas on the lam from other towns, especially New York, and is used interchangeably with Providence, R.I., for that. When one of your authors was assaulted by Sicilian hoodlums in the pay of Mafia tycoons last spring at Bill Miller's Riviera in New Jersey, New York police investigating the crime were tipped off that the sluggers were being sheltered in Baltimore's Little Italy, where they were feted as honored guests at a two-week wedding blowout for the daughter of one of the richest and most powerful Sicilians there. More recently, Tony Rotondo, a Brooklyn ex-convict wanted on suspicion of being the torpedo who slew Bill Drury, was found in Baltimore.

In recent years Baltimore has had an infiltration of Puerto Ricans. It is in handy sea communication with the Caribbean. It has also considerable air traffic with that area and at a cheaper rate than New York's. The affinity between the Mafia underworld and the new Puerto Rican migrants quickly developed, as it did in East Harlem. Young Puerto Ricans are employed as dope-peddlers, pimps, and torpedoes. Their colony is not large as yet. What it lacks in size is made up for with Latin enthusiasm.

Baltimore's Negro population is around 300,000. On the whole, the colored folk there are more orderly than their neighbors in the District of Columbia. Maryland is still a Southern state and its whites will stand for just so much. But Maryland's Negroes have the right to vote and they have been taken in hand by the professional do-gooders, the New Dealers and other such ilk, who often work hand in hand with the underworld. The result is that the Negro, the Italian and the Puerto Rican votes are often enough to tip the balance in local elections and perpetuate the criminal rule.

This is expressed on all levels with "fixes" necessary and available for everything from a special license number which will exempt you from arrest to the go-ahead for a bagnio. (When you see a Maryland license ending in three zeros, you know the car is an untouchable.)

The town's gambling czars are some Comi brothers, some Corbi brothers, all Italians, and George Goldberg, big in numbers.

Tom Shaw, original owner of the swank Club Charles, also was important in the gambling firmament until the Sicilians muscled in, taking a part of his night club as well. Nick Campofreda, a local radio sports announcer, was put in as permanent M.C.—not good either.

The Century Athletic Club on Baltimore St., was in the fight promoting business, as well as the central clearing house for bets. The Mafia had tried long and hard to declare itself in, always without success.

The deal was consummated three years ago, after a couple of swarthy boys from Brooklyn "stuck" it up. Every newspaper printed the story, but the cops denied it happened.

The Club has surrendered its fight charter, and is now simply a gambling place. Five leaders of the Sicilian colony are James Caranna, Frank Gattuso, Tom Lafata, John Maurice, and Joe Palozzolo. They control the potent minority votes—through threats and payoffs—and dictate to Baltimore's political leaders.

The town's top Democratic politicians are Bill "Boss" Curran, a lawyer, and Jack Pollack, former bootlegger, now in insurance. He runs the 4th District. Pollack was once arrested for murder but never indicted.

They split recently over patronage. Curran nominated his man for Governor, but Pollack threw his weight to the G.O.P. candidate, thus putting a Republican in the State House for the third time since 1864. He is expected to remember his political debt to Pollack.

The new Governor, Theodore Roosevelt McKeldin, was the last Republican mayor of Baltimore. He had Pollack's nod then, too.

The Governor can be a nuisance in Baltimore if he wants to, but never does. City police heads are appointed by him, not by the mayor. Beverly Ober, the incumbent commissioner, is "social," and acceptable. Anyway Maryland law provides a set term for the top cop. McKeldin is expected to keep his snoot out of Baltimore—he needs it for re-election; and its Democratic legislators—who control the legislature—to pass his measures.

A powerful Democrat is Senator Herbert R. O'Conor. The R is for Romulus. O'Conor is a member of the Kefauver committee. Locally he works with whatever faction is in power.

George Muller, 4th ward boss and State Racing Commission Inspector is a local czar.

Juke-boxes, vending-devices, slot-machines and other Frank Costello monopolies are handled locally by Joseph Corbi, of the brothers, out on bail at this writing after being arrested by the F.B.I. as one of the chief operators of an international lottery ring.

Senator O'Conor is the sponsor of a new plan to bring in 36,000 Italian immigrants forthwith, mostly from Sicily. The Baltimore underworld hopes to route most of these to Maryland. But New York's Republican Senator Ives has boosted the ante to 130,000. There are more Italian voters to appease in the Empire State.

The importation of Sicilians, legally and illegally, under the padrone system, is again growing. Huge numbers of aliens have been brought into the country and settled in certain key spots dominated by the Mafia, where they work off their fare and keep, usually by acting as dope-peddlers, numbers-runners or sluggers, or selling their daughters into white slavery.

Now let's catch up with our mythical refugee from Washington, who comes to Baltimore for only one purpose—and that's no good. You can be sure he finds what he wants in Baltimore. It's got everything that's no good.

The visitor's first impression is of a dirty old town, with ancient, smoke-grimed structures and narrow, rambling streets, one-third of which are still illuminated by gas-lights—with Welsbach globes!

Baltimore is overrun by rubes. And the dress, manners and

customs of most residents appear provincial. Washington is a city of hicks, too, but it is a yokel cosmopolis, with farmers drawn from all sections of the country, leavened with some civilized folk and foreigners.

Baltimore is the market for more chicken-farmers than any other of our cities. It is the place, therefore, where they come to raise the kind of hell a chicken-farmer would.

Washington women on the average seem smart and well-dressed compared to those in Baltimore. Yet Baltimore has some famous high-fashioned women's shops which bring customers up from Washington. But the street types don't patronize them, for they walk around in cheap house-dresses and shapeless coats of cloth, plush and phony fur.

This is the more surprising because Baltimoreans are the most finicky shoppers in the world. As we write this, the local department stores insert a pleading full-page ad in the papers:

"Gentle Reader . . . Over 11,000 purchases daily are sent back to Baltimore stores. NO OTHER CITY EVEN COMES CLOSE to our percentage of returns. . . . Think how thousands of sales people lose productive time making over 3,000,000 sales a year that come back."

Baltimore has a Skid Row that turns your stomach even in Baltimore, where so much of the burg looks like one Skid Row. Next door to and around the corner from some of the best hotels, cafes and department stores, you will find nude strippers, B-girls, hostesses and whores. Guttered drunks and street-walkers may be the badge of the Bowery elsewhere; here they are a common sight on every street.

The visitor heads for one of a half-dozen hotels, all but one of which are almost as ancient as the city itself. The newest, the Lord Baltimore, is almost a quarter-of-a-century old.

The hotels are cozy, but musty. The elderly Belvedere, once the class joint, is now part of the nation-wide Sheraton chain. Its cocktail lounge is the only social hang-out left. The Emerson and the Southern are doddering old ladies. There is an air of laissez faire in Baltimore which extends to the inns. If you are quiet and gentlemanly about it, they probably won't throw that broad out of your room. For it is a friendly town, as you will have many occasions to find out. Everyone talks to you, half the girls you meet want to go to bed with you. The name of its new airport is Friendship International.

When Judy Coplon worked for the Department of Justice

she was considered the most amenable gal there, which made her the most popular. Harold Shapiro, a good-looking assistant attorney general, dated her frequently. It was testified at her first trial that they went together to Baltimore, where they spent a night in a room in the Southern Hotel.

Judy admitted that, but claimed she did not undress. Shapiro was an unhappy witness against her, because many thought he had acted for the government to lure her—kissed and told.

He moaned to friends in Baltimore, "It happens to lots of guys. But not everyone has a G-Man under the bed."

The first item on the tourist's agenda after he gets out of the hay is East Baltimore Street, part of the main commercial thoroughfare. From Gilford Avenue to Fallsway it is Hobo Heaven. You know when you are getting to what you want to find when you see a Salvation Army meeting on a street-corner, in front of a barker for a burlesque house. Other towns have honky-tonk lanes, too, but this is the only one where it is the main attraction.

Skid Row starts as soon as you walk past the Emerson and Southern hotels. You are right in the middle of it—a good half mile of avenue lined on both sides with burlesque theatres, cheap bars, low-class night clubs, novelty stores, shooting galleries, penny arcades, flop-houses and second-hand clothing stores. All burlesques and some saloons have hawkers who will pull you in by main force if you hesitate or stop to look at the pictures.

The most famous dump in town is a basement dive called the Oasis Club. Years ago, when we first visited it, it specialized in a rowdy floor-show, with a chorus of elderly relics, their drooping bosoms unencumbered by brassieres. It is now a strip-joint selling a parade of nudes, some "refined" with bubbles or fans, pretending to "tease." Many peelers make $1,000 a week. But not these in Baltimore. The Oasis is non-union. The maximum salary is $35. They earn the rest of their living sitting out with male customers. We had seen crummy shows before, but nothing quite like the Oasis. Yet, when we stepped around, we found it tame for the course.

In Chicago, where nudes run wild, they never work at floor level. They are lewd on raised stages or on platforms behind bars. At the Oasis and a good many others in Baltimore, they work on the floor. If you are sitting at the ringside, you can reach out your hand and tap the babe on her bare behind. And she'll love it.

One or two Oasis girls strip completely, without G-strings, plaster or anything on. The m.c. mouths continuous patter of dirty talk in which he encourages the customers to tickle the girls—anywhere. The girls talk back to the patrons, jump on their laps, stick their bare backsides in their faces, in the spirit of good clean fun.

Max Cohen sold the Oasis to Sam Levin. He agreed to get out of the strip business. But he immediately opened another room, around the corner, called the Miami. Levin sued for breach of contract and collected $50,000. The competition between these two sewers opened the town up wider than it had been in decades. Each tried to outdo the other in nudity. But a girl can't take off more than all. Meanwhile, other strip dives found themselves outstripped and had to meet the new mode.

The Miami is around the corner from city hall and police headquarters. The mayor can turn at his desk and look into the Miami, and many other dives. This is one of the most vicious and lawless areas in the world. The mayor of Baltimore, whose present term expires in May, 1951, is Thomas D'Alesandro, Jr., a Democrat. He was chosen Permanent President of the U.S. Attorney-General's Continuing Conference on Crime and Corruption last winter.

Mayor D'Alesandro was, before his election as the city's chief executive, the "Mayor of Little Italy." His rise to the seats of the mighty, did not turn his head. He refused to move from the slums where he had always lived, at 245 Fawn St. Instead he rebuilt his home into a modernistic mansion, a show place surrounded by hovels.

Next door, and connected, is a new commercial building in which the Mayor operates his insurance business and his wife her home-beauty treatment supply company.

If the Mayor returns late from a banquet, political meeting or night session of the City Council, he will not be forced to travel through dark and deserted streets. For the immediate vicinity of his home is the bright light section of Little Italy, where neon-lighted restaurants run all night, and serve liquor in tea-cups, and some openly in orthodox set-ups.

Kid Julian runs one such place nearby, a mob hang-out.

It is interesting how Baltimore's Mayor was chosen to head the Conference on Crime over mob-fighting Mayors Bowron, of Los Angeles, and Morrison, of New Orleans. We know the inside. We covered the inaugural meeting in Washington at which all problems were solved in two hours, after President Truman opened it with a pep talk in which he said there'd be no crime if everyone read the Bible and stopped for traffic lights.

"Look at me," he said. "I am the most important man in the world. Yet I instruct my chauffeur to stop at all red lights."

That night the President's car went through 17 en route to a banquet at the Statler.

Mayor D'Alesandro's honor came after he read an intelligent paper to the delegates. It came as a surprise that D'Alesandro had such a fine grasp on the subject. It came to him that way, too.

You see, when he read it, it was the first time he had seen it. It was written for him by a Baltimore newspaperman.

The location of the deadfalls in Baltimore reminds us of Galveston, where the gambling and red-light districts, controlled by Syndicate-allied bosses Sam and Rosario Maceo, are also contiguous to the offices of the law enforcement authorities.

The Miami Club is on the main floor of a building which advertises "Rooms Upstairs." It has some of the most disgusting acts we have ever seen. Girls in the show will sit out with you on request. Every time you pay for your round of drinks—they require you to pay after each round—the sitter asks you for a dollar tip. The girls who work in the show get no commission on these drinks. But if they don't have a drink in front of them all the time they risk being fired. Their base pay, as "entertainers" runs from $20 to $35 a week. The rest they make from the tips and from deals arranged for after work. Some of the girls in the show aren't bad lookers. We spoke to one young Puerto Rican, named Aida, who could have gone places in New York if she had any spunk or talent. Here all she did was walk around the floor without a stitch on. Off her it looked good.

The m.c. at the Miami, when we got nauseated there, was a fairy. Some of the older dames in the show are lesbians. Many fags frequent the place. The girls told us all that freely, though not free.

The rest of the customers are servicemen, riffraff, sightseers and drunks. One seldom brings his wife or girl friend to this place. One of the nights we were there we saw two policemen and a lieutenant in uniform, sitting at a table drinking, surrounded by girls. At the next table was a wizened little old fellow tossing dough away on the broads. We figured him for a chump. But he turned out to be a retired Baltimore police captain who quit so rich that he can afford to spend $500 a night, that way.

Many of the lower-paid employes of the British and French embassies in Washington hang out at the Miami. Occasionally some of these girls are brought to Washington when low down high-jinks are wanted. The Miami advertises regularly in the Washington dailies.

The waitresses at the Miami seem to be independent con tractors. Tables are not assigned. Customers are continuously solicited for orders by dozens of different ones. Each carries a purse and you settle with her after every round. She pays cash at the bar for it. It seems any girl who wants to can come in and hustle drinks this way without being hired. Some wear slacks, others street clothes, and a few sport cheap evening gowns. They will sit with you with no coaxing. One of our waitresses sat down and said, "My tables always buy me a drink."

At the Miami Club we often saw men seated with girls from the show or waitresses and making obscene passes—not in booths, right out on the open floor.

But the ultimate in lowdown shows goes to Kay's, on Frederick and Baltimore Sts., across from the Oasis. There is nothing like Kay's anywhere, and we've seen them all. The dance-floor is about 15 feet square, all tables on the floor. Practically every girl in the show works naked and does raw routines within reaching distance of those at ringside. The women, with words and motions that wouldn't be allowed in Fultah Fisher's boarding-house, solicit men from the floor. One of the most startling dirty acts we've ever seen was done by a woman billed as Moana. She introduced it as her "Whore Dance."

Here are some of the sights of East Baltimore Street:

At Number 116, a couple of doors from the Emerson Hotel, is an amusement arcade where the kid pick-ups come. Those who like them so can walk off with 13-year-olds.

The first thing you notice is the profusion of stores and shops and stands selling "sanitary rubber goods" and other immediate accessories. In the lobby of the Globe Burlesque Theatre is a sign reading, "SALAMI—RUBBER GOODS."

A sign in the window of 424 East Baltimore reads "TRY

OUR HAMBURGER — SANITARY RUBBER GOODS — SHOOTING GALLERY IN REAR."

Most of these novelty stores and newsstands also sell dirty pictures, including series of snaps showing strips. In one we recognized a New York chorine we know. On sale are playing-cards with naked females on the faces.

In the window of the Maryland Gift Shop, in addition to a lavish display of "rubber goods" and salacious pictures, are switchblade knives. The newsstand at Gay and Baltimore Streets has "rubber goods" on display beside newspapers and the usual pictures. Gordon's Novelty Shop, at 428 East Baltimore Street, hands out a business card with a drawing on the reverse side showing a short-skirted cutie standing next to a young soldier in a rainstorm, with the caption: "Don't forget your rubbers."

Though we saw "rubber goods" displayed in at least 40 store windows, not only on Baltimore Street, but in other parts of town, we can't remember seeing so many pregnant women anywhere else. In New York one seldom sees such displays, even on the streets.

Many Baltimore Street joints are pointedly pick-up bars. One is the 408. Another is the Midway Bar, where the local hoodlum hot-shots hang out. Harry's Bar has strippers and pick-ups. Katherine's Bar goes in for a couple of cheap teasers and a lot of cheap whores working the tables. Next door to Katherine's Bar is a sign, "Rooms one dollar a night."

Down a couple of blocks in the Victoria Hotel, a tawdry assignation joint, is a dive called Bettye Mills Night Club. It was once known as the Stork Club, but Sherman Billingsley brought suit. It has a couple of long bars where soiled strippers work on platforms, above the bartenders. While you sit on the stools, dames come over and ask you to buy them drinks. This doesn't surprise anyone, because they do it in every low joint in town. Such places have female bartenders, and many lean over and kiss customers. If not too busy, they come out and sit with the trade.

One bartender at Bettye Mills is a character known as Mitzie, a plump little broad, a retired stripper. She has a running line of patter. If you give her a dollar tip she will pull up her skirt, pull down her panties and stash the bill in full sight of the customer.

In the men's room is an ad which reads: "Sanitubes for defense, protect our Army and Navy."

Bettye is the town's chief call girl madame, operating through the hotel switchboard.

The Village Bar, 12 Harrison Street, around the corner from Baltimore, is a pick-up dump with B girls, hustlers and barmaids who go through the customers, and we mean just that. Three of us saw a guy get rolled. He was a good-looking, well-dressed young fellow, obviously plastered. A whore in an evening gown sat next to him and pawed him with both her hands. Then she got up, went to the women's room for a minute, then took a seat by herself at the far end of the bar. When the cluck woke up, he frisked his pockets for his poke. It was gone. Still in a daze, he wandered around the room looking for the dame. She didn't give him a glance. He wandered off, befuddled.

Even the better places have circular bars. We figured that out—they are better for pickups. You can look at the girls from front, then motion them. But in most places you don't have to motion. They practically attack you. Not even in Chicago are they so voracious. They don't ask you to buy a drink. They move right in and order.

Few Baltimore B girls work on commission. Most of them live on their tips, which they solicit after they've bilked you for drinks. The procedure is for a girl to move in next to you, order without asking, then get ready to blow if not propositioned and demand a dollar tip for her "company."

Some saloons which specialize in better-looking ones give them $5 a night and they keep their tips and anything they can make after hours. Entertainers must cadge drinks to keep their jobs. No commissions.

Baltimore has a 2 A.M. closing, which except in Little Italy is generally observed—one of the few laws that is. These easy hours give the girls plenty of time to pick up money after work. A strange sight is East Baltimore Street a few minutes before 2 A.M. It is lined with walls of men waiting for the frails to come out of the bars, strip dives and burlesque houses. These are not pimps or dates, but men on the hunt who saved drink-money and put a ceiling on the commodity. Hundreds of pick-ups are made this way every night, openly in front of the few cops there on patrol.

Streetwalkers pace in front of the filling-station at Baltimore and Fallsway. They are very low-grade stuff. Asking prices start at five bucks and waver to what they can get.

Parlor-houses have about disappeared from Baltimore, as from most cities, but there is a line of them in the 600 block, on West North Avenue. There's one in the 1000 block of N. Charles, also one next door to the Blue Mirror.

Most of the dives are on Baltimore St. and in the vicinity, but there is no monopoly there. A store next to May's department store, in the retail shopping district, has a window display of "sanitary rubber goods" and switch-blade knives. Ditto is a shop known as Blizzards, on Eutaw Street, which advertises a bargain, "Three dozen latex, one dollar."

There's a strip-dive, the Picadilly, around the corner from the Lord Baltimore Hotel, in the midst of the financial and retail district. It has pretty lowdown floor-shows and swarms with hustlers who work the bars. We saw one cute bartender there, calling herself Val, about 18, from some mountain town in Tennessee. For a dollar tip she'd let you play around and never slap your hands.

The joints on East Baltimore are bad—but on the outskirts of town, on the Pulaski Highway at Fayette Street, you find places not patronized by tourists, bums or sailors, but by local kids. You see nude floor-shows at the Ambassador, on Fayette, and at De Carlos, on the Highway, that would make Baltimore Street bums blush.

The Big Mob operates or protects the dives. It owns many of the good places, too. Every dump and purveyor of filthy pictures now has a sign in the window: "Re-elect D'Alesandro."

The better region is along Charles Street, where the more expensive specialty and antique shops and the few better-class night clubs and lounges are. Among them is the Club Charles, part of the circuit which includes the Copacabana in New York, the Chez Paree in Chicago, and clubs in Saratoga, Miami, Las Vegas and New Orleans, which play such acts as Sophie Tucker and Joe E. Lewis. When the heat isn't on, a game runs in the back room of the Charles.

Less elaborate is the Chanticleer, but far above deadfalls in the other part of town. It boasts good floor shows and "name strippers." Among the good cocktail lounges in this district are the Coronet and the Blue Mirror. These are places where men take their own girls or their business associates. They provide no entertainment, but usually have a musical trio behind the bar.

As the 2 o'clock closing ordinance is generally obeyed, a problem in Baltimore after hours is to find a place to drink on the premises. But liquor package stores sell until 2 A.M., and most licensees are permitted to sell for off-premise consumption, too—a procedure practically unknown in other parts of the country. So, if you still want a drink at 2, you buy a bottle and take it with you.

Ask a cab-driver where you can get a drink after hours and he will know only of two spots—outside of Little Italy—Sue's and Hector's. Sue's is a lowdown dump. Unless you are known, all you can buy there after the deadline is beer, which is also illegal. If they know you, they will sell you rotgut liquor.

Hector's is not quite so bad, but it closes Saturdays.

The night after we were given a courtesy card to the Press Club, 100 West Fayette Street, it was raided for selling liquor at 3:30 A.M. to non-members.

There are many cheating private flats and remodeled homes, especially on Charles St., where chumps are steered from the Club Charles and the Chanticleer, for girls, booze and stud poker.

Bell-boys and hackies can steer you to anything. Baltimore cab-drivers have to scrabble for a living. The legal rates are about the lowest in the country. You can go almost anywhere in town for a quarter and tips are meagre.

Gambling is plentiful and easy of access. There are horse-rooms on Eutaw Street, across from the Public Market. Most of the rooms, however, are in the outlying sections of South Baltimore and Northeast Baltimore. We found three running in the 1900 block of Greenmount Avenue and others in the 2400 block, the 2500, 2700, 2800, and 3300 blocks of Greenmount Ave. There was wide open gambling in the 1800 block, the 2000, 4300, and 5500 blocks of Hartford Road, as well as the 5200 block of Bel Air Road.

Casinos and horserooms run openly across the County line in Anne Arundel, and a regular scheduled limousine service is maintained to transport suckers.

The cars leave at frequent intervals from Redwood and South Sts., and the Biltmore Hotel, Fayette and Paca.

Some of these suburban gaming hells are guarded by armed men stationed in pill boxes commanding the gates.

There are thousands of one-armed bandits and gambling devices in the city, where they are illegal even by local option. At this writing, the city itself was in the gambling business with a game room in the new Friendship International Airport, eight miles south of the city, in Anne Arundel County, where slot-machines are tolerated by illegal local option. But the airport is owned by the City of Baltimore, which is officially on record against slot-machines.

Into the game-room of the airport came something new in the way of trying your luck. It is a combination cigaret-vender and slot-machine. You can buy cigarets at the usual price, 20 cents. But if you want "action" you put in a nickel instead of the 20 cents, and hope to get up to 20 packages of your favorite brand—or nothing. The Frank Costello enterprises are giving the machine its first tryout under this blessing of legality.

The gambling payoff in Baltimore is made through the police. North Side cops get $10 a week for their services, those on the South Side only $7.50.

Sergeants rate $25 and lieutenants $50, with higher officers greased accordingly.

The cops collect the take from the numbers men and book-makers and deliver it to their higher-ups, who then transmit the "documents" to the gang collector.

One reason for this complicated business is a shrewd point of law to get around the income tax laws. The government will not allow a deduction for graft to public officials but if the payoff is taken off the top before the mobsters get theirs, then all they need to pay on is what they receive, the net.

Baltimore is a way-station on the international underground railroad that transports narcotics. Considerable foreign stuff comes in through the port. It is also brought down from New York in quantity and stored in the Italian and Negro sections, awaiting transportation in smaller packages to the District of Columbia.

Local street sales of narcotics are concentrated on Pennsylvania Avenue in the Negro district, where individual caps of heroin, morphine and reefers are available cheap. Puerto Rican and Italian peddlers work the white dives in East Baltimore Street, where they sell to whores, strippers and B girls, many of whom use it and others sell it.

Baltimore's Little Harlem—Pennsylvania Avenue—is more

peaceful than the Negro section of any other large town we ever gandered.

The cops don't let the colored places get away with anywhere near what they act blind to in the white spots on East Baltimore. Some of the cleanest and best night clubs in town are the black-and-tan resorts in the Pennsylvania Avenue district. Though whites are welcome, they seldom visit them.

Gamby's is an orderly colored night club with fine Negro entertainment and a small but excellent line of tan chorines. There was no stripping here, though one pretty wench, billed as an exotic dancer, shook swiveled hips but took off nothing. It occurred to us that we had never seen a Negro stripper anywhere. The girls of that race refuse to vulgarize themselves in public to the extent that many white girls do. Not only was Gamby's show clean and entertaining, but the customers, all colored, behaved well and were better dressed than the social sewage we saw in most of the white dives.

We saw no soliciting here. But there was a one-armed bandit in the bar. Willie Adams is the numbers boss of Darktown.

The Negro joints close on the dot, and then the streets fill up with thousands of laughing, shouting, usually sober merrymakers. White policemen patrol the streets in pairs, but at ease. We saw one buck pull a razor on his sugar in front of Gamby's. Two white cops in a squad car drove off.

Baltimore has a large homosexual population, which is swelled by visiting fairies from Washington. On mild nights you can find them in Mt. Vernon Place, under the Washington monument, where they pick each other up and make liaisons. A favorite gathering place is the Plaza Bar, formerly Longfellows, at Madison and Charles. They also patronize Ball's and the Harem, the latter a corny night club with two entrances, one leading to a stag bar with a sign on the door, "For Men Only," and a place on Mulberry near Howard. The lesbians hang out at the Earl Club.

Baltimore follows the trend of most large cities, other than New York, in that its best people never go to cafes in town. When they feel the need of night life they come to New York. When they want to drink and dance in Baltimore, they do it at house parties or at country clubs. So most of the patrons of Baltimore liquor dispensaries are the lowest classes. The few better rooms, like the Club Charles, cater to the sporty set, big spenders, gamblers, buyers and salesmen and trippers up for the night from Washington.

When the Charles has a first-rate attraction it advertises in the Washington papers. For a couple of years the ancient Ford's Theatre in Baltimore was the only house within 150 miles of the District offering legitimate shows. Ford's gets top road companies and attracts show-lovers from Washington, who drive up for a sea-food dinner, for which Baltimore is famous, an evening at the theatre, then take in the cabaret at the Club Charles.

Baltimore's big night life season begins when the races at Maryland's famed tracks bring in loose money from all over the country. Then the town is brilliant, gambling is rampant and the whores cash in on bonanza.

The city is the center of the so-called "Minor League" racing circuit. There are five half-mile tracks in Maryland, which run almost all year, with unknown plugs and has-beens, raced by "Gypsy" horsemen. These are a unique breed. They own one or maybe two nags, which they may have picked up for dog-meat money. They train them themselves and often are their own jockeys. It is not uncommon for them to live in the stables with their horses and even travel from track to track on the horses' backs. The entry fees at these tracks are as low as $10 and a $100 purse is something to shoot at. The shenanigans at these tracks, controlled by the gamblers in Baltimore, are atrocious.

This smudgy picture of the Baltimore that embraces the visitor brings up the question: How Come?

This city of H. L. Mencken has long prided itself upon rebellion against what most of its citizens believe to be an invasion of their private rights. Prudery was never profitable in Baltimore. The Prohibition Amendment was deported as an undesirable alien.

One old-timer said, "You think this is something? You should have been here 50 years ago!"

Baltimore, the mid-Continent seaport, is one of the most provincial of Eastern cities. In some of its set ways it is a backwash to the colonial days and the cavaliers.

Yet Baltimore is the "big city" to thousands of hillbillies from the nearby mountains of Western Maryland, Virginia and West Virginia, and the poor white trash of Maryland's Eastern shore counties on the seaboard, and Delaware. They are the folk who trade and settle in Baltimore.

It took us some time to figure out why there were so many pretty young girls whoring in Baltimore. If they left home to sell it, why didn't they go on to New York? Research showed they came from the nearby hills and farms; even those with roots deeper in the South or in the reaches of West Virginia came to Baltimore because that was as far as their small savings or imagination could get them. Some planned to make the major league when they saved up a roll, but they were the exceptions.

One girl put it up to us frankly. All she had to offer was all she had. New York, the word has spread, is closed to hustling hucksters. New York's market trades through switchboards for smartly turned-out call gals, models, chorines, pent-house patooties. A rosy-cheeked milkmaid in gingham dress, with no capital, would be pinched and jugged if she winked to a Sand Street sailor.

The hungry harlots on Baltimore's streets and in its stinking saloons come there because the whisper back home is that it's the place to go to. Often procurers have brought them and started them, or they are beckoned by bims who are there. "Bread of infamy" has more raisins than home-baked loaves.

After soliciting at the bars a while, some get ambition. They see strippers don't even know how to walk across a stage, a requisite in even repellent Chicago. They need only take off clothes, and all gals know how to do that.

Few, if any strippers, except at a couple of places that import semi-names, were ever in show business before. Pretty soon they're local celebrities, with a special following. These nude numbers are heart-breaking to Broadway-wise guys who've known the best. Few have looks, none have wit, and at $35 a week most of these stag-show strumpets are overpaid.

Like New York, New Orleans and San Francisco have flavor, Baltimore exceeds both as a ship port, yet it has little appeal for travelers.

Seafaring folk whose vessels bring them into Baltimore's fine harbor are an unromantic lot. No important passenger ships call. Those that do carry steerage. Its freighters are cattle-ships and oil-tankers.

In the thousands of uniform flat-front red brick homes with

the balustradeless white stoops, unique to Baltimore, live good, solid people, white and Negro.

The department of political skulduggery, though, in the Free State metropolis, is a streamlined model, oiled up and with all the gadgets.

Baltimore is exceeded in population only by New York, Chicago, Philadelphia, Los Angeles and Detroit. It has passed Boston, St. Louis and Cleveland, and is growing. It is a combination of an anachronism and a boom town. Labor is flocking in to work its mushrooming airplane factories, huge wholesale trading houses, needle-trade shops and ship works. These are mostly people without roots.

But Baltimore is getting the gravy that overflows from crowded Washington, the hot money out for the kind of fun not tolerated in the District. Baltimore is somewhat in the state of development Chicago knew four decades ago. That city's political morality is still primitive. The same trend is manifest in Baltimore. Yet crimes of violence and serious felonies are not as pronounced as in either Washington or Chicago.

Most citizens are openly on the side of the law-breakers, too; the concepts of liberty and non-interference play into the hands of the hoodlums and the harpies.

At this writing, any and all forms of vice are tolerated and protected. There is a price for everything, and it's not much. In fact, it costs only $500 to jump to the top of the police promotion list.

PART FOUR

THE LOWDOWN
(Confidential!)

36. INSIDE STUFF

*T*HE SHARPIE who got tired of selling the Brooklyn Bridge moved into the District and now sells the Washington Monument.

Suckers aren't born at the rate of one a minute, Washington never does anything on time; but the Union Station and the airfield pour them out day and night. And God made them marks. For they are either simpletons with cow-dung on their boots or they are the con-man's dream, the lunk with larceny in his heart. Those who don't come to Washington to gawk come to get. And the little chiseler is a setup for the bigger chiseler. The characters in "The Gilded Age," by Mark Twain and Charles Dudley Warner have shaved off their beards, but otherwise are still with us. Men with grandiloquent schemes, who think a Congressman from their county can land them a $10,000,000 contract for the quick conversion of a barn, are ready-made for the polished pros who can wrap that up for them and who set themselves forth as "expediters."

They confide, sotto voce, that they have connections which they can't even breathe about; they hint with delicacy that certain people must be reached, and for that purpose advance funds must be placed in hand, after which the expediter will gladly accept a small commission on the completed deal—as, if, and never.

That is only one, but the main one, of the lines. Nowhere else are there so many men and women who live in luxury and are guilty of vagrancy. In a community of nonproducers, where there is a minimum of tangible exchange, the nature of man breeds agents and agents' agents, because the liveliest industry is "getting to" people who can or could deliver golcondas.

Those who are not big-time enough to know people can know people who know people, and do nicely on the far fringes. They case a "prospect" and work him on whatever he is after. His principal occupation will be waiting—waiting; thus he will have the time as well as the temperament to be plucked. In that atmosphere the crudest con-games flourish. Never trust a stranger in Washington. Gyp-and-clip carney operators who are run off the lot because they can't shill a rustic to a ten-cent wheel of fortune, come here and take executive vice-presidents.

A. Swindlers with Swank

Beware of smooth-gabbing guys who drive around in big black limousines with chauffeurs and live in costly apartments staffed with butlers, housekeepers and valets. Some may be on the up-and-up. But, what with taxes and cost of living, few square shooters can afford such luxury.

A few we know:

One has an "in" in the reservation departments of the big hotels. He is tipped off to the prospective arrival of a wealthy chump. This is how he worked one case: When Mr. Money arrived at the airport, the grifter had him paged, then introduced himself with a bunk story, such as being a friend of the hotel manager, who had asked him to pick up the boob. The lamb lamps the limo and is sure the glib gypster who is giving him a lift is okay. The wire has been properly briefed on the stranger's habits. He knows he'd go for a little life, so he suggests they go to his suite for a slug. In a little while, a couple of babes happen in. Soon everyone is drunk and undressed. That's when the pictures are ground out. One metal-manufacturer went for $35,000, left town next day.

Another sold the famous Muscle Shoals Dam to a former Congressman from Nebraska for $50,000. He used Henry Ford's name as a reference and flashed a phony letter from him authorizing the sale.

Some years ago, in another administration, this same tip-and-tosser tried to sell forged documents to the President and

Vice-President and other high officials. He said they were found in the clothes of a dead man on the street. The papers, if genuine, were so hot they would have blown up the government.

If someone tells you he can let you in on the inside of a hot oil deal, and then introduces you to a couple of "prospectors" who just arrived from Kentucky, call the cops, especially if one is an Indian with long plaited hair and the other is dressed like a vaudeville comedian's idea of a Southern Colonel. These fast workers make a splendid living peddling queer securities from an office on the sidewalk in front of the Ambassador Hotel, at 14th and K. They have a fabulous well in Kentucky, and they guarantee it is producing. It is. One barrel a day.

They mooch strictly person-to-person. They do no business through the mails, so they are clear of the Post Office and the SEC. Many of their meat are middle-aged and elderly women, widows with a small amount of insurance or a modest business like a rooming-house preferred. But they will tackle tough touches, approached originally by dames.

Watch out for anyone you meet in a hotel who offers to get you a dame. Odds are you will end up in a barrel, running second in a badger-game. The boys tried it on a Washington newspaperman recently, but for once they saw the back of the eight-ball. Not only didn't the reporter have any money, but he knew the right cops. He ended up borrowing a century-note from them.

B. Fortune-tellers

Reading the future is big business and strictly sanctioned by law, at an annual fee of $250.

Wives of high officials, members of Congress, and society dames are pushovers for this kind of flimflam, and fork over sums to astrologers, palmists, psychics, clairvoyants, and other such miracle-mongers. Many government officials furtively consult fortune-fakers. (Look at the state the country is in now.)

These thimble-riggers advertise openly. Most of them state "Licensed by the District of Columbia," which convinces the morons they have been investigated and certified by government authorities.

One dame, Madame Harrison Astor, states ". . . prides herself on the fact of being the only palmist in the world who during her stay in England has been officially summoned to the

St. James' Palace to read for his late Majesty King Edward VII."

Martha Mar Vell, who advertises herself as a palmist, clairvoyante, medium, spiritualist and practitioner of spirit ember and Egyption sand divinations, haughtily warns, "Please observe hours."

Many fortune-tellers are on the con, hoodwink the superstitious into investing in shady enterprises; they often do not even go that far, but relieve them directly of money to cure the evil eye and the hex.

Some legislators and high officials make no moves without consulting their favorite psychics. That is why they are licensed here, whereas in other cities, when they get by, it is sub rosa.

Some oracles who boast august personages or their wives in their clientele are in the pay of foreign governments, Communists, lobbyists or fingermen for thieves. Lawmakers or law enforcers come to the mediums or diviners to seek advice from the spirits or the stars and get what the swindlers have been paid to tell them.

Gypsies never had it better. Most of them don't bother to buy licenses. As this was being written, a gypsy fortune-teller was under indictment charged with using such props as torn diapers, a red candle and a department store ladies' room, to skin three Washington housewives of $450. Police said Julia Nichols would show up at a woman's home, announce she was a church-worker, then tell the housewife she was hexed. She would ask for money, a handkerchief or diaper. She would tear the cloth in half, fold the money in it and depart to have it "blessed." And blessed if she would return!

Rituals were involved, the police said. In one case Miss Nichols allegedly placed a silver dollar in a glass of water and told her victim to park the tumbler in a bureau drawer. In another, she allegedly enclosed the money in a diaper, with flour, salt, and a length of the housewife's hair. In a third case, police said, the gypsy led a victim from her home to a department store rest-room before taking her money. In another, she allegedly left a housewife's apartment with the currency after giving her a red candle to light and telling her to recite the Lord's Prayer.

C. Free Loaders

A shrewdie can live here forever on the cuff. A gate-crasher, if well-dressed, can be choosy about eating and drinking gratis. Every day there's a profusion of breakfasts, lunches, cocktail parties, dinners and late suppers thrown by lobbyists, corporations, officials, pressure groups, embassies and social climbers.

Admission is by invitation, but bids are sent out broadside. Organizations and lobbyists exchange mailing lists, even take names out of directories. Almost anyone who cares to get on such a roster can. Once on, his name makes all others. If he isn't entered, it is simple to mooch an invitation from someone who has one, because few use them. Few large affairs are well guarded. It takes little ingenuity to walk in nonchalantly and act like a belonger.

The gate-crashers turn up in the unlikeliest places, maybe breakfasting at a press conference given by ladies of the W.C.T.U., lunching at a radio salesmen's convention and dining, in tails and white tie, at a debutante's ball.

Beds, and what goes with them—gals—can be stiffed, too. Those who make the lobbyists' lists are invited to the wild parties in the hotels and mansions, where all that is on the house.

A friend of ours, a Congressman, told us this story. He was walking down Connecticut Avenue, past the Mayflower Hotel, on his way to dine at Harvey's. He bumped into an acquaintance, a press agent from New York, who insisted the Congressman eat with him. "I'm going up to a swell private party at the Mayflower," he said. The Congressman went along, had a wonderful meal, with wine and cigars, and soon pretty blondes began to mix. The satisfied legislator turned to his friend and said, "Gee, this is a swell party. I'd like to thank the host. Who is he?" The press agent said, "Damned if I know. I've been trying to find out all night."

D. The Introducers

Nowhere else on earth, including New York, are there as many guys who make their livings introducing people. These articles thrive because they are personality-plus ghees with guts, who know right people, and if they don't they go through the motions. If you want to meet someone—cabinet officer, army brass, congressman, fixer, or social hostess—these birds will introduce you—no hoke. They can get you into the White House to meet the President. They play poker with General Vaughan.

These fellows are functional. They are the catalysts who bring various elements together. When they assume a contract from an industrialist to introduce him to a bureau chief, they serve for the bureau chief, too, by introducing him to the industrialist from whom he will get favors in return for favors.

Some of the introducers work for straight fees. Others, smoother, are taken care of in politer but more lucrative ways, such as getting on the inside for a hunk of stock or a chance to buy government surplus for peanuts or other charming get-rich-quick methods.

You can be introduced to charming ladies, too. Polished procuring is a polite profession. No lush-rolling or extortion involved. It is honest pimping. Yet, little Rollo, there are still some honest gentlemen in Washington.

37. TIPS ON THE TOWNS

Booze

WASHINGTON consumes four times as much hootch as the entire state of Maryland, including Baltimore, which alone has 200,000 more population. The most popular kind of liquor is bourbon, suh, with rye next. Only fairies, English diplomats, New Yorkers and spats-wearers drink Scotch.

The legal liquor closing for on-premises consumption in the District is 2 A.M. on weekdays and midnight on weekends. Only beer and light wine may be sold on Sundays. Baltimore sells until 2 A.M., seven nights a week, though some saloons which do not serve food and which pay a lower license fee must close their bars at one. (But you can sit there until 2 to finish anything you bought earlier.) Only beer and light wine may be sold for on-premises consumption in Virginia. The closing hour is midnight. Prince Georges, Md., has a law similar to Washington's—seldom observed.

Legal boozing age in the three jurisdictions is 21, though minors over 18 may drink beer in Maryland and D.C.

But there's something about the climate—everyone looks older than he is.

Cabaret Info

Most District area night clubs do three shows nightly, at 8, 10:30 and 12:30, and two on Saturdays and Sundays, at 8:30 and 12. The hotel grills do two, at 8:30 and 12.

The burlesque joints in Baltimore grind continuously until 2.

Few Washington night clubs impose a cover charge. All have minimums, usually a dollar or $1.50. The hotel cafes, when presenting expensive attractions, usually put on a couvert up to $2.

It's agin the law and the rules of the American Guild of Variety Artists to permit female entertainers to sit at tables with male guests. The hotels and the better Washington night clubs enforce this. The others wink at it. There is no attempt at observance in the Maryland suburbs or in Baltimore.

Checks and Chicks

When the cutie in the checkroom hands you back your hat, don't think for a moment she keeps the tip you slip her. She works on a straight per diem for a concessionaire, who pays the restaurant or hotel by the year. But if she doesn't turn in a tip for every hat, she loses her job on grounds she swiped the money or she is so stupid or icky that she gets stiffed. For many years, the minimum hat check in New York by habit has been two bits, but the hoosiers who come to Washington get lavish with a dime or sneak off ignoring the plate with the decoy coins entirely. The concessionaire figures 18 cents as the average tip and on that basis he checks his employes. The gals learn how to pinch part of the loot from liberal tippers, though their uniforms are made without pockets. Photo concession girls may keep their tips, but cigaret girls have to turn theirs in.

Clip Joints

Beware of the invitation from the stranger you meet at the bar, who suggests you go to a friend's place after hours for liquor and gals. There are at least 300 clip joints running in Washington, most of them in the colored neighborhoods, in private houses and flats, where you can get booze of a sort after-hours; but it may be spiked with knockout drops and you will wake up rolled and robbed—if you wake up at all. Baltimore clip-dives operate more closely to the orthodox custom. As soon as you sit down in a hideaway, a couple of bimbos rush to your table and order drinks. When you are ready to go, you get a bill that includes the month's rent. If you don't come across, you'll be lucky to get out with a broken nose.

Dancing

If your specialty is the rumba or samba, don't expect to find a partner in Washington or Baltimore, They'll do a shaky fox trot to that music. The codgers still do the old conservative dances. The youngsters are jive maniacs.

At this writing, there are no public dance halls in Washington where you can meet partners, but, though table hopping is supposed to be de trop, you won't have any trouble getting dames on the loose to dance with you. As in Baltimore, they will solicit you for dances, even if that's all they're after.

All night clubs, but few hotels, present dancing on Sundays in Washington and Maryland.

For matinee and cocktail dancing consult the appendix or the daily papers.

Dates

If you still can't get yourself a girl after having read this book, we don't think you're trying. But here are some easy ways:

Ask the bell captain.

Refer to appendix for a list of dance studios.

Call Clara Lane, Friendship Center, Republic 3504 (Washington), for personal interview.

Get a manicure.

Read the newspaper ads for dances run by the State Societies. Join a church or the Y.

In the summer, go to any beach or take a ride on a Potomac steamer.

Strike up a "Haven't I met you somewhere" with any girl you see in a cocktail lounge or a hotel lobby. For that matter, your chances are good with almost any girl you see anywhere in Washington. She may say no. We bet you five to three she won't.

Dining

We will recommend no restaurants here. A list of best-known places in Washington and Baltimore will be found in the appendix. We guarantee none. But Baltimore goes in for good food in the good places, while Washington doesn't know what fine cuisine is. Meals are cheaper in Washington than in New York. Baltimore, with some of the finest restaurants in the country, charges even less.

Most people dine early in both towns. Some of the best restaurants close for the night at 8 or 9. This is the Keokuk touch.

Washington politicians hang out at Harvey's and the Occidental. They don't mind the insults. Some of the better food is at Olmsted's. The taxpayers foot the losses of the dining-rooms in the Senate and House of Representatives.

Baltimore politicians dine in the back room of the Emerson; the ward heelers eat at Bickford's, called "No. 10 Downing Street."

There are no swank dining places of the grade of El Morocco, the Colony or 21 in Washington or Baltimore. The elite in government service eat lunch in their own private dining-rooms and dinner at their clubs.

Divorce

The divorce rate in the District, as well as in Maryland and Virginia, is considerably below the national average, though the grounds are not particularly oppressive. At this writing there are 4,000 divorced males in the District of Columbia and 8,000 divorced females.

All three jurisdictions require one year's residence before beginning a divorce action, which eliminates them from competition with Nevada or Florida. If the grounds are out-of-state, it's two years in D.C. You have to wait six months after a District decree before remarriage.

Grounds for divorce in the District are adultery, desertion for two years, conviction for felony, and living apart five years. Maryland adds impotence and insanity. Virginia also grants divorce for impotence, pregnancy of wife at time of marriage and wife's unchastity, as well as all causes specified in the District.

Some smart lawyers know how to beat the residence provisions, but if you can afford that kind of a lawyer you're much better off going to states that specialize in hot-cake divorces.

Guns

You require a license to carry a concealed weapon, but no one enforces the law if you keep a dozen machine-guns in your house. The courts have ruled you are not carrying a concealed weapon if you have a gun in the glove compartment of your car or if you have an unloaded one in your pocket, even if you have cartridges on you. Cops can't pinch you without a search warrant.

The Federal Small Arms Act, enforced by the Alcoholic Tax Unit of the U.S. Treasury, imposes a $300 tax on transfer of certain firearms and forbids any felon to carry a pistol. But this is practically unenforceable in the District, because of the niggardly appropriations of Congress and the disinclination of federal judges to sentence anyone for anything.

Hotels

In most towns we warn first-time visitors to beware of cab drivers who steer them to hotels they don't want to go to. But Washington hotels are usually so crowded, you're lucky to be steered. We have seen people sit in lobbies from early in the morning until midnight, while the clerks phoned all other hotels, trying to take care of the overflow.

Do not come to Washington unless you have made a reservation in advance. Be sure the reservation is confirmed. A few hotels are part of nationwide chains, among them the Mayflower (Hilton), the Hay-Adams (Manger) and the Statler. You can probably make your reservations and have them confirmed in your own home town.

Hotel rates are high. The cheapest single room in the first-class hotels is $8, and that faces the garbage cans. Modest suites are $20 a day, and you pay at least $25 for anything decent.

But Washington abounds with cheap assignation hotels, where you can take a broad for the night for three bucks, no baggage required. In Baltimore you can find this kind for as little as one dollar a night.

Few good Washington hotels have any qualms about your morals. If you are raided because that gal isn't your wife, it is because the house dick and bell captain have their own stable of fillies and they get no cut-in from outside competition. The "security officer" (refined designation for a house dick) of one of the oldest and most famous hotels in Washington, near the White House, was recently fired because he ran a shakedown racket, putting the bite on guests who brought dames in.

(*Inside stuff:* Smart guys start charge accounts in hotels and have their bills mailed to their offices. That way, if they suddenly make a date, they can call and have a room prepared for them. Hotels do not like to cash checks for strangers, but will for those with charge accounts. It is a specific crime to defraud an inn-keeper.)

Washington and Baltimore hotels, unlike those in northern cities, are not required to serve or admit Negroes.

(Unless you are expecting a guest, do not open your door if someone raps on it. Many people have been robbed, raped or assaulted that way. When the girl with the nice voice phones and announces she's from Harris & Ewing, the photographers, and read you were in town and wanted to take your picture, don't think you are a celebrity. This firm goes through all registrations, plays for the chumps. After you pose for their photos, a glib salesman sells you a dozen. We wouldn't have minded, but they phoned us at three in the afternoon, and we never get up until four.)

(*Tips:* And that's the only way you'll get along in any hotel —with tips, big ones. If you can't get a room, slip the room clerk a sawbuck. Liberal handouts to the bellhops, doormen and elevator boys will help you get service, also pave the way for the things that hotels aren't supposed to supply, but always do.)

Limousines

We told you about the smooth con-men who travel in shiny chauffeur-driven limousines. The cars are easy to obtain. All smart travelers rent them wherever they go. They cost $5 an hour, which is usually cheaper than cabs for any considerable use. They are available at any hour. The chauffeurs are well-trained and in uniform. The cars are brand new Cadillacs or Packards, indistinguishable from a millionaire's private car, except that the D.C. license plate begins with the letter "L." Look in the phone book or ask the hotel porter to get you a car or phone Haines, HObart 8460, ask for James Conley, the best driver in town. Minimum tip one dollar an hour, unless you're a skunk. In Baltimore, phone Belvedere, LE 8888.

Marriage

It's much cheaper and easier without rice and old shoes here, but you will always find a few old-fashioned people who like it the hard way. If you are one who has to be respectable, we will give you the lowdown on how to go about it in the area.

(*Note:* Common law marriages are valid in the District. They are not in Maryland and Virginia, though the former state, while prohibiting such marriages for its own residents, will recognize as binding any such entered into in the District.)

The marriageable ages in the three jurisdictions are 16 for girls and 18 for boys, with parents' consent; 18 and 21 in D.C. and Maryland, without consent, and 21 and 21 in Virginia. Marriages between first cousins are permitted in all three.

Maryland and Virginia forbid marriages between whites and Negroes or Orientals. Virginia also proscribes American Indians. There are no racial restrictions in the District.

Maryland and Virginia require medical certificates before marriage, but Washington doesn't. So, if you flunk your Wassermann, come to the District. The waiting time between issuance of license and ceremony is two days in Maryland, four in the District, and none in Virginia. Maryland requires that all marriages be solemnized by a clergyman, which is pretty prissy for that state, where you can get so much without marrying at all.

Both the District and Maryland permit one party of a proposed marriage to take out a license without the consent or knowledge of the other. Sometimes overly-eager ones take out these licenses (which are published) as a means of bringing final pressure on the other person. Recently a 21-year-old Marine shot himself to death after a minister refused to marry him and an unwilling maiden who had not been aware a license was issued.

Washington men are the choosiest in the country when it comes to picking wives. The marriage rate is falling yearly. In 1950, 10,729 licenses were taken out compared to 10,885 the year before and 12,156 in 1948. Meanwhile other cities are reporting increases. These figures are even worse than they read. Many transients come to wed in the District, to avoid blood tests elsewhere or to boast they were hitched in the nation's capital.

Medical

Osteopaths, chiropractors, naturopaths and other such un-orthodox healers are permitted both in the District and Maryland and are allowed to precede their names with the honorific "Dr." Many Washington residents from Los Angeles, the Southwest and the moronic regions where faith healers, layer-oners-of-hands, herb doctors and other such quacks are common, are now living in Washington and provide a boom market for the irregular curers.

One of Washington's biggest medical problems is V.D., because of the shifting, transient nature of the population and the unusual Negro percentage. Last year, more than 16,000 cases of gonorrhea were reported, and 507 new cases of syphilis. Fifteen people died of unchecked syphilis.

Midday Manners

Both as a world capital and as an Eastern city, Washington's manners and modes, on paper at least, could be supposed to resemble those of New York. But it is in a warmer belt and much of its resident population originated in other sections of the country, where habits are different, so some compromise of customs is common.

Washington women generally follow the New York style of not wearing hats. But the men wear lids all year around, even on the hottest days.

The women wear suits for daytime in winter and print dresses in summer. Men wear dark suits in winter, but, because of the deadly heat, don such tropical outfits as Palm Beach, seersucker, crash and linen in summer. Like most yokels, a sharp crease in the sleeve means a well-pressed suit.

A Washington woman never wears slacks on the street. When you see any dame so attired, you know she arrived by bus on a sight-seeing jaunt.

Midnight Manners

Few women wear hats at night. Those who do are visitors. Most men wear dark suits but compromise good taste with god-awful loud ties. Customers of the classier rooms, i.e., the hotel grills, are apt to overdress. You see more people wearing evening clothes than in New York, where such frummery is now worn only on occasions when required, like a formal ball or the opening of the opera.

All restaurants and night clubs, regardless of season, require men to wear coats, though some of the more popular-priced ones do not demand ties in the summer.

Protocol

If you are a climber, or the wife of a government official, social precedence and correct social forms are more important in your life than the Sermon on the Mount. When in doubt about whether the governor of Nevada sits ahead of or in back of the minister of Costa Rica, you should consult Mrs. Carolyn Hagner Shaw, WIsconsin 3030.

Taxi Talk

The first thing that amazes the visitor is the terrific number of cabs on the streets. There is no limitation by law and, at this writing, there are 9,000. Cabs do not have meters, but operate on a zone system, the first charge 30 cents anywhere within the zone, or 20 cents a head for two or more passengers. They are asking for an extra dime a zone. The out-of-towner is always puzzled figuring out how the owner of the cab gets a fair shake from the driver, with no meter to check up on him. It was Congressman Tom Blanton who slipped riders into all bills to ban meters in the District.

What happens is that every hackman is an independent contractor. He rents his cab by the day, for which he pays $6, which includes insurance, tires and advertising. He buys his own gas and oil, which comes to another $3.50 a day. He keeps everything above that outlay. When business is bad, he swallows the loss himself. He can keep the cab 24 hours a day, and he usually drives it home at night and starts out in the morning in it. Some older cabs are rented for less, as low as $3.50 a day. These are used by men who hack in their spare time, such as policemen, chauffeurs, and government employes, who act as cabbies for four or five hours a day.

Washington law not only permits cabbies to double up passengers, but requires them to do so. Your taxi will not leave Union Station until it has a full load going in your direction. When Washington cabs go to the airport in Virginia or the suburbs of Maryland, they make a flat rate. They are not permitted to pick up return passengers outside the District. Maryland and Virginia cabs which come into Washington must return home empty.

Despite the huge number of cabs, it is almost impossible to get one at around five, when the government offices empty, or whenever it rains. The rates are so cheap, many Washingtonians find it costs them only a nickel more to go to their destination by cab than by bus or street-car. Few locals ever tip. Cab drivers fall all over out-of-towners.

If you are having trouble hailing a cab, the best place to get one is outside a hotel or a popular restaurant or night spot, for they will be driving up to these places with passengers. If you are caught at the Capitol and can't get a cab, go over to the Congressional Hotel, across from the House Office Building, where the doorman can usually snag one for you. Don't forget a tip. Our favorite cabbie is Harold Ramsburg, EM 2438, and you can hire him by the hour.

Tipping

While on that subject, don't act like a rube, a Southern cracker or a dope. Most hotel, restaurant and transportation employes are practically dependent for their livings on gratuities. Ten percent is no longer enough. Your waiter should get 20 percent, even more in a high class place where each waiter has only a few tables. Don't forget the captains and headwaiters, especially if you want a good table.

Traffic Tickets

We always got our parking and speeding tickets killed by Congressmen's secretaries. That is one thing they are good for. Congressmen are the rulers of the District; when their secretaries call the District Commissioners or the Chief of Police, they get a respectful hearing.

Congressmen, themselves, are immune from arrest when Congress is in session. They are provided with special plates over their own license tags reading "Member, 82nd Congress." Smart Congressmen seldom use the special plates. They say that when they do, traffic cops always bother them, then suddenly pretend they noticed the plates for the first time, after which they let the Congressman go, making it appear they are doing him a great favor. The next day they show up in his office asking for a favor—a promotion, probably.

Transportation

You can get to Washington by train, plane, bus, auto, bike, or merely hitch-hiking. Train service, while frequent and fast, is generally lousy. From New York on the Pennsylvania there is only one first-class train, the Congressional Limited, which makes the 226 miles in 215 minutes, but it's a shell of its old self, when it was all Pullman and extra fare. The Congressional is one of the few day trains in the country which runs complete cars of drawing rooms. These are always full, with lobbyists, officials and their dames, and other heavy drinking parties, spending the three and a half hours as pleasantly as possible. (*Note:* No liquor is served on trains in Pennsylvania on Sundays.)

The two best trains from the West are the B & O's Capital Limited and the Pennsy's Liberty Limited from Chicago. The Capital is an all-Pullman streamliner and carries a through car to Los Angeles, which connects with the Santa Fe's Chief in Chicago.

Railroad and plane tickets to and from Washington are difficult to get, especially on key days of the week. Traffic moves to Washington on Sunday nights and Monday and away on weekends, beginning Thursday. At those times a little judicious tipping of hotel porters is advised. Railroad and plane employes are forbidden by law to take gratuities, but who's going to do anything about it if they find a $10 bill neatly folded in their breast pockets?

The Washington Airport, though in Virginia, is only 15 minutes from the center of town. Baggage is unloaded considerably faster than in other airports. But the Union Station is a madhouse. Sometimes it takes a half-hour for your bags to get out to the taxi stand, if you can get a red cap at all. Then there is another wait for a cab going your way to fill up. (*Note:* The railroad exacts a 25-cent charge for each parcel carried by the red cap. He doesn't keep that. You are expected to tip him on top.)

(*Inside Stuff:* There are special airplane and railroad ticket offices for members of Congress in the Capitol Building.)

38. CONFIDENTIAL GUIDE TO
WASHINGTON AND BALTIMORE

Alcoholism Treated: The per capita consumption of hootch here is the highest in the world. If you raise it still more call: (Washington) Greenhill Institute, CO 4754. (Baltimore) Baltimore Clinic, LA 1200.

Amusement Parks: Where lonely people meet. The rides are fun, too. (Washington) Glen Echo Park and Marshall Hall Park. (Baltimore) Bay Shore Park, Gwynn Oak Park and Carlins.

Art Instruction: Learn to paint nudes in the nude. (Washington) de Burgos, ME 1039; Kane, ST 7917.

Astrologers: If you're wondering what Congress is going to do next. (Washington) Mabel Bowles, HO 5017. They're outlawed in Baltimore.

Baby Sitters: Some people still bring their brats with them. If you're that dumb after reading this book, call: (Washington) Part Time Mothers, DI 2300; or Courtesy, EX 5050. (Baltimore) Samuels, HO 4303; or Villa, CL 1931.

Bail Bonds: The fee is $75 for each $500. If you work for the Big Mob, the price is just half. Call: (Washington) Weinstein, ME 9292; Jones, ME 8123; Ryan, RE 7661 and O'Conor, ME 5500. (Virginia) Weinstein, WO 6700. (Baltimore) Statewide, BR 8200 and Walker, SA 6333.

Barber Shops, All Night and Sunday: If you failed to make a date before midnight, why do you want to get shaved so late? (Washington) Robinson's, 829 14th St. (Baltimore) East Baltimore St.

Baseball: The Washington Senators never get anywhere, but they always make money. That's because Washingtonians come from every part of the country and liberally patronize Griffith Stadium when their old home teams are in town. All week-day games are at night. Baltimore is larger than half a dozen major league cities, yet it only has a minor league team, the famous Orioles. Night games, too.

Blacksmiths: Left-Wingers insist conservative Congressmen are still in the horse-and-buggy stage. This proves it. If you're looking for a smithy, try (Washington) Capital, 4706 Rhode Island Ave.; Del Grosso, 424 New Jersey Ave. (Baltimore) Adams, 2628 Boston; or Phillips, 645 East 25.

Boating: (Washington) Potomac Boat Club, foot of 36th St.; Dempsey's Boat House, 3600 K St. (Baltimore) Atlas, foot of Broadway; Ward Brothers, Deal, Maryland. And don't forget the excursion and night boats on the Potomac and the Chesapeake.

Bookmakers: Must you ask?

Bridge Games Found: The experts claim the game is all skill, but with us it's purely luck—bad. (Washington) RE 9886.

Burlesque: For what New York can't have—see page 263.

Carnival Suppliers: Maybe you've always wanted to own a paddle wheel, a bingo layout or a Jap rolling ball game. Merry-go-rounds and ferris wheels, too. (Baltimore) Superior, ED 3737 and United, LE 6239.

Cats Boarded: In case your pussy is shy, this place has a lady attendant. (Washington) Williams, SH 6923.

Chaperones: Most unattached ladies are so ugly they don't need this. But if you don't trust your cutie call (Washington) DI 2300 or EX 8596. If no answer, call us.

Chinese Cooking; How to Learn: Personally we don't know why you want to, but if you got a yen for moo goo gai pan and don't like the way it's prepared in the marts of trade, try Washington School, EX 0265.

Cleaners, One Day: When the Fair Dealers finish spending your dough, you probably will have gone to the cleaners. But if you have a suit and you've got to get it back the same day, try your hotel valet or (Washington) Central, 1405 H or Century, 633 F, cleaning done while you wait. (Baltimore) Premier, Monroe and Windsor, same day.

Colonic Irrigation: Just in case. (Washington) Warcoff, RE 0872; Riggs, ME 2388; Washington, BI 7701. (Baltimore) Keller, LE 6862.

Comfort Stations and Rest Rooms: When you gotta go, you gotta go. (Washington) Pennsylvania Ave. between 13th and 14th; Library Park; Lafayette Square; the Capitol and all public buildings. (Baltimore) Lexington Market.

Detective Agency, Colored: That's not where we got our info. (Washington) Keystone, RE 8913.

Detective Agency, Confidential: They can find anything except what's happening to the taxpayers' money. (Washington)

Bradford, NA 4610; Burns, NA 7681. (Baltimore) Pinkerton, MU 2770.

Drags, Costumes For, Also Wigs: (Washington) Jack Mullane, 714 11th St.

Drug Addiction Treated: Uncle Sam will do it free if he catches you first. Otherwise (Baltimore) Relay Sanitarium, phone Elkridge 40, or Pinel, phone Ellicotte City 362.

Drug Stores, All Night: If you run out of lipstick at 3 a.m. (Washington) Peoples, Thomas Circle, HO 1234. (Baltimore) Morgan & Millard, Baltimore and South Sts., SA 4233. For 24-hour prescription service, phone Arbutus 2019.

Emergency Information: (Washington) Birth Control Clinic, 715 E St., SW, NA 4780. (Baltimore) Planned Parenthood Association, 1028 North Broadway, DR 1681.

Escort Services: To accompany the lonely. (Washington) DE 8000.

Fashion Shows: Some guys surprise their wives and ask to come along. See the pretty models Thursdays at six in the Willard lounge; Fridays at six, Mayflower lounge (Washington). In Baltimore—Wednesday luncheon at the Belvedere.

Friends, to Meet New Ones: How lonesome can you get? Call (Washington) The Just For Fun Club, DE 2500 or Clara Lane, RE 3504 (Baltimore). Visit the Baltimore Friendship Club, Charles Street.

Frustrated, are you? (Washington) Curt Miller, 1406 G St.

Gambling: See page 207.

Ghost Writers: Some Congressmen write their own. (Washington) Henderson, NA 4576.

Guns and Firearms: After reading this book, you may want to defend yourself. (Washington) Lorch, 1010 Vermont; Temblers, 913 D. (Baltimore) Baltimore Gun Smith, 218 So. Broadway.

Handwriting Expert: In case she forged the embarrassing love letters call (Washington) Dr. Newton J. Baker, DI 7070. If you really wrote them don't bother.

Limousines: So you want to put on the swank. (Washington) Haines, HO 8460, ask for James Conley. (Baltimore) Associated, HA 5494; Belvedere, LE 8888.

Manicurists: No matter how easy it is to get others, most traveling men still prefer the finger-nail mechanics. They're on duty in every hotel and large barber shop. Some will come to your room.

Manure: This has absolutely nothing to do with the subject, unless it's what you think about when you hear your Congressman's speech. We said Washington is a small town and we mean it. You can get it by the shovelful or the truckload from American, GE 2440. (Baltimore) Town and Country, HO 0906.

Maps: We don't know what this has to do with this book, because none of the cartographs they sell are confidential. On the other hand, a lot of phony foreign spies buy them over the counter and send them home as the genuine article filched from the files. See classified phone directory.

Marital and Sex Problems: This book is guaranteed to cure them for some, cause them for others. (Washington) Lurie, CO 1331; Psychological Service, OL 1980.

Masseurs: If you read what we wrote about the Hopkins Institute you will know why we don't want to get mixed up with the F.B.I. on this one. However, if you still insist on getting a massage, refer to the classified phone book. Most are legit.

Models' Agencies: All girls like to pose. Some get paid for it. If you want to be a model or hire a model see (Washington) Phyllis Bell, ST 2353; Fashion Show, NA 6590; Models Bureau, DU 1000; Ralston, RE 0069. (Baltimore) Academy Models, PL 4454; Model Agency, PL 4019. (*Inside Stuff:* Some model agencies try to sell you lessons, photos and make-up instead of securing work for you. Have nothing to do with them.)

Out-of-town Newspapers: The news is bad all over. (Washington) 14th and New York. (Baltimore) Calvert and Fayette.

Palmists: In Washington, when she says, "Give a little girl a great big hand," she ain't the ghost of Texas Guinan. If you want to have your palm read, try Astor, ST 0698; De Long, ME 5234; Gentry, EX 3075. Illegal in Baltimore.

Personal Services: We mean such things as running errands, answering your phone and doing your dirty work. (Washington) Buddie's, MI 9034.

Personality Developed: They laughed when he walked into the drawing-room. After he took lessons, they wouldn't let him in the drawing-room. But if you've got a personality like a dead fish, try (Washington) Colt, OV 4531 or Parker, ME 2299.

Post Office, All Night: Just in case you want to write home for dough. (Washington) General Post Office. (Baltimore) Calvert and Fayette.

Pregnancy Tests: If your luck is dubious. (Washington) Professional, NO 2944.

Psychics and Mediums: Guaranteed to put you in touch with your great aunt (Washington) Wright, AD 4249; Mar Vell, HO 5017. No lost souls admitted in Baltimore.

Psychologists: Some people were born goofy, others went crazy reading this book. No matter how you got that way, call (Washington) MacBaugh, OL 1980 or Dupont, HU 7979. (Baltimore) Kaufman, BE 5640 or Schor, LE 5445.

Punch Boards: If you would like to set up a little gambling racket back in your home town, you can buy the paraphernalia in Baltimore from A & A, 715 Ensor or Royal, 618 East Baltimore.

Secretarial: Some people call them because they want to dictate in their hotel rooms. Others have hopes. We do our own typing. Look in the classified phone directories under "Stenographic."

Shooting Galleries: Some Washingtonians practice their marksmanship on the streets. If you want to do yours indoors go to (Washington) 9th St. between Pennsylvania and G or (Baltimore) East Baltimore St.

Shopping Service: Some guys don't do anything they shouldn't when they're away from home. Others bring their wives beautiful gifts. (Washington) Embassy, EX 7158; Ideas Unlimited, ST 0082. Phyllis Bell, ST 2353 will help women who have no confidence in their own taste to buy their clothes. (Baltimore) E.Z., SA 0295. All department stores maintain such services.

Slot-Machines: Some people buy them for their game rooms. Personally, we'd like to own a two-bit one-armed bandit in the Times Square subway station. Whatever purpose you want one for, you can buy them in (Washington) at the Game Room, 1538 Connecticut Ave.; Atlas, 1360 H St. NE or Silent Sales, 1771 Columbia Road. (Baltimore) A & A, 715 Ensor; Premier, 214 South Howard. It's illegal to transport across state lines.

Spiritualists: They talk to the departed. (Washington) Brewer, EX 3075; Worsley, LI 3-3557. (Baltimore) If they call themselves fortune tellers they're taboo. But Madame Matthew,

ED 1260, is a "spiritual advisor." So is Madame Collins, SA 4745.

Stags: Why anyone should have to go to one to see naked dames is beside us. However, if you want to hire such babes to perform in the District or in Baltimore, phone (Baltimore) Sponsler, MU 0271.

Sucker Lists: Have you anything to sell by mail? (Washington) Intelligence Bureau, 1311 G, has "wealthy" list of government executives, home-owners, teachers, graduates, businessmen and women, etc. for D.C. and suburbs. (Baltimore) call Webb LE 5671.

Tattoo Artists: If your girl friend likes pretty pictures, try (Washington) 8th St. SE or (Baltimore) East Baltimore St.

Telegraph Office, All Night: Washington 708 14th NW, phone NA 7100—Baltimore, 108 E. Baltimore, LE 6300.

Theatre Tickets for New York and Philadelphia Shows: When the road won't come to you, you've got to go find it. Always reserve your seats in advance, because if the show's any good you can't get 'em, and if you can you won't want to see the show. (Washington) New York Service, NA 5575; Stabler, RE 7307; Willard Hotel Agency, NA 5575. (Baltimore) New York Service, SA 2100.

Toupees and Wigs: When you blow your top. (Washington) Emil, 1221 Connecticut Ave.; Hepner's, 612 13th St. (Baltimore) National, 334 North Howard.

Worrier, Professional: Before you lose your hair, consult (Washington) Thelma Hunt, RE 4600 or Clifton, AD 4550. They're willing to get bald, for a fee.

And now turn to

PART FIVE

THE APPENDIX
(Confidential!)

A. HEADWAITERS

This and a sawbuck gets you an insult.

AMBASSADOR HOTEL (NA-8510) Hi-Hat: Joe Brito
CARLTON HOTEL (ME-2626) Congo Room: Stephen
COLONY RESTAURANT (ST-8165): Orlando Connio
MAYFLOWER HOTEL (DI-3000) Lounge: Alfred Leggett
OLD NEW ORLEANS (RE-7284): Ivanhoe Wills
OLMSTED RESTAURANT (ME-8055): Gus Kooles
SHOREHAM HOTEL (AD-0700) Palladian Room: George and Alfred. Blue Room: Paul
STATLER HOTEL (EX-1000) Embassy Room: Nick
WARDMAN PARK HOTEL (CO-2000) Caribar Room: Leslie Matke

BALTIMORE

CLUB CHARLES (VE-8020): Tommy McGee
EMERSON HOTEL (MU-4400): Walter Katzli
LORD BALTIMORE HOTEL (LE-8400) Oak Room: Mr. Cavalier
SHERATON BELVEDERE HOTEL (MU-1000): Antone
SOUTHERN HOTEL (SA-1600): Nick Brown

B. GUSTATORY GUIDE

Listed, but not necessarily guaranteed.

FOR COCKTAILS:
  Anchor Room, 12th & H, NA-9220 (servicemen and pick-ups)
  Cafe Caprice, Roger Smith Hotel, NA-2740 (government workers' hangout)
  Chelsea Room, Hotel Carlyle, N. Capitol & E, EX-7670 (gathering place for Southerners)
  Hay-Adams Lounge and English Tap Room, 800 16th St., NW, ME-2260 (respectable)
  Hi-Hat, Ambassador Hotel, NA-8510 (pretty babes)
  King Cole Room, 820 Conn. Ave., ME-3935 (flashy crowd)
  Mayflower Lounge, Conn. Ave. & De Sales, DI-3000 (political)
  Statler Hotel, 16th & K, EX-1000 (cosmopolitan)
  Washington Roof, 15th & Penn., ME-5900 (summer)
  Willard Hotel, Penn. & 14th, NA-4420 (pretty babes)

FOR DINING:
  Alfonso's, 1403 L St., ME-7803 (excellent New York cuisine)
  Allies Inn, 1703 New York, NA-0523 (famous cafeteria, high prices, elderly ladies favorite)
  Allison's Little Tea House, Arlington, Va., OT-7900 (popular suburban luncheon spot; government workers)
  Arbaugh's, 2606 Conn., AD-8980 (spare ribs)
  Cannon's Steak House, 1270 5th NE, LI-3-8685 (in the market place but high class)
  Ceres Grill, 1307 E, NA-9427 (government clerks like its good food at low prices)
  Colony, 1737 De Sales St., ST-8165 (elegant)
  Collingwood, On the Potomac, OV-1521 (suburbanites' delight)

Duke Zeibert's, 1730 L, ST-1730 (new and popular steak house)
Hall's, 1000 7th St., SW, ME-8580 (sea food on the waterfront)
Fan & Bill's, 1132 Conn., RE-9856 (New York style)
Harvey's, 1107 Conn., NA-2860 (sometimes the best. Famous for sea food and celebrities)
Hogate's, 9th & Maine, SW, RE-3013 (tourists' paradise)
Hot Shoppes, all over (Washington's most famous drive-ins)
Louis, Ted, 2655 Conn., HO-3222 (local stand-by)
Michel's, 1020 Vermont, RE-1356 (Bohemian atmosphere)
Mrs. K's Toll House, Silver Spring, SH-3500 (bucolic atmosphere)
Naylor's, 951 Maine SW, NA-9659 (sea food where the boats come in)
Normandy Farm, Potomac, Md, WI-9421 (delightful suburban atmosphere)
Occidental, 1411 Penn., DI-6467 (hangout of five percenters and upper bracket officials. Too crowded for service)
O'Donnell's, 1207 E, RE-2102 (almost everyone comes for the sea food including Charlie Ford)
Olmsted's, 1336 G, DI-8235 (with that wonderful Luchow cuisine from New York)
Pierre, Conn. & Q, DU-0666 (the ladies like this)
States, 516 N. Capitol, FR-9443 (for tourists)
Tally Ho, 810 17th St., ME-3218 (popular for luncheon)
Water Gate Inn, On the Potomac, BI-9256 (government girls consider this a treat)
FOR DINING & DANCING:
Caribar Bar, Wardman Park Hotel, Conn. Ave. & Woodley Rd., CO-2000
Casino Royal, 14th & H, NW, NA-7700
Congo Room, Carlton Hotel, 16th & K, ME-2626
Lotus, 727 14th St., NW, NA-4766
Lounge Riviera, Hotel 2400, 2400 16th NW, CO-7200
Madrillon, 15th & New York, DI-4561
Mayflower Lounge, Conn. & De Sales, DI-3000
Old New Orleans, 1214 Conn. Ave., RE-7284
Pall Mall Room, Raleigh Hotel, NA-3810
Palladian Room, Shoreham Hotel, AD-0700
Rainbow Room, Hamilton Hotel, DI-2580
Shoreham Hotel Terrace, Conn. & Calvert, AD-0700
Statler Hotel, 16th & K, EX-1000
FOR DINING IN BALTIMORE:
Asia, 710 N. Howard, VE-8193 (Chinese)
Baum's, 320 W. Saratoga, SA-7196 (steak and sea food)
Belvedere Hotel, MU-1000 (better hotel)
Candle Light Lodge, Frederick & N. Rolling, CA-9754 (country dining)
Cathay, 110 W. Saratoga, LE-7985 (Chinese)
Chesapeake, 1707 N. Charles, VE-7711 (steaks)
Dubner's, 6427 Harfd Rd, CL-6459 (sea food)
Emerson Hotel, MU-4400 (politicos' hangout)

Gannon's, 3150 Frederick, GI-6147 (sea food)
Haussner's, Eastern & Clinton, EA-8365 (unique German with an art gallery)
Hollander's, 10 W. Oliver, LE-9869 (steaks)
Marconi's, 106 W. Saratoga, PL-9286 (French-Italian)
Marling House, 20 E. Fayette, SA-4460 (steaks)
Maria, 300 Albemarle, SA-9366 (Little Italy)
Marty Welsh, 17 E. Fayette, SA-3639 (steaks)
Miller Brothers, 119 W. Fayette, LE-2826 (the town's biggest)
Nate's & Leon's, 850 W. North Ave., MA-2400 (this is Baltimore's Lindy's. Hangout of show folk)
Park Plaza, Charles & Madison, BE-4000 (hotel dining room)
Pierre's, 704 N. Howard, LE-3506 (high class French)
Pizza's, 300 S. High, MU-1327 (Little Italy)
Roma, 900 Fawn, LE-8065 (Little Italy)
Rossiter's, 1001 S. Hanover, LE-9196 (sea food)
Shellhase's, 412 N. Howard, MU-6783 (H. L. Mencken's favorite)
Sussman and Lev, 923 E. Baltimore, MU-6321 (kosher)
Walker-Hasslinger, 1701 N. Charles, VE-9410 (steaks, sea food)
White Rice Inn, 320 Park Ave., MU-6790 (Chinese)

C. DINING AROUND THE WORLD IN WASHINGTON

CHINESE:
Cathay, 624 H, RE-3330
Chinese Lantern, 14 F, LI-9534
Dragon, 1329 G, ME-3218
Good Earth, 1609 K, NA-0441
Gung Ho, 1406 G, ST-6339
Orient, 1715 Wisconsin, AD-4700
Ruby Foo's Den, 728 13th St., NA-3565
Peking, 5522 Conn., WO-8079
Yet Ho Restaurant, 714 11th St., NA-9379
ENGLISH: Old English Tap Room & Lounge, Hay-Adams House, 16th & H, ME-2260
FRENCH:
Aux Trois Mousquetaires, 820 Conn., RE-2619
Bonat's Cafe, 1022 Vermont, RE-3373
La Salle du Bois, 1800 M, RE-1124
Maxime's, 1731 Conn., AD-9811
Napoleon's, 2649 Conn., CO-8955
GERMAN:
Hammel's, 416 10th St., ST-9301 (one of Washington's best)
Old Europe, 2434 Wisconsin, OR-7650
GREEK:
New Athens Restaurant, 1741 K, DI-4081
Old Athens, 804 9th St., ME-9582
ITALIAN:
Aldo Cafe, 1143 New Hampshire, RE-9510
Alfredo's, 1724 Conn., HO-9729

A-V, 607 New York, RE-0550
Ciro's, 1705 De Sales, ME-1434
Gusti's, 1837 M, RE-0895
Roma, 3419 Conn., WO-9833 (dining under the stars)
Villa Nova, 5 F, TR-8978
MEXICAN & LATIN AMERICAN:
  Copacabana, 1711 Eye St., RE-9668
  El Mexico, 2603 Conn., HO-4550
NEAR EAST: The Sheik, 2317 Calvert, HU-4343
ROUMANIAN: Roumanian Inn, 8151 13th St., RE-6434
TURKISH: Dardanelles, Falls Church, Va., FA-2171
SCANDINAVIAN: New Smorgasbord, 2641 Conn., AD-9659
VIENNESE: Little Vienna, 2122 Penn., RE-9316
YIDDISH:
  Holfberg's, 7822 Eastern Ave., GE-5878
  Jones Delicatessen, 1123 S, CO-3786, NO-9862
  Pomerantz, 1782 Columbia Rd., CO-4413, CO-8738
  Randy's, 1113 15th St., RE-0661 (the Rueben's of Washington)
  S & L Kosher Delicatessen, 1205 7th St., NO-4633
  Uptown, 3500 Conn., OR-1040

D. BARE BABES

Where to find 'em. Or where to keep away from 'em, which is harder.

WASHINGTON

Kavakos, 8th & H
The Players, 5th & K

MARYLAND SUBURBS

Chesapeake, 3804 Bladensburg Rd.
Club La Conga, 9412 Baltimore Blvd.
Crossroads, Bladensburg at Peace Cross
Hilltop, 5211 Marlboro Pike
Senate Inn, 5704 Marlboro Pike, SE
Waldrops, 4318 Rhode Island Ave., NE

BALTIMORE

Ambassador, Fayette & Washington (low)
Bettye Mills, 704 E. Baltimore
Chanticleer, Charles & Eager (high class)
Copa, 21 W. Baltimore (ditto)
Kathleen's, 612 E. Baltimore
Kay's, Baltimore & Frederick
Miami, Fayette & Frederick (low)
Oasis, Baltimore & Frederick

E. LUPO'S LOG BOOK

Being some notes to file away where your wife won't look.
Backstage Phone No.: The Capitol Theatre, RE-7193. Star's dressing room call RE-1000 and ask for extension 305.
Boy Meets Girl Dance: Every Saturday, Victory Room, Hotel Roosevelt.

District Age of Consent: 16.

Lipstick Stains Removed (No Odor): Texas, phone MI-9301.

Lonesome Gals: Friday and Saturday nights at the Officers' Service Club, 1624 21st St.

Florist, All Night: Charles Chisley, 603 4th St., ME-8709.

Tourist Courts: On the Baltimore Highway.

F. THE INNER CIRCLE

These are extracts from a master list of 800 names submitted to the Kefauver Committee of the U.S. Senate by Narcotics Commissioner Harry J. Anslinger in June 1950.

Since this list was compiled by Commissioner Anslinger some of the subjects on it changed their addresses—some to a much warmer climate.

NEW YORK

SAVERIO, Frank, Alias Frank COSTELLO: (International List 310) This subject holds the No. 1 position among major criminals in the United States today. He is a member of the Grand Council of the International Mafia and ranks among the "top ten" of the organization. Costello, as he is usually known, controls the gambling interests in New York, New Jersey, Louisiana, Florida and California, collaterally with interests in Colorado and other western states. His gigantic coin machine operations which extend through many sections of the country have gained him the title "The Slot Machine King." The subject is reputed to be interested in all the major criminal activities conducted by the Mafia and other organized criminals throughout the United States. He is regularly seen in close association with wealthy and influential persons and powerful political figures on both state and national levels. The political success of candidates sponsored by Costello in New York and Louisiana, which have included some of the highest officials of both states, are attested facts.

DOTO, Joseph A., alias Joe ADONIS: (International List 79) This subject is one of the most important figures of the Mafia organization in New York City, a member of the Grand Council of the International and a powerful leader in the national underworld. For several years Doto has controlled gambling and other rackets in New York, New Jersey and collaterally in the west and Pacific Coast. He is a national figure in the organization, beyond question. In addition to his gambling interests, Doto long has been known as an important smuggler and distributor of narcotics. He maintains a home at 1020 Dearborn Road, Palisade Park, Fort Lee, N. J. He travels extensively. He is of Italian descent and was born at Passaic, N. J., in 1902.

MANGANO, Vincent or Vicente: (International List 211) Subject is an important member of the Grand Council of the International as well as of the national organization within the United States. He is reputed to derive a sizeable commission on all gambling and other rackets in which the organization is engaged. He professes inability to speak English. Mangano also controls the labor unions on the Brooklyn docks and has connections

with underworld operations along the waterfront engaged in smuggling and distribution of narcotics throughout the United States. Subject is closely associated with top members of both the international and national Mafia organizations. He is of Sicilian descent and so far as records reflect was born in New York in 1887. His address is 254 President Street, Brooklyn.

MANGANO, Philip: (International List 208) Although of less importance than his brother, Vincent (above), subject is a highly influential member of the Mafia in New York City. He is closely associated with leading members of the organization there and throughout the United States. He was born in Italy in 1900 and became a naturalized citizen of the United States in 1925. He lives at 1126 Eighty-fourth Street, Brooklyn.

PROFACI, Joseph: (International List 274) Subject is a member of the Grand Council of the International. Although there is much indirect evidence that subject's criminal activities have included smuggling, counterfeiting, extortion, narcotics traffic and murder, he has no record of convictions.

GENOVESE, Vito: (International List 130) Subject is an important member of the Grand Council of the International and is powerful in the underworld of New York City and the national tie-up. He is associated with virtually all the influential Mafia members in New York and with key individuals of the organization throughout the United States. He is a notorious gunman and at one time was linked with one of the most extensive narcotics operations in the country. In 1939, Genovese fled to Italy while sought by Kings County, N. Y. authorities in connection with Murder, Inc. He was returned to the United States in 1945 and subsequently was acquitted of a murder charge by a New York jury. Subject's criminal activities include murder, smuggling, extortion, theft and gambling. He lives in an expensive home in Atlantic Highlands, N. J.

CARFANO, Anthony, aka Augie Pisano: (International List 031) Subject is a highly important member of the national Mafia and is a powerful leader of the underworld in its transcontinental connections, as springboarded from Brooklyn and Miami. He has been linked actively in the conduct of major drug smuggling operations, with horse booking, the race wire and other gambling. He was a former partner of Charles (Lucky) Luciano and was a close associate of the late Al Capone. Carfano has accumulated considerable wealth and lives lavishly. In recent years he has been associated closely with Vincent (Jimmy Blue Eyes) Also in operation of exclusive gambling establishments in the Miami area. These resorts are known to be hangouts for major underworld figures of the nation when they are in Florida. His summer home is 85 Clayton Avenue, Long Beach, N. Y., but usually he lives in various swank hotels in New York and Florida.

MORETTI, Quarico, aka Willie MORETTI: (International List 235) Subject is an influential member of the Grand Council as well as the national organization and is one of the chief lieutenants to Costello. He is the recognized leader of the New Jersey operation and is associated with all the heavy rackets. He is considered to be a man of substantial wealth. He is of Italian descent but probably was born in this country. (Note: Subject is paretic and highly unstable, hence his position today is known to be precarious because of various ill-advised decisions which have been costly to the organization recently.)

ANASTASIA, Albert, 842 Ocean Pkwy, Bklyn

BARRA, Morris—aka Mickey Mouse— Lorillard Place, Bronx

BONANNO, Joe—aka Joe Bananas—114 Jefferson, Bklyn (See Colo.)

BONASIRA, Anthony—aka The Chief— 1117 83rd, Bklyn (SE202)

COPPOLA, Mike, NYC (Int. List 052)

LANZA, Joseph, NYC (SE193)

LASCARI, Michael, 1111 Park Ave., New York City

LI MANDRI, Michael—aka Mimi, Marco— 325 E. 58th St., NYC (Int. List 187) (NYS 2719) and Calif.

LIVORSI, Frank—aka Chuck—NYC (Int. List 193) (NYMV 123 B) (NYS 4997)

LUCHESE, Thomas—aka Three-fingered Tommy Brown—106 Parsons Blvd., Melba, L. I.

MAGARDINO, Stefano, 1809 Whitney Ave., Niagara Falls

RAO, Vincent, 19 E. 80th, NYC

STROLLO, Anthony—aka Tony Benda & Tony Bender—NYC (Nat. List 392)

TEXAS

MACEO, Sam: This person is a very important member of the Mafia in Texas and an extremely powerful and nationally known figure in the underworld. He is associated with leading Mafia members and other major racketeers throughout the United States. Maceo was born in Italy in 1894 and came to the United States at an early age. Prior to 1920, he worked as a barber in Galveston, Texas; however, during the Prohibition era, he became the leader of a group of liquor and narcotic smugglers who operated in that vicinity. Following the repeal of prohibition, Sam Maceo and his brother, Rosario, continued their drug smuggling activities and at the same time "muscled in" on the gambling racket at Galveston. Within a reasonable length of time, the Maceos were in control of the gambling racket in that area, and as a result of their diversified activities they became very wealthy and also influential in politics. In 1937, Sam Maceo was reported with 87 other defendants in our Case File

SE-131, involving an extensive narcotic smuggling enterprise. However, Maceo was acquitted by a jury on this charge. At the present time, the Maceo organization has control of all gambling rackets in Galveston which consists of dice, roulette, handbooks, policy, bingo, corno games and slot machines. They also own several night clubs and bars and two hotels in Galveston. Sam Maceo is a naturalized citizen of the United States.

ANGELICA, Binaggio: This individual is an important member of the Mafia Society of Houston, Texas, and is closely associated with influential members of the organization throughout Texas, and in the states of Louisiana, Missouri, Illinois, New York and Florida. He has long been an important narcotic smuggler and distributor and on October 20, 1938, was sentenced to ten years in prison for violation of the narcotic laws in connection with our Case Files Texas-9349 and SE-131. Angelica was formerly identified with Mafia activities in Pennsylvania and was arrested in Philadelphia in 1932 for "blackhand" extortion. The subject was born in Italy and is a naturalized citizen of the U. S. He resides at 1906 State Street, Houston, Texas.

ATTARDI, Alfonso: This man is an important member of the Mafia Society in Houston, Texas. He was a former associate of Nicolo Gentile, the former national arbitrator of the organization and was associated with other members throughout Texas and in the states of Louisiana, New York and Missouri. Attardi was co-defendant in our Case File SE-131, NYS-5198 and Texas-9225 and on January 10, 1940 was sentenced to 8 years in Federal prison in the latter case.

MISSOURI

DI GIOVANNI, Joseph: This man is the head of the Mafia society for the state of Missouri, and without question is the most feared and influential man in the Kansas City underworld. Di Giovanni, who is now one of the wealthiest Italians in Kansas City, came to the United States as a poor Sicilian immigrant in 1912. He began his career as the leader of a small group of extortionists and within a short time was the leader of the Mafia element in Kansas City. During the Prohibition era, Di Giovanni and his associates controlled the manufacture and distribution of all contraband liquor in this area as well as the raw material used therein, and in the early thirties, his group organized the narcotic syndicate which operated in Kansas City until 1942. At the present time, Di Giovanni owns and operates a wholesale liquor business known as the Midwest Distributing Co. at 1109 Cherry St., and also owns a chain of retail stores known as the Happy Hollow Liquor Stores, Inc. He resides at 410 Gladstone Blvd.

BALESTRERE, James: This individual is the head of the Mafia Society at Kansas City, Mo., and is second in command in the state. Balestrere is often referred to as the "Mystery Man" of local politics by the Kansas City Star and has been known to exert considerable influence in both state and national circles. For a number of years, Balestrere was the leader of the North Side Democratic club which controlled the entire Italian district as well as the greater portion of the northeast section of the city. In 1943, Balestrere went into so-called retirement and installed an associate, Charles Binaggio, as the club head. On April 5, 1950, Binaggio was assassinated. During the interim, Balestrere and his superior, Joseph Di Giovanni, have directed all matters, political and otherwise, from the background.

DI GIOVANNI, Peter: This individual occupies a position of great importance in the Mafia society at Kansas City, Mo., due to the influence of his brother, Joseph, who is state head of the organization. He resides at 502 Campbell St. and was a stockholder in the former "Kansas City Narcotics Syndicate."

DE LUCA, Joseph: (Nat. List 102) This man is a very influential member of the Mafia Society at Kansas City, and one of the most vicious characters in the underworld of that city. He was the head of the former "Kansas City Narcotics Syndicate" and during the Prohibition era was one of the largest bootleggers in the state of Missouri. De Luca resides at 2840 Forest St.

GIZZO, Anthony Robert: This subject, usually known as Tony, is an influential member of the Mafia and long has been regarded as Balestrere's first lieutenant. He personally looks after Balestrere's business enterprises and is said to have a small interest in each. In addition, Gizzo is the owner of one of the largest horse books in Kansas City. He is a close associate of the Fischetti brothers in Chicago, Joseph Profaci of Brooklyn, and Carlos Marcello of New Orleans. He is frequently a liaison man for the Kansas City Mafia between these points.

IMPOSTATO, Micolo: (Nat. List 189) This subject is a very influential member of the Mafia at Kansas City and reputedly holds a high seat on the International Council. He is a known professional "killer" and is known to have been brought to Kansas City originally from Springfield, Ill., as an enforcer for the local Mafia. Impostato was the general manager of the former "Kansas City Narcotics Syndicate" and on April 13, 1943, was sentenced to two years in Federal Prison for violation of the Narcotics Laws. He lives at 32 Warner Plaza, Kansas City.

COLORADO

DIONISIO, Robert Victor: This subject is an important and influential member of the Mafia at Trinidad. He is a son of the late Rosario Dionisio, who formerly was head of the society in Southern Colorado. The name Dionisio is well known throughout Southern Colorado in that the family long has been notorious as so-called "black-handers." The Dionisios have been investigated by numerous law enforcement agencies in connection with bootlegging, bombing, gang killings, etc., but for the most part have no criminal records. Robert Dionisio was indicted and convicted in 1938 at Trinidad on fraud charges growing out of misuse of public funds. He was one of 12 so convicted. Subject was born in Lucca, Sicula, Sicily, and came to the United States when he was 17. He operates a grocery at 1002 Arizona St., and also has an interest in a tavern. He resides at the Arizona St. address.

BONANNO, Joseph, Trinidad, Colo., and Brooklyn, N. Y. (Bonnano also has a home at Tucson, Ariz.)

MISTRETTA, Anthony, Denver (NY-E 105)

CALIFORNIA

RIZZOTTI, Antonio (Alias Jack Dragna): This subject, usually known as Jack Dragna, is a member of the Mafia in Los Angeles. He is a powerful figure in the underworld and has the reputation of being a big time gambler and racketeer. He is a member of the notorious Rizzotti or Dragna family. Dragna's home is 3521 Beechwood Avenue, Los Angeles.

LI MANDRI, Michael (Alias Mimi Li-Mandri): This subject is a very important member of the Mafia and an influential figure in the California and New York underworld. He is associated with leading members of the Mafia throughout the United States and for many years has been a major trafficker in narcotics. Li Mandri is known to have been a leader of a gang which was engaged in smuggling of narcotics from Mexico to the United States and processing it into heroin. He maintains a home at 335 E. 58th Street, NYC.

MAUGERI, Salvatore: This man is an important member of the Mafia in the San Francisco area and is closely associated with influential members of the organization throughout California, New York and New Jersey. He has been an important trafficker in narcotics many years and formerly was a partner with Charles La Gaipa in an extensive narcotic smuggling enterprise on the Coast. Maugeri was sentenced to 10 years in prison, Nov. 30, 1944, for narcotic law violation (SE 204 and Cal 3368). Other important associates of Maugeri in this case, in addition to La Gaipa were Joseph Tocco, Charles Alberto and Joseph Dentico. Maugeri also has a record of counterfeiting, with one conviction in 1935, for which he was sentenced to two years in prison. He was born in Italy, Sept. 13, 1892, and is a naturalized citizen of the United States. His legal address is 378 23rd Ave., San Francisco.

TOCCO, Joseph: This individual is an important member of the Mafia in California and New York. Prior to his imprisonment he divided his time between the two states. He was a member of an extensive narcotics ring operating in New York and on the Coast. On Aug. 16, 1944, Tocco was arrested in possession of 630 ounces of opium and 8 ounces of morphine at Chicago while en route from California to New York. He was sentenced to 10 years imprisonment the following Nov. 30 (see Case Files Calif. 3368 and SE 204). His legal residence is 315 E. 114th St., NYC.

MILANO, Tony, 9451 Sunset, Hollywood

NANI, Sebastiano, San Mateo

ROSELLI, Johnnie, LA

SICA, Joseph, 627 N. Griffith Park Drive, Burbank (ditto above)

FLORIDA

TRAFFICANTE, Santos: This subject was head of the Mafia at Tampa for many years and still holds an influential position in the organization there. In 1946, Trafficante was replaced as head of the local organization by Salvatore Scaglione through the intervention of the Diecidue family, who have long opposed the subject. During the period from 1929 to 1942, Trafficante and other members of the Mafia in Tampa, New Orleans, New York, St. Louis and Kansas City were involved in an extensive narcotics racket. This enterprise was broken up by the arrest and conviction of eleven defendants, two of whom were members of the Tampa organization. (See Case File 202). His address is 3010 North Blvd., Tampa.

DIECIDUE, Apphonso: This individual is the father of Antonio, Thomas and Frank

Diecidue and is an important figure in the Mafia at Tampa. However, in view of the fact he now is 78, a large portion of his influence has been delegated to his eldest son, Antonio. The latter is alleged to dictate all policies of the Tampa organization. Alphonso is and has been for many years the head of the Unione Siciliano in Tampa. It has been well established that this organization is substantially the same as the Mafia. He has long been closely associated with important Mafia figures in NYC, New Orleans, Chicago, Kansas City and St. Louis. The subject formerly engaged in extensive narcotic, alien and liquor smuggling operations and is reputed to receive dividends from the proceeds of all gambling and bolita in the Tampa area. His home is at 46th and E Sts., Tampa.

DIECIDUE, Antonio: This subject is a close personal friend of Vincent Mangano of Brooklyn and is probably the most influential member of the Mafia in Tampa. He is closely associated with important members of the organization in NYC, New Orleans, Chicago, Kansas City and St. Louis. For a number of years, Diecidue opposed Santos Trafficante as leader in Tampa and finally succeeded in deposing him in 1946. Salvatore Scaglione, or Scagliano, who was sponsored by Diecidue, now heads the organization there.

ITALIANO, Salvatore: (Int. List 154) This individual, usually known as "Red," is an influential member of the Mafia at Tampa. During the period from 1929 to 1942, Italiano and other members of the Tampa Mafia were engaged in an extensive liquor, narcotics and alien smuggling operation. This was broken up by the arrest and conviction of eleven persons, two of them relatives of Italiano. (See Case File SE202). Italiano was convicted in 1929 of a narcotics charge. He is a naturalized U.S. citizen, born in Belmonte, Italy, Oct. 19, 1896. His citizenship was revoked but he regained it in 1947. Italiano is closely associated with top members of the Mafia in Chicago, New Orleans, Kansas City and St. Louis. He owns a beer firm known as Anthony Distributors, Inc., 1707 20th St., Tampa, and lives at 2801 Nebraska Ave.

LOUISIANA

MARCELLO, Carlos: (La 1M) (La 15M) This subject is head of the Mafia in Louisiana and advanced to that position in 1947 when Francisco Paola Cappola, the former leader, was deported. Marcello is closely associated with Frank Costello and with other important figures of the organization in Texas, Missouri, Illinois, California and Florida. He is associated with Costello and Kastel in the Beverly Club and reputedly owns the New Southport. Marcello also owns the largest coin machine company in Jefferson Parish, known as the Jefferson Music Co. He lives now at Marrero, La.

KASTEL, Philip: This individual is a very important member of the Mafia and an extremely powerful figure in the rackets. He is the main representative of Frank Costello in Louisiana and is in charge of the syndicate's gambling and coin machine enterprises. Kastel is closely associated with leading members of the Mafia in Louisiana, New Jersey, New York, Florida and Illinois. He owns a palatial home in Florida but lives for the most part at a suite in the Roosevelt Hotel, New Orleans.

CARROLLA, Sam or Silvestro (deported in 1947) (now in Tijuana)
CAPPOLLA, Francisco Paola (deported in 1949) (now in Tijuana)

MICHIGAN

LICAVOLI, Pete: This individual is one of the most prominent members of the Mafia in Michigan and a very powerful underworld figure of national reputation. He is a member of the notorious Licavoli family of Detroit and St. Louis, whose gang was in competition with the Purple Mob and eventually supplanted and liquidated that group. The subject is associated with leading members of the Mafia and other important racketeers throughout the United States. Although he maintains a legal residence at 1154 Balfour Ave., Grosse Pointe, he spends a great portion of his time at the Grace Ranch, Box 521, Route 2, Tucson, Ariz.

MELI, Angelo: This subject, usually known as Genni Meli, is an important figure in the Detroit Mafia and is closely associated with Angelo Polizzi, et al. He is a notorious racketeer and underworld character, acquiring his reputation when he was leader of a mob with Jo Barzoli, known as the Meli-Barzoli mob in the Prohibition era. In recent years he has been engaged in night club operations, gambling and other rackets in Detroit. He has a record of 15 arrests. 13 of them for felonies and two misdemeanors, ranging from murder to being a disorderly person. These cover the period 1919 to 1944. He has only one conviction—carrying concealed weapons. He lives in an elaborate home at 1060 Devonshire Road, Grosse Pointe.

BOMMARITO, Joe (Scarface), 7540 West Seven-Mile
LUCIDO, Sam, 1507 Sunningdale, GP
MASSEI, Joe, Detroit and Miami

OHIO

MILANO, Frank: This subject is a member of the Grand Council of the International and is head of the organization in Ohio. Although he maintains legal residence at 375 North Hawkins Ave., Akron, he spends a great amount of his time in Mexico, where he has extensive business interests. Among these is a 45,000 hectare ranch called "La Columbia" located near Vera Cruz, and the controlling stock of two corporations—the Tehuacan Lumber Co. and the Columbian Plantation Oil Co. Milano has a long criminal record dating from 1913, involving two charges of murder and a number of arrests for counterfeiting. He is a nationally known figure in the underworld and an associate of Lucky Luciano, Al Polizzi, Frank Costello and other outstanding Mafia leaders in the United States, Mexico, Cuba and Italy. Milano was born in Sicily and is a naturalized citizen of the United States. He spends the greater part of his time at his apartment at Atenas, No. 31, Mexico City, D. F.

POLIZZI, Alfonso: This subject, usually referred to as Al, is an important and influential member of the Mafia and is believed to rank second in the organization in the state of Ohio. He was a former business partner of Frank Milano and is closely associated with members of the organization throughout Ohio, Michigan and Florida. Polizzi is a very powerful figure in the underworld and is greatly feared.

CAVALLARO, Charles: This individual is a member of the Mafia in Youngstown.

He is associated with members of the organization throughout the state and in New York, Illinois, Pennsylvania and to a lesser degree elsewhere. Subject has been arrested on several occasions on such charges as extortion and liquor law violation and has been a suspect in other criminal investigations. He has operated gambling houses in Youngstown and his last known address was the Pick Ohio Hotel there. He was born in Italy and entered the United States illegally on May 1, 1921, at New Orleans, as a stowaway aboard the *SS Cerco*. His FBI number is 1144812.

ANGERSOLA, Fred, Cleveland
ANGERSOLA, John, Cleveland

ILLINOIS

DELUCIA, Paul: This individual, usually known as Paul (The Waiter) Ricca or Ricci, is an important and influential member of the Grand Council of the International and a powerful figure in the underworld. He is a former member of old Capone organization in Chicago and is one of the defendants in the Brown-Bioff case. DeLucia received a ten-year sentence in connection with that case and was paroled in 1949. Subject is closely associated with the Fischetti brothers in Chicago and with members of the Mafia throughout the United States. He maintains legal residence at 812 Latrobe Ave., River Forest, Ill., and has a country estate at Berrien Springs, Mich. He is associated with Jack Guzik and they are reputed to be the most influential gangsters in the Chicago area.

ACCARDO, Anthony: Subject lives at 1431 Ashland Ave., River Forest. He is an influential member of the International. He classifies himself as a betting commissioner and confines his activities almost exclusively to gambling operations. He is a former member of the old Capone organization and is presently associated with the Chicago syndicate—DeLucia, Guzik, the Fischetti brothers, Murray Humphries and others. In November, 1948, Accardo was tried on charges of conspiracy to defraud and for concealing material facts. He was acquitted.

FISCHETTI, Charles, Rocco and Joe: These brothers are very important members of the Mafia at Chicago and are members of or associated closely with the International. They are cousins of Al Capone. The Fischettis are interested in gambling operations and various other rackets. Their connections with top Mafia members extend through Illinois, Missouri, New York, New Jersey, Michigan, Ohio, California and Florida. They have gambling casinos in the Chicago area, Indiana and Southern Wisconsin, Kansas City, East St. Louis and in Florida.

CAPEZIO, Anthony, alias Tough Tony: This subject is mentioned in Case Files Ill. 5909 and SE 202, the latter in the investigation into the death in Chicago of Carl Carramusa.

DE GRAZIO, Rocco alias Gramps: Subject figured in Ill. 5909 and in SE 202. He was an important member in the old Capone mob. He has been convicted of income tax violation and served 18 months. He currently controls all gambling in Melrose Park. He is closely associated with the Mafia.

CAMPAGNA, Louis alias Little New York: Subject is an important member of the Mafia at Chicago and is said to be a member of the International. He is a close personal friend of De Lucia with whom he currently is associated, as well as with Guzik, Humphreys, D'Andrea and Charles Gioe. Campagna is closely connected with all influential members of the Mafia in Illinois and has connections with top-level members in New York, Indiana and Michigan. He was born in Brooklyn, Sept. 23, 1900, and came to Chicago during the ascendancy of the Capone mob. He began his criminal career in Chicago and was sentenced in 1919 for bank robbery. In 1945 Campagna was convicted and sentenced in the Southern District of New York to 10 years in the Brown-Bioff case. Later paroled. During the interim he was arrested numerous times but evaded prosecution. Campagna has two farms on Rural Route 1, Berrien Springs, Mich., which he has owned since 1932 and which he rents out to tenants.

GIOE, Charles alias Cherry Nose: Subject is mentioned in files in connection with the International. He was a former member of the old Capone mob and was convicted with several others in the Brown-Bioff case. Now on parole.

IMPOSTATO, Nicolo: Subject formerly lived in Springfield, Ill. He has been identified with various narcotic traffickers since about 1938, in New York, Kansas City and Tampa. Convicted in Kansas City for violation of immigration laws as outgrowth of a narcotics investigation.

D'ANDREA, Philip: Subject is an influential member of the Mafia. His uncle, Anthony D'Andrea, was head of the Mafia in the Chicago area some years ago. Philip formerly a big shot member of the old Capone mob was convicted in the Southern District of New York in the Brown-Bioff case and is presently on parole.

CAPONE, John, alias Mimi, Chicago
CAPONE, Matthew Nicholas, Chicago

WISCONSIN

CAPONE, Ralph (formerly of Chicago). Now living in Mercer, Wis., where he operates the Rex Hotel and Billy's Bar, a gambling establishment.

MASSACHUSETTS

BUCCOLA, Philip: Subject is the leading Mafia figure of Boston and of the state, probably for the entire New England area. A native of Palermo, he migrated to this country about 1920 and became a prominent sporting events and fight promoter in Boston. He operates the Goodwin Athletic Club. He is intimately associated with Lucky Luciano and leading New York and Florida figures of the Mafia.

IACONE, Frank, Worcester

RHODE ISLAND

CANDELMO, John, Providence
PATRIARCA, Raymond, Providence (also Patriaca)

N. J. and PENN.

ACCARDI, Sam, Newark and Bloomfield
REGINELLI, Marco, Phila. and Camden (SE 226)

(Many of the above were similarly mentioned in other testimony before the Kefauver Committee.)

INDEX

CPSIA information can be obtained
at www.ICGtesting.com
Printed in the USA
BVOW06s1414120917
494672BV00016B/197/P

9 781163 820797